THE HOBBIT PARTY

Jonathan Witt and Jay W. Richards

The Hobbit Party

The Vision of Freedom That Tolkien Got and the West Forgot

Foreword by James V. Schall, S.J.

IGNATIUS PRESS SAN FRANCISCO

Cover photograph by Eva G. Muntean

Cover design by John Herreid

ISBN 978-1-58617-823-9
Library of Congress Control Number 2014908647
Printed in the United States of America ♾

To our wives, Amanda and Ginny, and our children—
without whom we would know precious little of the Shire.

CONTENTS

FOREWORD

Jonathan Witt and Jay Richards were fortunate men. They read Tolkien while they were still boys. I did not encounter Tolkien until I was into my sixties. No doubt, the reading of Tolkien at any adult age makes you young again. But it also makes you wonder if you are wise, with the kind of wisdom we find in Bilbo, Frodo, Sam, Gandalf, and the forces of good that populate Gondor and the Shire. The tales of Tolkien assure us that our desire to "live happily ever after" is not wholly in vain. Yet, no books bring home the sense of loss and doom that we often experience in our souls more vividly than *The Hobbit* and *The Lord of the Rings*. Witt and Richards seem to have caught the spirit that animates this most famous of the "second creations" that we contemplate in our literature.

As the twenty-first century rolls on, we find that we have the original tales of Tolkien, including his unfinished ones. We also have myriads of commentators who have undertaken, as they suppose, the delicate task of clarifying for us what Tolkien was "really" about. We have, in other words, a literature about literature. It goes without saying that no one reads Tolkien without gaining some insight into himself, the cosmos, and God. And yet, many interpretations of Tolkien's work did miss the mark, often widely. Witt and Richards deftly take us through these efforts that too often explain Tolkien by explaining him away. This is why it helps to have wondered about Tolkien since one was a boy. The recalled magic enables us to see through the explanations that, in effect, miss what Tolkien was about.

The title of this book deserve comment. "The Hobbit Party" might refer to a movement, even a political party. The distributists, the ecologists, the hippies, even the Marxists and the atheists, as well as the Catholics and other such believers and reasoners, have all claimed

Tolkien for their own. The stories we read in Tolkien are nothing if they are not about journeys and marches. Yet, the stories are ultimately about home and staying at home, about the hope that we never have to leave our homes once we have discovered where we are finally intended to dwell.

But our homes and families are under siege in this world, often by politicians and political parties we ourselves support. As this book suggests, we are more threatened with "soft" democratic tyrannies than with the blatantly bad ones. At first sight, we seem to suffer from our own greed or lethargy. We do not want to take the trouble to acknowledge who is for us and who is against us. Reading Tolkien makes us more vividly aware of the scriptural admonition that our struggles are not just about flesh and blood but about principalities and powers (see Eph 6:12). The father of lies is right at home in a world in which we lie to ourselves about *what is* so that we can proceed to do what we want.

But a "party" can also mean a gathering together of friends and family to rejoice in what is worth celebrating. At celebrations and parties, we give gifts and receive them. Why do we do this? It is not because we are bent on supplying to others what they do not have. The economics of the Shire makes it clear that the things we need we should make and acquire for and from others by fair exchange. If large markets make it possible to feed, clothe, and house many others, well and good. We were intended to discover what works and put aside what does not.

But something beyond necessity hovers over the tales of Tolkien. The important things are not really necessities. Indeed, we ourselves need not exist. The best things are given to us. It is a sign of character to be able to accept gifts from others, including from God himself. The Mordors of this world are places where all gifts cease. The eye that sees everything allows no privacy. It allows no place wherein we can be ourselves. The Hobbit "Party" by contrast is a scene of joy and abundance, of the time when all else is done, a time for listening to tales that explain who we are.

And yet, that there is evil in the world cannot be denied by most sensible men. It is the truth that hovers over all mankind. It provokes us. Each of us must take our stand. It is on this stand that we will be judged. We find ourselves living our lives in a divine plan that we, like Bilbo and Frodo, would just as soon avoid. We think that because we are among the insignificant of this world it will pass us by. None of our deeds, we think, can be great, because we are so small. Tolkien tells a different tale. The divine plan follows not just the paths of universal history and the great heroes of this world, but the detours of Nazareth, Tarsus, and Tagaste, where Augustine, in his teens, read Cicero. Seemingly insignificant places are often where the real events that define our essential being took place.

But the great battles of history are not insignificant either. It is not an evil to resist evil. Tolkien, as we read in these sober pages, was not a pacifist, nor did he glorify war. But he fought in the trenches of World War I; he knew the horror of war. He also knew what happens when we lose a war. The good side does not always win. And we can choose not to fight against an enemy who does not understand what man is. So, as Witt and Richards remark, Tolkien did understand a freedom that, once given to us, also requires our choosing to understand and defend it.

Evil is indeed the lack of a good, but it is also the lack of a good that should exist in a free being, angelic or human. Once a free being chooses himself over the order of things, he works to corrupt what is good in others. The Hobbit Party could not be what it was unless what we understood, chose, and yes, if need be, fought for made some ultimate difference.

We tend to forget that our freedom is itself a result of the divine creation that made us what we are. God did not want a world in which nothing that any one did made a difference. Personal freedom makes those who possess it unique and different. They are what they choose. But their choices are not simply left alone, unnoticed or unresponded to by the divine freedom that brings all things to the good if it can. The one thing that it cannot do, and this awareness dogs the journeys of the characters in *The Lord of the Rings*, is to deny the freedom of those who choose to reject God. They are allowed their choices. And they, in defending their self-chosen world, seek to draw everyone else within it.

If the drama of our lives did not really have something at stake, the very possibility of a happy ending, the whole meaning of existence would evaporate. What this book is really about is the worlds that we choose in response to the divine gifts of reason and will. Such a world contains tragedy and suffering, even of the innocent. But it remains rooted in joy, that final result of choosing what is good, even if we have to suffer for our choice. The "second creation" that Tolkien offers us illuminates the first creation in which we exist. It is in the first creation that we are initially created. Through our choices, we respond to the gifts of life and reason. Eternal life, the only life that lasts, is "the Hobbit Party" for which we exist, with its joys.

James V. Schall, S.J.

ACKNOWLEDGMENTS

This book is the fruit of many years, so it's impossible to acknowledge everyone who has helped us. Here we list just a few who aided us in the push to shape and bring the book to press. First we want to acknowledge Mark Brumley and the team at Ignatius—willing to walk with us down a path into Middle-Earth that many another feared to tread. We also want to thank Amanda Witt for her editorial input and encouragement at various stages; Adam Bellow for early encouragement and input on positioning the work; Ginny Richards for helpful feedback in the middle phase; Dante Witt for reminding us about an intriguing connection between Tolkien and Plato; and Elise Hilton and Holly Rowley for helping us review the galley proofs. Additional help and encouragement came from new friends and old, including Joel Salatin, Marcus Daly, Bruce Chapman, Steve Buri, Michael Matheson Miller, Kris Mauren, and Fr. Robert Sirico.

Chapter 1

In a Hole in the Ground There Lived an Enemy of Big Government

Until Aragorn's impassioned speech in defense of the West at the gates of Mordor in the 2003 film adaptation of J.R.R. Tolkien's *The Return of the King*, it hadn't occurred to a lot of people that Middle-Earth was anything more than an entertaining fantasy world created by a slightly pudgy English professor with a fondness for pipe tobacco. But in the wake of 9/11, Aragorn's speech struck a chord. Many concluded that the author behind the epic was surely a passionate defender of Western civilization. Others insisted that the Oxford don had in mind only the West of his fictional Middle-Earth, not the sordid and polluted Western civilization of our age.

There's some truth in both of these views, but what's interesting is how little has been written about the political and economic dimension of Middle-Earth. Tolkien's fantasy world is bursting at the seams with politics and political maneuvering, and its creator had unusual, even surprising opinions about politics and economics, and yet there have been no major books dedicated to the subject.[1] Here's how Tolkien scholar Joseph Pearce characterizes the situation:

> If much has been written on the religious significance of *The Lord of the Rings*, less has been written on its political significance—and the little that has been written is often erroneous in its conclusions and ignorant of Tolkien's intentions. There are exceptions, but alas, they are merely the exceptions that tend to prove the rule. Much more work is needed in this area, not least because Tolkien stated, implicitly at least, that the political significance of the work was second only to the religious in its importance.[2]

Exploring such matters will help us better understand and appreciate Tolkien's novels. It's also valuable, we believe, because the Oxford professor has considerable wisdom to offer on these matters—wisdom the free peoples of the West neglect at their peril.

It's a cliché in political commentary to say that "we stand at a crossroads". Actually, our culture blew past the crossroads some time ago and is well on its way to a devil's bargain with Saruman and his gang of "gatherers and sharers". If you watched *The Lord of the Rings* films and haven't had the chance to read the novel through to the end, then you haven't yet met these "gatherers and sharers". A later chapter of this book will introduce you to them in all their meddlesome glory, but for now we'll just note that their spirit and power is alive and well in the West today, such that there are no easy roads back to a society of free and responsible people. What Tolkien does, what his novels can do, is beckon us up the rocky path of hard choices—the only path back to freedom still available to us.

The Free Hobbit

Any person who has read *The Hobbit* and *The Lord of the Rings* can gather that their author was no fan of tyrants. What many people don't realize is that Tolkien was a lifelong enemy of big government in every form, not just the harsher forms we find in Soviet Communism, German Nazism, or Italian Fascism, but also as it manifested itself in British democratic socialism and the mongrel state capitalisms in other parts of the West, where central governments collude with big business to squeeze out the up-and-comers and reward special interests. The novelist who once described himself as a hobbit "in all but size"[3] was socially and politically conservative even by hobbit standards, and his conservatism was closely bound up in his deeply Christian, and specifically Catholic, vision of man and creation.

Tolkien had the subtle, cautious, and meticulous mind of a good scholar, but there was nothing murkily nuanced in his attitude toward political power. As he put it in a letter to his son Christopher, "My political opinions lean more and more to Anarchy (philosophically understood, meaning abolition of control not whiskered men with bombs)."[4]

His allergy to concentrated political power extended even to terminology that might subtly serve such power. "Government is an abstract noun meaning the art and process of governing and it should be an offence to write it with a capital G or so as to refer to people", he wrote. "If people were in the habit of referring to 'King George's Council, Winston and his gang', it would go a long way to clearing thought, and reducing the frightful landslide into Theyocracy."[5]

Add to this the fact that Tolkien was also a conservative Catholic in twentieth-century Britain, and you have the makings of a thinker far out of step with the rank-and-file intellectuals of his time and ours. The intellectual establishment of his day hated God and loved Big Brother. Tolkien loved God and hated Big Brother. Unlike the many self-appointed "radicals" in lockstep with spirit of the age, he was the true radical—the round peg in the square hole of modernity.

The secular left's relationship with Tolkien has been complex. In some cases, it's involved an attempt to co-opt him. Robert Stark, for example, seems to when he comments that "while they have vast differences in ideology and values, both Tolkien in his works and the cultural Marxists of the Frankfurt School laid the ideological ground work for the 1960s counterculture movement, which most political thinkers characterize as left-wing."[6]

Marxist literary critic Jack Zipes goes further, telling readers that "Tolkien's unconscious secularization of religion brings him close to" a "Marxist viewpoint of religion" and that "there are unusual similarities between orthodox Catholics and orthodox Marxists."[7] Zipes needs to bone up on his knowledge of Catholic teaching, which for a century and a half has consistently opposed socialism, and Marxism in particular. Consider two encyclicals, one from just before Tolkien was born, and the other published when Tolkien had been teaching at Oxford for six years and was working on *The Hobbit*. In *Rerum Novarum* (1891), Pope Leo XIII defended the "inviolability of private property" and wrote bluntly that "it is clear that the main tenet of socialism, community of goods, must be utterly rejected".[8] And in *Quadragesimo Anno* (1931), Pope Pius XI wrote, "Socialism, if it remains truly Socialism ... cannot be reconciled with the teachings of the Catholic Church because its concept of society itself is utterly foreign to Christian truth." Or as he put in the same encyclical, "No one can be at the same time a good Catholic and a true socialist."[9] Tolkien, a staunchly orthodox Catholic and proponent of small government, surely agreed. Indeed, his distaste for socialism was so far reaching that in one of his posthumous stories he used it as a metaphor for the debasement of language. There, one of his characters speaks of "misusing an established word, robbing Peter to relieve the poverty of Paul", of "lexicographical socialism, which would end by reducing the whole vocabulary to one flat drab Unmeaning, if there were no reactionaries."[10]

How could one miss all this? Claims that Tolkien was a fellow traveler of more sophisticated Marxist thinkers trade on an either-or fallacy. A critic shows that Tolkien opposed this or that element of modern capitalist society and from there jumps to the conclusion that Tolkien supported key features of some leftist alternative, ignoring another alternative that Tolkien actually embraced.

Others on the left, rather than co-opting Tolkien, tried simply to ignore him, hoping the man and his work would soon pass into oblivion. Another and more aggressive strategy was to dismiss his imaginative work as escapist fluff. Some sixty years on, many academics still view Tolkien as insufficiently progressive, cynical, or nihilistic to be taken seriously, but the effort to consign his work to the dustbin of secondhand pulp fiction has met a variety of obstacles. First, Renaissance scholar C.S. Lewis and English poet W.H. Auden came to Tolkien's early defense, making it difficult to simply ignore the Oxford professor. Another obstacle was Middle-Earth's growing, and often wildly enthusiastic, throng of admirers around the globe, both inside and outside academia. Initially, *The Lord of the Rings* struggled in the face of expensive paper prices, but sales rose steadily through the 1950s and then caught fire on college campuses when released in affordable paperback form in the 1960s.

The Lord of the Rings and *The Hobbit* together have now sold as many as a quarter billion copies worldwide, behind only *A Tale of Two Cities* on the list of all-time bestselling novels. Surveys regularly list *The Lord of the Rings* as the novel of the twentieth century and Tolkien as the author of the twentieth century. And while these surveys could be written off as merely reflecting the stunted taste of the masses, a raft of academic studies in the past several years has built up the case for Tolkien's position as an author to be reckoned with.

The Fantastic

If you're reading this, you're probably already a Tolkien enthusiast, with none of the hang-ups noted above. However, there is one other thing that could prevent even the most ardent of Tolkien lovers from exploring Tolkien's insights into matters political and economic: the conviction that Tolkien didn't mingle his art and his private political views, and that while Tolkien's novels are perfectly worthwhile, they are timeless fantasies without political or economic significance. Such a conclusion contains a shard of truth but not the whole truth.

Tolkien hated didacticism in storytelling, so you won't find his political opinions shouting at you from the pages as you might in, say, *Atlas Shrugged* or *The Grapes of Wrath*. Tolkien insisted that his novels were not allegories of modern life. The races, characters, and events of the stories were not meant to correspond neatly with the characters and events of World War II or the Soviet Union or to the rise and fall of this or that nineteenth-century robber baron. Tolkien did, however, allow that his novels had "applicability" to modern life.[11] As we'll show, he even suggested some specific political applications.

You see, Middle-Earth isn't some never-never land without connection to the real world. Middle-Earth, as Tolkien himself explained, is just his term for "the inhabited world of men ... round and inescapable".[12] Middle-Earth isn't a photograph of our world, of course. Better to think of it as an imaginative painting of our world, estranging things around us that have become too familiar and familiarizing realities strange and fantastic.[13] As Tom Shippey argues, Tolkien was doing what was actually common among twentieth-century literary authors, "writing about worlds and creatures which we know do not exist"[14]—not to ignore reality but to see it anew.

Shippey, who occupied the same chair at Oxford that Tolkien occupied, labels this mode "the fantastic", and in searching out the reasons for its prominence in the twentieth century, he notes that several pioneers of this mode were military veterans, "present at or at least deeply involved in the most traumatically significant events of the century, such as the Battle of the Somme (Tolkien), the bombing of Dresden (Vonnegut), the rise and early victory of fascism (Orwell)." These and other respected authors—Franz Kafka, Jorge Luis Borges, Ursula K. Le Guin, Thomas Pynchon, Kingsley and Martin Amis, Ray Bradbury, Anthony Burgess, Walker Percy, Don DeLillo, Gabriel García Márquez, and Italo Calvino—worked within the fantastic mode, not to ignore reality, but to comment more effectively on the traumatic and dislocating events of their times.[15]

The novelist as artist, like the poet, is struggling to speak of things that are almost unsayable, to write about aspects of the human experience that are hard to convey with power and clarity by more ordinary means.[16] The great medieval philosopher and theologian Thomas Aquinas wrote that beauty consists of depth, elegance, and clarity. By clarity he didn't mean drab, easily digestible newspaper prose. He meant almost exactly the opposite. Saint Thomas' word translated here as *clarity* is the Latin word *clarus*, which means bright, shining, illustrious, and evident. Authors in various ages and genres have pursued this radiant clarity by a diversity of means. The seventeenth-century metaphysical poets wrenched the English language in shocking and fanciful ways to achieve clarity. Shakespeare scandalized the neoclassical critics by mixing tragedy and comedy and violating the unities of time and place. From pagan Homer to Catholic Hopkins we could go on and on with examples of authors working outside the proverbial box in pursuit of the bright, shining, and illustrious.

In the first half of the twentieth century, nineteenth-century realism was the old box for aspiring novelists, and the great writers of the fantastic climbed out of it in pursuit of a depth and clarity they didn't think they could achieve within the conventions of "realism". And we stand by the scare quotes. Prince Hamlet's comment applies just as well to the nineteenth-century authors working in this mode as it does to his good friend Horatio: "There are more things in heaven and earth ... than are dreamt of in your philosophy" (1.5.166–67).[17]

The Hobbit Party explores some things in our world Tolkien hoped to bring to light through the fantastic world of Middle-Earth, things bound up in the human drama, including the nature of good and evil, freedom, law, power, and authority, and the mysteries of death and renewal. These in turn bear on questions political: What is the highest form of freedom? What is the relationship of law and order to liberty? What is political freedom? Is it worth pursuing? Can it be sustained in the face of human evil? Does power inevitably corrupt? What are the necessary supports of a free society? Our journey through Tolkien's imaginative world will shed light on each of these questions.

Tolkienomics

We should address one final objection, namely, that surely we have little to gain by exploring a fantasy novelist's thoughts on questions of political economy, since he wasn't a political economist. Here it is important to recognize that political economy isn't ultimately about graphs or mathematical equations, however much some have tried to reduce it to such things. It's about human beings acting in society according to certain rules, and the principles we discover as a result.[18] It would be a grave mistake to limit ourselves to the mathematical world of econometrics to gain economic insights. In fact, much of modern economics is misguided because, as it obsesses over this graph or that model, it gets the human person wrong. Tolkien got the human person right, and with it much that has been forgotten in certain economic circles about what does and doesn't work in organizing society.

Political economy is an integrative discipline, and Tolkien was an integrative thinker of a high order. Put another way, his insights into the free society are worth tending to because he was a man of wisdom and wide-ranging knowledge and experience.

Tolkien spent many years working quietly as a professor at Oxford University, and yet he lived anything but a sheltered life. He lost his father when he was four and his mother when he was twelve. He fought in the trenches of World War I, lost all but one of his closest friends there, married and raised a family, saw the industrial revolution disfigure his pastoral childhood home, and sent two sons off to World War II. He developed close friendships with leading intellectual figures such as C. S. Lewis, and distinguished himself as a renowned philologist, becoming familiar with Latin, Greek, French, German, Italian, Spanish, Old and Middle English, Finnish, Gothic, Old Norse, modern Welsh, Medieval Welsh, Dutch, Danish, Norwegian, Icelandic, Lithuanian, Russian, Swedish, Lombardic, Middle Dutch, Middle High German, Middle Low German, Old High German, and Old Slavonic, and with them many truths about the sources of Western civilization that were in danger of being lost. Tolkien was a gifted scholar and writer who studied English and Western culture down to its roots while also facing some of its worst horrors as well as his share of personal griefs. His novels and letters bear the fruit of that deep and varied experience.

Entering Middle-Earth

When the two of us first encountered Middle-Earth as teenagers, we weren't looking for politics or economics or theology or literary theory.

We were looking for a good adventure story and perhaps a bit of relief from the flat, dusty landscape around us on the Texas High Plains.

We both read *The Hobbit* and *The Lord of the Rings* for the first time when in junior high. We had been friends since first grade, but were attending different schools at the time. I (Jay) was without literary acquaintances at my school to test my reading, so I got it in my head that Bilbo and the hobbits were more or less covered with hair and suffered perpetually grubby fingernails from living underground. (I'm still surprised to see the clean-shaven Frodo and Bilbo in the movie adaptations.)

Jonathan had the advantage of fellow Tolkien enthusiasts at his school, meaning his first experience in Middle-Earth was a less solitary affair.

I (Jonathan) still remember the joy of discovering Middle-Earth—finding the colorful boxed paperback set on the shelf at Hastings bookstore, my first entering the Shire, my arriving at school each morning where a couple of my friends, seasoned Tolkien geeks, would query me about whether I'd reached the trolls yet, had Bilbo found "the precious," had I reached the Lonely Mountain, had I met Bilbo's nephew Frodo, had I met Sam Gamgee, had I made it to Bree, Rivendell, Fangorn Forest, Gondor, Mordor, and I either shushing them or diving into the conversation, depending on which emotion predominated at the moment—the dread of spoilers or the desire to share the imaginative experience.

I also remember the first time I reached "The Scouring of the Shire" chapter near the end of *The Lord of the Rings*. I enjoyed reading about the humble hobbits pulling together to overthrow the spiteful tyrant who had despoiled their Shire; and yet the budding little critic in me couldn't understand why Tolkien had tacked such an anticlimactic and shabby bit of villainy onto the end of his majestic epic.

After all, the novel had pitted the greatest forces of Middle-Earth against each other. They had followed the "one ring to rule them all" to the very Cracks of Doom and seen its final destruction. And then, after the epic clash between good and evil, after the glorious victory celebration in Gondor with a royal wedding tossed in for good measure, after all of this, the hobbits make the long journey back to the Shire only to find that a washed up wizard has taken over their lovely Shire and begun mindlessly hacking down trees, destroying the graceful homes built into the side of the hills, and throwing up a series of ugly huts in their stead.

Only later did it become clear to the two of us that the events described in this curious chapter bespoke a present evil, one less dramatic and violent than a Hitler or a Stalin, but in a way more dangerous to the free society because more insidious. Growing up during the last chapter of the Cold War, we knew that the twentieth century had been, in its darkest moments, an arresting illustration of what Friedrich Nietzsche called "the will to power". But we began to see that Tolkien was hinting that modern life also exhibited a less imposing if more curious urge. Call it *the will to ugliness*—the curious tendency, amid unparalleled prosperity, to embrace a host of things that are tasteless, deadening, depraved, or some combination of all three.

Economists and cultural critics have offered prescriptions for this will to ugliness, but many of them involve what Tolkien adamantly rejected: giving the political class more power than it already has. The desire to remedy cultural decay is worthwhile, but if we're going to do more good than harm, we need to test any prescription against a foundational truth that Tolkien wove throughout his imaginative work: we are all fallen creatures, and that includes every political leader we might appoint to run some centralized plan for building a better society. This is why Tolkien steadfastly opposed the trend—strongly in evidence in the England of his day—to place more and more power in the hands of politicians in the hopes of hastening social reform. He resisted it through his personal correspondence, speeches, and as we'll see, by weaving his opposition into the warp and woof of Middle-Earth.

Today, even many lovers of freedom and virtue have been led to support big top-down solutions for what ails society. Inevitably these quick fixes involve ever greater power in the power centers of the world. Tolkien rejected these big plan prescriptions, but not from a lack of concern for the downtrodden and dispossessed. He was deeply worried about where Western democracy was headed and about the many people it was damaging. But he believed the way to confront cultural decay was, well, culturally—in other words, not through government edicts or government planners or government "sharers", but through the leavening work of great and good art, through discourse grounded in truth and reason, and through the hard, patient work of modeling whatever is worth rescuing and cultivating in civilization. Exploring his insights will take us into some rarefied terrain, but our first stage is more modest: through a green, round door into a humble corner of Middle-Earth called Hobbiton.

Hardly Any "Government"

As every lover of Tolkien knows, *The Hobbit* begins in a hobbit hole, not a nasty, dirty, bare hole, but a comfortable home that—except for its being underground and round of door—feels a lot like a Victorian middle-class home. And yet *The Hobbit* isn't set in Victorian England or any other part of nineteenth-century Europe. It seems to be set in some ancient period before the advent of Christianity. Or is it the Middle Ages with its swords and horse lords and chain mail? Maybe—but that wouldn't account for some of the technological conveniences that didn't arrive until well after the Middle Ages.

Where we are, of course, is in the fantasy realm of Middle-Earth—and more specifically, the Shire of Middle-Earth, and even more specifically, in the thoroughly comfortable, thoroughly bourgeois home of hobbit Bilbo Baggins. (Hobbits, remember, are a sturdy, sociable folk about half the height of men, conservative by taste and temperament, with hairy, leathery feet, a fondness for pipe tobacco, and a custom of eating six meals a day.) Mr. Baggins will soon be swept away from his comfortable home and into various uncomfortable adventures involving dwarves, elves, dragons, and various other creatures pleasant and unpleasant. We will follow him on his way. But while the bachelor gentleman is still idling about making tea and imagining that his life is going to continue on in its sensible rut, let's duck out of the round front door of his hobbit home, take a stroll up and down the lanes, and see if we can get a feel for how Hobbiton and the larger Shire are run.

Having ambled around enough to digest the exquisite mix of farmland, pasture, and grove; having taken in the charming homes with their round windows and doors set into the slopes of the valleys of the Brandywine and its tributaries; and having strolled over to the Green Dragon pub and caught up on the latest gossip as the sun is easing toward the western horizon, something almost as peculiar as the size and hairy feet of the hobbits should begin to dawn on us: this gentle civilization appears to have no department of unmotorized vehicles, no internal revenue service, no government official telling people who may and may not have laying hens in their backyards, no government schools lining up hobbit children in geometric rows to teach regimented behavior and groupthink, no government-controlled currency, and no political institution even capable of collecting tariffs on foreign goods. "The Shire at this time had hardly any 'government'", we eventually learn. "Families for the most part managed their own affairs."[19]

We do not have to search far and long for an explanation as to why the author might have wished to create a society of this sort. Tolkien, as we have seen, said that his "political opinions lean more and more to Anarchy (philosophically understood, meaning abolition of control not whiskered men with bombs)." As he went on to add, "The most improper job of any man, even saints, is bossing other men. Not one in a million is fit for it, and least of all those who seek the opportunity." With the Shire, Tolkien had created a society after his own heart.

Hobbiton—Tech Hub

Tolkien was by taste and temperament a staunch traditionalist. Among his fictional creations this is perhaps most clearly hinted at in Lord Elrond and the elven realm of Rivendell, where first Bilbo, and later Frodo and his companions, take refuge on their journeys. In a letter written probably toward the end of 1951, Tolkien commented that "Elrond symbolises throughout the ancient wisdom, and his House represents Lore—the preservation in reverent memory of all tradition concerning the good, wise, and beautiful."[20] But one doesn't need access to Tolkien's letters to register his esteem for this realm. His fondness for this "Last Homely House east of the Sea" is palpable from the warm narrative descriptions of it; from the positive role it plays in the two quests (first Bilbo's and later Frodo's); and from the high esteem it is held in by such "good guy" characters as Gandalf, Bilbo, Frodo, Sam, and Aragorn. One could almost say that Rivendell was Tolkien's Oxford University as it ought to have been—a contemplative, scholarly, and intellectual community reenchanted and purged of the antitraditionalism that had begun to infect the institution in Tolkien's day.

The picture that emerges from these various lines of evidence is unambiguous: the novelist who once described himself as a "hobbit (in all but size)" was conservative even by hobbit standards. He prized many of the things that were vanishing or had long ago vanished from England and the West, he disdained the rise of a monolithic global consumer culture, and he expressed a strong distaste for various modern innovations, such as the internal combustion engine. Making sense of the man who was Tolkien means recognizing this traditionalism. If you overlook it, you really don't have in view the master of Middle-Earth. At the same time, it's easy to miss the man by exaggerating this side of him.

Tolkien was no Luddite who rejected all technology. Look closely at that most pastoral corner of Middle-Earth, the Shire, and something curious emerges, curious at least for a fictional culture set in a faraway place seemingly before the spread of Christianity. First, many of the things we find in the Shire were, in our world, invented long after the advent of Christianity, during the last five hundred years of Western development. Since we view Middle-Earth from the age of cell phones and global Web surfing, it's easy to overlook this, as well as the fact that the Shire is one of the more modern places in Middle-Earth.

Tom Shippey suggests that hobbits function as bridges to the more ancient and fairy-tale world of Middle-Earth beyond the Shire. Hobbits cultivate tobacco and are said to have invented the habit of smoking it in pipes (a custom not introduced to Europe until the Renaissance). They are in the habit of an afternoon tea (very English and Victorian). They have the mail delivered (begun in England in the 1830s), and they have butchers who deliver meat to the door ready for cooking. As for Bilbo, he keeps fairly exact time, at one point exclaiming that "I didn't get your note till after 10.45 to be precise." He feels "he cannot leave home without a pocket-handkerchief." He longs for bacon and eggs, "a characteristically modern and characteristically English menu." And at one point he "gropes for matches for his pipe (friction matches were invented in 1827)."[21]

As for his home, "it is in fact, in everything except being underground (and in there being no servants), the home of a member of the Victorian upper-middle class of Tolkien's nineteenth-century youth, full of studies, parlours, cellars, pantries, wardrobes, and all the rest."[22] You see the pattern. The Shire enjoys numerous innovations that, in our world, came about through the creative dynamism of Western capitalism; and it possesses several legal and economic features of a market economy in what we might call its ideal form, features that include freedom of exchange and association, secure property rights, sound money, and a minimal government focused not on regulating and redistributing but on maintaining the rule of law. The Shire, in sum, is enormously free and enjoys a host of innovative conveniences that such freedom gave rise to in our own world.

"Petty, Complicated, Detailed"

Now contrast the Shire's system of government with our own. The nineteenth-century French social philosopher Alexis de Tocqueville studied the contours and tendencies of the American system and, looking ahead, limned a portrait of what he feared was coming. "I see an innumerable crowd of men, all alike and equal", he wrote. Above them "stands an immense and protective power which alone is responsible for looking after their enjoyments and watching over their destiny. It is absolute, meticulous, ordered, provident, and kindly disposed." It's a ruling power, he continued, that "spreads its arms over the whole of society, covering the surface of social life with a network of petty, complicated, detailed, and uniform rules" until it "reduces each nation to nothing more than a flock of timid and hardworking animals with the government as shepherd."[23]

Tocqueville was farsighted. More than a century and a half after he penned those words, the modern administrative state does cover "the surface of social life with a network of petty, complicated, detailed, and uniform rules", regulating everything from the kind of cooking oil we are allowed to have in our restaurant fries to how and where and with whom we can arrange to treat our physical ailments.

A little patch of the Upper Midwest illustrates what we mean. I (Jonathan) live outside of Grand Rapids, Michigan, in an old two-story farmhouse surrounded by rolling farmland, orchards, woodland, a handful of neighbors within a five minutes' walk, and four vividly distinct seasons that I'd only seen in pictures growing up in Texas. My little corner of western Michigan is beautiful, and I count my blessings. Still, it isn't quite the Shire in terms of freedom.

Thanks to zoning rules, I'm permitted to own a horse. I would also be completely within my legal rights to keep a pack of large, snarling dogs and half a dozen roaming cats. But for some reason I'm not allowed to trade in the large horse, snarling dogs, and wandering cats for a single, small Dexter cow or milking goat to provide grass-fed beef or fresh raw milk for my family. This should strike any sane person as strange. Either of these (Dexter cow or goat) would be gentler on my three acres of grass than a horse. Either of them would mow my lawn much more quietly than my gas mower. Either of them would provide a higher quality fertilizer for our vegetable patch. And neither of them would be as likely to attack my neighbors as the perfectly legal pack of snarling dogs. So why can't I have a cow? No one I've asked seems to know. It's the law, that's all—a law apparently made, sometime in the obscure past, by people who wanted to own dogs, cats, and horses, but didn't want to protect the freedom of people who prefer pets that earn their keep.

Meanwhile, in town, a group of citizens recently decided to fight a local law that prohibits the keeping of laying hens inside city limits. A city commissioner agreed to sponsor the amendment and, after extensive research, the proposed statute was written. It allowed people to keep up to five laying hens in their backyards. It didn't permit roosters in the city, just the quietly clucking female variety of chicken, creatures far quieter than your typical dog. (My wife and I once lived a full year next door to laying hens before we realized they were there.) The proposed new statute also specified various health and safety measures to prevent predator, rodent, and odor problems, and proposed a five-year probationary period, after which the whole issue would be reexamined. A pretty sensible initiative, right? Most people thought so. Public hearings were held, and those who spoke up were largely in favor of approving the ordinance—so much so that many considered approval a done deal. Hooray for locally grown food; hooray for sustainable lifestyles.

And yet, when the city commission voted, the result was a 3–3 split that, under Michigan law, meant defeat. What happened?

One commissioner argued that, despite the evidence of the public hearings, most people didn't want chickens in the city limits; another declared the statute a dangerous slippery slope: "If someone wanted to have turkeys, on what logical ground would we deny them that right?"[24] he asked.

Then there's the issue of cronyism. In a master's thesis on the subject, Traci D. Joseph points out that the most vocal opposition to the proposed change came from the Michigan Poultry Alliance and one area poultry farm. They argued that the livelihoods of large poultry farms would be put at risk if city chickens got out of hand, developed diseases, and communicated those diseases to birds at the farms (located on average forty to fifty miles away). Some insisted this was highly unlikely, including Jason Otto, a graduate student at Michigan State University in the agriculture and natural resources program, who pointed out that "there's no published evidence of airborne spread over long distances and no significant correlation can be found between backyard flocks and commercial farms."[25]

"It is worth noting again that those in the opposing group fell primarily within groups that held positions of power in one way or another", Joseph writes. "The overwhelming majority of residents spoke publicly in favor of the proposed ordinance, and the proposal was considered a citizen-led movement, yet it did not pass."[26]

Now, obviously we don't want to wantonly risk our food supply; but there's no compelling evidence that chickens in the city would in fact risk it. And as Michael Pollan argues, concentrating our food supply in a few hands poses its own risk.[27] What's definitely at risk is personal liberty.

Yes, I'm on a hobby horse. But horses are the only large animal I'm allowed to own, so indulge me a minute longer. Here's the question: Did the commissioners who voted against the hen proposal ever stop to ask themselves, "What moral right do I have to deny my fellow citizens the freedom to responsibly maintain a small number of laying hens in their backyards?" And how did the land of the free reach a point where the meddlesome regulation could sit on the books for years without sparking an uproar? It's one more sign that we are disturbingly close to becoming the society of soft despotism that Tocqueville predicted. We have been trained to sing about liberty while blithely acquiescing to policies and politicians that deny liberty.

To see how arbitrary all these rules are, consider Jay's zoning situation in Western Washington.

Until recently, I (Jay) lived right in the middle of fussy, urban Seattle, just far enough from downtown that we had a small backyard. We *could* have up to eight hens on our property (though we didn't really want any). In all likelihood, this liberated zoning rule has to do with the eccentricity of the Northwest, rather than a love for freedom, since Seattleites happily hyperregulate all sorts of other activities and would promptly execute a neighbor they caught failing to recycle.

Now, we're not saying that all zoning and city planning is bad. Zoning rules can enhance people's freedom instead of suffocating it. If a suburban neighbor decides to use his eighth-of-an-acre backyard as a hazardous waste pit, or decides that his front yard is the perfect place to run a hundred-decibel concrete demolition business in the wee hours of the night, he's violating his neighbors' property rights, plain and simple. Sane, modest zoning laws serve as a safeguard against such violations. The point then isn't to cast zoning into the outer darkness, but to emphasize that the "land of the free" has grown alarmingly comfortable with denying freedom to its neighbors when it suits the majority—or the minority who holds the greatest lobbying power. Most of us, sadly, simply accept this situation. One example: both of our families have homeschooled, and at one point a woman told one of our wives, "Isn't it nice that the government will let you do that?" We have come to assume that everything—even our children—belong to the state.

Do you see the night-and-day difference between the current regulatory state of affairs and the Shire of Middle-Earth? There is rule of law and government in the Shire, but it is a highly limited government that begins and ends in self-government. The "Shirriffs" aren't there to interfere with people's property rights. Just the opposite. Unlike the "gatherers and sharers" who later seize control of the local economy, the Shirriffs of Bilbo's day do not even wear uniforms and focus mainly on returning farm animals that have strayed onto another's property. Notice what this work is aimed at preventing—the animals' owners from unintentionally infringing on the property rights of others.

Set the Shire beside the so-called free economies of the modern age, and right away it becomes clear that the Shire is more low tax, limited government, and open market than the so-called capitalist societies of today. Millions of readers who have fallen in love with the Shire have been attracted by its pastoral beauty, by its whimsical round windows peering from the sides of its green hills, and by its charming inhabitants. But surely another of its appeals—sensed perhaps only vaguely or unconsciously by many readers—is the Shire's palpable air of freedom, of *ordered liberty*. One of the most attractive features of this land of small people is that it is also a land of small government.

There is a clue here to understanding Tolkien's vision of the free society.[28] The Shire is consistent with Tolkien's stated preference for government that is less about meddling and more about protecting people's basic freedoms. Notice how different that vision is from the rigged game of international corporate-government cronyism that is with us today, and that was alive and well in the Europe of Tolkien's day. While it purports to lift up the weak, this big, invasive form of government always seems to end up privileging the well-connected and fueling more cronyism, since lobbyists are drawn to the halls of political power by the knowledge that a bureaucratic class sits in the middle of every market exchange bigger than a—well, it's hard to think of anything small enough nowadays. As a girl and her parents in Bethesda, Maryland, learned in 2011, even lemonade stands aren't small enough anymore.[29] When the hand of the state gropes forth to control an economy, few things are small enough to go undetected.

Tolkien understood this acutely, and his leading hobbits eventually learn it, too.

Chapter 2

Adventure, Inc.

Hobbiton and the Shire have charmed millions of Tolkien readers, and as we saw, hobbits enjoy an enormous amount of political and economic freedom as well as several technological conveniences that, in our world, came to us through the creative ferment of free enterprise. This is significant—but we don't want to make too much of it. The Shire isn't a capitalist society in the way we normally think of that term, and Bilbo Baggins isn't a capitalist. Bilbo learns to be industrious, but he is not an industrialist; he learns to be an entrepreneurial risk taker, but he is far from an entrepreneur. The bourgeois bachelor isn't even a diligent shop owner or trader. What is Mr. Baggins? He's a country-village gentleman, and like the properly prosperous country gentlemen of Tolkien's late Victorian youth, Mr. Baggins of Bag End has enough inherited wealth to pick and choose his leisure and his labor as it suits him. Whether it's making himself tea, blowing smoke rings on the lawn, reading up on the history of the elves, or tinkering away with quill and pen on some writing project, he can undertake whatever endeavor he chooses and let the profits, deadlines, and quarterly reports go hang.

So at the outset of the novel we have a pastoral village with no banks or bankers, no stock markets or stockbrokers, no heavy industry or titans of heavy industry, and at the center of it a middle-aged country gentleman in seemingly permanent retirement. One could almost say the only notable thing the opening scene has in common with capitalism is the Shire's remarkable degree of political and economic freedom.

One could say this, but it would be a mistake. You see, there's something almost ostentatiously capitalist sitting in plain sight in the opening pages of *The Hobbit*. It's easy to miss because when we come upon it, we're busy orienting ourselves to a world very different from our own, one with a troupe of dwarves with long, plaited beards; a magical wizard with a tall, pointy hat; a lot of talk of dragons and lost treasure; and, for a host, a hole-dwelling creature called a hobbit. But if we shift our focus a quarter turn, we'll notice something quite distinct from these fantasy elements, something right out there in the open: a business consultant bringing together two parties to create a formal contract.

True, the arrangement calls for the fantastical hobbit creature to travel over and under hill and misty mountain, past elves, trolls, and goblins, and to confront the abominable fire-breathing Smaug. But again, don't let the fantastical obscure the mundane: in the opening pages of the novel, a person named Gandalf mediates a contract negotiation between a Mr. Bilbo Baggins and a Thorin Oakenshield and Company. The upshot is a legal document:

> Thorin and Company to Burglar Bilbo greeting! ... Terms: cash on delivery, up to and not exceeding one fourteenth of total profits (if any); all traveling expenses guaranteed in any event; funeral expenses to be defrayed by us or our representatives, if occasion arises and the matter is not otherwise arranged for.[1]

It ends with a call for a meeting in the town of Bree at "11 A.M. sharp. Trusting you will be punctual." Thus is the central plot element of the novel launched by a commercial bargain complete with shareholders, two scheduled meetings, a modest life insurance provision, a signed contract and—in good businesslike fashion—an emphasis on punctuality.

The matter would be of only passing interest if it weren't connected to a larger theme running throughout *The Hobbit*: the importance of manners, custom, and doing things "properly". A signed contract is, after all, a customary way of making a commitment between two or more parties, and the contract Bilbo and the dwarves settle on isn't a self-contained incident. It's made possible by a broad fabric of customs and formal interactions we're introduced to in the first two chapters of the novel—the whole tradition of hospitality and its attendant demands on host and guest; various formulaic greetings; a concern with the reputations of gentlemen and noblemen; the norms surrounding spoken and written agreements; and matters as relatively trivial as the norms of good housekeeping and, specifically, the regular dusting of mantels. Take these things away, and the contractual agreement never happens.

Moreover, the adventure that unfolds from the initial contract at Bag End involves a sustained focus on custom, propriety, punctuality, property rights, the rule of law, and a capacity for trust that extends beyond family and clan. These are elements economic historians have highlighted as crucial to wealth creation and the rise of enterprise economies, beginning in the monasteries and city-states of northern Italy in the Middle Ages.[2] Later chapters are focused on themes more obviously connected to questions of political economy: market freedom in Middle-Earth, the rings of power and the corrupting effects of political power, the Just War tradition, a critique of socialism implicit in a late chapter of *The Lord of the Rings*, and the relationship of the Shire to contemporary movements like localism, distributism, and neo-agrarianism. In a book about the political-economic vision of Tolkien, the easy thing would be to spend all our time on this low-hanging fruit. But this book—like Tolkien—is as much about root and soil as fruit and flower, and to grasp Tolkien's political-economic vision we must see why he believed that propriety, honor, and tradition—particularly that of Christendom—were crucial to sustaining freedom and a flourishing civilization.

Good Morning and Good Manners

As *The Hobbit* opens, Bilbo is taking in the morning air on his front porch when along comes an old man with a gray cloak, silver scarf, pointed blue hat, and a staff. Bilbo immediately invites the stranger to share some pipe tobacco and enjoy the morning together. The stranger, of course, is the wizard Gandalf, and he isn't there to blow smoke rings or talk about the weather. He's "looking for someone to share in an adventure".[3]

On hearing this, Bilbo decides that this stranger isn't quite "his sort", tells him "Good morning!" a second time, and explains that they don't want any adventures in these parts and that he would have better luck "over the Hill or across the Water".

"What a lot of things you do use *Good morning* for!" Gandalf says, since now Bilbo obviously means by it "that you want to get rid of me, and that it won't be good till I move off." The retort strips the tact right off of Bilbo's gentle attempt to nudge the fellow on his way.

Taken aback, Bilbo commits his first blatant deception of the novel, denying that he meant any such thing by "Good morning!" It's deceptive, but notice that Bilbo's reaction isn't to escalate what was the beginning of an argument, but to defuse it by returning to a more hospitable tone, even if a bit on the starchy side. "Not at all, not at all, my dear sir!" he says. "Let me see, I don't think I know your name?"

The hobbit's response is both an invitation for the two of them to get to know each other better, and an indirect way of pointing out that the man is a complete stranger, after all, and it's a little cheeky of him to stride right up to Mr. Baggins' front porch and immediately start in about "someone to share in an adventure".

Bilbo's error here, however, runs deeper than diplomacy shading into deception. As the old man is about to explain, Bilbo isn't talking to a complete stranger but to an old friend he's failed to recognize. What paved the way for Bilbo's error was an earlier and more basic error: Bilbo has allowed his capacity for hospitality to grow cramped. As a too-comfortable hobbit nestled in his spacious home in the heart of Hobbiton, he's happy to show hospitality to "his sort". What has atrophied is that more muscular and expansive hospitality needed for entertaining the strange and wonderful, a capacity indispensable if he is to thrive amid the many surprises, meetings, and challenges of the coming adventure. The respectable, comfortable, tea-at-four side of Master Baggins of Bag End has grown overly dominant, while the poetic, adventurous side, inherited from his mother, has grown flabby from disuse.

Sensing the problem, Gandalf goes right to work.

"I am Gandalf and Gandalf means me!" the wizard exclaims to the startled hobbit. "To think that I should have lived to be good morninged by Belladonna Took's son, as if I was selling buttons at the door!"

"Gandalf! Good gracious me!" the hobbit blurts, realizing his mistake, and with genuine excitement begins recounting the many strange and wondrous things Gandalf did, gave, and told about on his visits to the Shire long ago. There are no battles or mysterious maps or magical treasures in this little scene. All the same, it's a critical moment in the plot. In revealing himself to Bilbo, the old wizard kindles back to life something in the hobbit that will carry him over and under sky and mountain, into the lair of a great, green dragon, and ultimately into the role of a most hospitable, and most urgently needed, peacemaker.

But first Bilbo will have to survive the following day's teatime.

Raining Dwarves

The following afternoon Bilbo is just settling down to tea and cakes when there comes "a tremendous ring on the front-door bell". Bilbo assumes it's Gandalf again, but when he throws open the door, standing before him is a bright-eyed dwarf "with a blue beard tucked into a golden belt". This fellow steps inside "as if expected", hangs his cloak on a nearby peg, and with a low bow says, "Dwalin at your service!"

Bilbo manages to return the greeting and, gathering himself, invites the dwarf to join him for tea. Keep in mind, the dwarf is a total stranger. The two sit down to tea. The doorbell rings again. It's another dwarf, older, who also steps inside as if invited and says, "Balin at your service!"

Flustered, Bilbo manages a "Thank you!" The narrator immediately informs us that this "was not the correct thing to say".

True, the narrator hurries to excuse Bilbo's faux pas by noting that the hobbit was knocked off his game by Balin's worrisome opening remark: "I see they have begun to arrive already." They? What does the dwarf mean by they? However, it is significant that the narrator even gently reprimands Bilbo for so subtle a lapse in courtesy (for saying "Thank you!" at an uncustomary moment), and right when Bilbo is demonstrating a level of hospitality far above the ordinary (welcoming in a second total stranger for afternoon tea). The gentle reprimand signals readers living in a less mannerly age that we are visitors in a realm of neatly starched, old-fashioned manners, one very different from our own.

This emphasis on good manners and correct form will recur throughout the novel in moments that often provide comic relief, though rarely in a way to suggest that they are inherently ridiculous. In the next paragraph, for instance, Bilbo has collected himself and is leading Balin to the table when the hobbit is suddenly struck by "a horrible thought that the cakes might run short, and then he—as the host: he knew his duty and stuck to it however painful—he might have to go without." The humor here is at Bilbo's expense, of course. A well-padded hobbit in the habit of eating six meals a day probably could do with the horror of a missed meal now and then, particularly cakes at afternoon tea. But it's Bilbo's inflated sense of impending deprivation that is being poked, not his decision to do his duty as a good host and go without. Although this bit of self-sacrifice is on a decidedly unheroic scale, he *is* putting others first, and the practice of doing so will find a heroic outlet as the novel progresses.

The Deal with Bombadil

Notice, too, the effort involved in being hospitable, as well as the role that duty and cultural expectation plays. Bilbo, for all his virtues, isn't effortlessly good. There actually is a character of wholly natural virtue in Middle-Earth, one who is on stage only briefly (in *The Fellowship of the Ring*). His name is Tom Bombadil, and he's a rather mysterious figure, neither man nor dwarf, elf nor hobbit. He seems, in fact, to be in a category with a single member: himself. Apparently older than the first man, he was around to witness "the first raindrop and the first acorn", and knew "the dark under the stars when it was fearless—before the Dark Lord came from Outside"[4] (a reference to the rebellion and fall of Melkor, one of the Ainur, who are akin to high angelic beings who existed before the creation of Earth). Bombadil is ancient, powerful, magnanimous, whimsical, and—unlike any other character in the novel—utterly fearless. Twice he comes to the rescue of Frodo and his fellow hobbits.

There has been plenty of conjecture about what Tolkien meant to convey in the curious figure of Tom Bombadil. Given that he is borrowed from Tolkien's earlier imaginative writings,[5] and given Tolkien's stated distaste for allegory, it's unlikely Bombadil is meant to represent some single thing or idea. We also have Tolkien's explicit remark that "there must be some enigmas" and "Tom Bombadil is one (intentionally)",[6] so it would be misguided to search for too neat an explanation for this character. With all of those qualifications on the table, however, we would like to suggest one possible way of regarding him: Tom Bombadil is, among other things, an exercise in one of the great theological what-ifs—what if God had created a species of flesh and blood, made in his image, but one that never reached for the forbidden fruit, never sinned, never fell? Would such a person be a naïve, insipid figure of innocence? No, because goodness does not require evil to complete it. Instead, as an intimate friend and steward of the Creator, he would be far more likely to develop something of the verve and fearless authority—the joyful exuberance, the playfulness, and magnanimity—of a Tom Bombadil.

Consider how he relates to the One Ring. Normally the ring turns its wearer invisible and begins to gradually corrupt him. There are hints that magically powerful characters need not become invisible while wearing it (for example, Sauron doesn't seem to be invisible before Aragorn's ancestor Isildur cuts the ring from his finger in battle). Also, some characters, such as the black riders who chase Frodo and his companions in *The Lord of the Rings*, can see a person who is wearing the ring. But there are no characters other than Tom Bombadil who appear to be immune to all of its effects, including its corrupting power—not good-hearted

Bilbo, not sacrificial Frodo, not humble Sam Gamgee, not even the noble characters Gandalf, Aragorn, and Galadriel.

But Tom Bombadil is different. He can see a person who is wearing the ring. He is not made invisible when he himself wears the ring. And he is so immune to the ring's charms that, as Gandalf explains to the Council at Rivendell, he would misplace it if entrusted with it. It holds all of the awe for him that a cheap plastic trinket might hold for a child more interested in playing with dogs and chasing birds. In essence, Tom Bombadil appears to be naturally good, much as we can imagine man would be if he hadn't fallen and had continued long in the habit of obedient communion with his maker.

In contrast, Bilbo and all of the other hobbits, dwarves, elves, and men of Middle-Earth seem to struggle with temptation and the potentially corrupting effects of the One Ring, and to struggle in more or less the same way that human beings of our world struggle with temptation. As Tolkien put it in one of his letters, "I have not made any of the peoples on the 'right' side, Hobbits, Rohirrim, Men of Dale or of Gondor, any better than men have been or are, or can be. Mine is not an 'imaginary' world, but an imaginary historical moment on 'Middle-earth' which is our habitation."[7]

It's true that Bilbo is made of deceptively sturdy stuff—morally and constitutionally—so the One Ring he later possesses works only very slowly on him. But it does work. To use the language of theology again, Bilbo is fallen. He is a creature made in the image of God and drawn by that original nature and common grace toward acts and impulses of profound goodness. But in the unexpected party at the beginning of the novel, and later in the story as well, the clear suggestion is that only through training and cultural expectations—through attention to what is and isn't *proper behavior*—is he able to rise to acts of magnanimous and even courageous hospitality. In the first event, Bilbo's good breeding sufficiently fortifies him to welcome in a troupe of strange dwarves, commit to going without teatime cakes if necessary, serve his unexpected guests a veritable feast, and, before it's all over, sign a contract for adventure.

Of Hippies and Hobbits

Sealing the contract requires diplomatic maneuvering on Gandalf's part but also a good deal of humility from Bilbo, who has to put up with being ordered about a lot by his guests, particularly Thorin, who, as royalty, is used to being waited on. It also requires a willingness to trust, a measure of precision (with Bilbo rightly insisting that the expectations be laid out "all plain and clear"[8]), and last and seemingly least, a measure of punctuality. This latter element is only seemingly least because punctuality is a cultural feature highly correlated with economic development. It's partly a proxy for things like the presence of accurate clocks and functional roads, but also for a due commitment to precision and respect for other people's time. Development economists have found that if a culture's members cannot be bothered to show up at something when and where they say they will, that culture rarely pulls itself out of extreme poverty.[9] Now, if you have taken a college anthropology course with a professor who thinks eighteenth-century philosopher Jean-Jacques Rousseau's fantasy of the noble savage is as real as garden soil, then you have been exposed to the common romantic prejudice against precision, neatly arranged meeting times, and the like. These, we are told, are the tyrannical bindings of civilized man, without which he might at last find his way back to his inner child and rejoice "undisguised and naked".[10] If we're ever going to thrive, in other words, we need to permanently relax and get on "island time". Tolkien was not of this mindset, nor did he share much in common with that '60s subculture which quickly embraced Middle-Earth: the hippies.

This brings us round to one of the great ironies of Tolkien's rise to prominence in the United States. *The Hobbit* made a respectable run in America upon its initial release, and *The Lord of the Rings* sold steadily in hardback during the 1950s. But it was the release of economical American paperback editions (first an unauthorized version, then an authorized one) that marked the beginning of its explosive popularity. That buying phenomenon was centered on American college campuses in the midst of the counterculture revolution, and the hippies, in particular, "really dug" Middle-Earth. (The hobbits, after all, were even into mushrooms, for goodness' sake!)

If one were to go just on these data points, it would be easy to conclude that Tolkien's imaginative world was the literary correlative of the whole countercultural phenomenon. "Indeed," Bradley Birzer comments, "Tolkien's association with the youth rebellion of that era is one reason why with a few notable exceptions, several generations of academics have viewed Tolkien's mythology as little more than a psychedelic 'sword and sorcery' story."[11] But this would be to fixate on the points of contact and miss the differences. William Ratliff and Charles Flinn make the point in their 1968 essay "The Hobbit and the Hippie":

> Both Professor Tolkien and the hippies reject (1) the "rationalist progressive" view of history as a series of distinct improvements over the past and (2) the materialist belief that matter is the ultimate determinant of all things.... Here is a kinship which might make a hippie feel at ease in the world of *The Lord of the Rings*. Yet even here the paradox remains just below the surface. For instance, the great respect for the past found in the trilogy has already been noted, and it is this respect which in part supports the rejection of the idea of continual progress. For the hippies, however, continual progress is denied because it conflicts with the exaltation of undifferentiated experience and with the state more usually associated with madness.[12]

Ratliff and Flinn further note that the happy, uncluttered life of Shire hobbits is the fruit of the Shire's "respect for quiet and good order which would be repelled by the frenetic behavior and art of the Hashbury community". Another difference: "It is surprising that the hippies have not noticed the esteem for age and for ancestors which is *so* characteristic of the inhabitants of the Shire."[13]

Then and Now

Hippies are mostly a thing of the past, and yet much of their outlook has made its way into the wider culture. Like hippies, and unlike Mr. Baggins and Mr. Tolkien, our age takes a generally dim view of custom, formality, and "good breeding". Some view such things merely as a way for the rich and well-connected to signal their exclusivity; others view it as a mask on the hairless apes we all pretend not to be—the superego trying to mask the Freudian id, that raw animal heart cribbed and cabined by the many inauthentic courtesies of "civilized" society. Some arrive at this outlook by following in the train of philosophers like Rousseau or John Dewey. Others do so by absorbing the works of various anti-traditional poets, literary novelists, painters, and composers. But most come to the attitude just by breathing in the air of the times, reflexively spurning formal manners and custom because they're associated with being "stiff", "unnatural", and "inauthentic". The end result is a mass culture drastically less formal than the Western world of half a century ago, and far less formal than most societies in ages past, including many technologically undeveloped ones.

Ken Myers suggests that this "shift toward informality, toward the abandonment of proprieties, is not, as many assume, simply a meaningless evolution of style", but instead is "deeply tied to suspicions about authority and about metaphysical hierarchy,... an expression of our culture's valuing of individualism and moral autonomy."[14] John McWhorter boils down the new outlook in his 2003 book *Doing Our Own Thing*: "At such a cultural moment, formality becomes repressed, boring, unreflective, and even suspect, while Doing Your Own Thing is genuine, healthy, engaged, and even urgent."[15]

In a similar vein, *Real Presences*, a beautiful work of literary theory by George Steiner, notes that the terms *civility* and *courtesy* have fallen into disrepair. Steiner sees the first term as "a charged word whose former strength has largely left us", and the second as so impoverished that he feels compelled to retreat to an ancestral word, *cortesia*. According to Steiner, this degraded view of custom and courtesy, far from being merely cosmetic, threatens our capacity to sustain culture and forge authentic connections with other people and peoples.[16] The loss of courtesy in the older and richer sense of the term signals a growing inability to connect with anyone but our own increasingly limited selves.

To grasp the full measure of the cultural shift, we can reach back into the Hebraic tributary of Western civilization and consider how lavishly the patriarch Abraham welcomed the three strangers, killing for them the fatted calf; or how a bit later in the book of Genesis, his nephew Lot took in two of them and was willing to protect them from the Sodomites outside his door, even at the expense of his own family. Would that happen today? It's certainly far less likely. And our tendency—however prudent—to bar our doors against strangers stands in stark counterpoint to a virtue essential to free societies: the capacity to be open enough to "the other" to begin building trusting relationships beyond family and clan—the capacity, in other words, to be hospitable to the strange and different.

The change is our loss, in more ways than we might expect. In welcoming strangers, Abraham and Lot entertained angels unawares.

From ancient Canaan, fast-forward to Christendom and a passage from Shakespeare's *Hamlet*. The ghost of King Hamlet has just confronted

Prince Hamlet. The prince's friend Horatio arrives a moment later and, before he and Hamlet can exchange more than a few words, the voice of the ghost booms from under the earth, demanding that they keep secret the ghostly visitation. Hearing the voice, Horatio cries, "O day and night, but this is wondrous strange!" Hamlet then replies, in words often quoted, "And therefore as a stranger give it welcome. / There are more things in heaven and earth, Horatio, / Than are dreamt of in your philosophy" (1.5.166–67).

The lines are often enlisted against an arid rationalism that makes no room for the transcendent, but notice something else in the exchange: Hamlet views hospitality to strangers as such a fixed cultural expectation that he uses it as an assumed premise when urging Horatio to welcome the strange and wondrous:

Implicit Major Premise: One should be open and welcoming to strangers.
Minor Premise: The ghostly visitation is a kind of stranger.
Conclusion: One should be open and welcoming to the ghostly visitation.

In a contemporary context, the argument wouldn't even make sense. *Give it welcome "as a stranger"? You mean talk to it through a door intercom? You mean keep moving down the sidewalk and try not to make eye contact?*[17]

Aurelie Hagstrom explores the link between hospitality and religion in her essay "Christian Hospitality in the Intellectual Community". There she characterizes Christian hospitality as "self-giving, embodying a way of being and thinking about the 'other' or the 'stranger' ", grounded in "the basic conviction that in welcoming others we are also welcoming God, and by welcoming God we are participating in God's reconciling love for the world, manifest in God's triune nature."[18]

The early twentieth-century English writer G. K. Chesterton, regarded as a key influence on Tolkien and C. S. Lewis, touches on these matters. In his indispensable book *Orthodoxy*, in the chapter "The Ethics of Elfland", Chesterton urges us to take a hospitable attitude toward tradition and inherited cultural riches, insisting that democracy, rightly understood, embraces the wise and respected voices of the past. "Tradition means giving votes to the most obscure of all classes, our ancestors", he writes. "It is the democracy of the dead. Tradition refuses to submit to the small and arrogant oligarchy of those who merely happen to be walking about."[19]

Chesterton then connects this openness toward the riches of the past with a capacity for welcoming in the strange and wondrous: "We need this life of practical romance; the combination of something that is strange with something that is secure. We need so to view the world as to combine an idea of wonder and an idea of welcome."[20] Chesterton says he initially thought he was developing something new in all this, an innovative "heresy", but then "when I had put the last touches to it", he discovered that it was Christian orthodoxy—what he refers to in the book's subtitle as "the romance of faith".[21]

A natural objection to our connecting this "romance of faith" to Middle-Earth is that there is no religion in the Shire. How could the "romance" of the Christian faith have anything to do with Bilbo's reasons for being hospitable and courteous?[22] But if we dig a bit, we find that the objection misses Tolkien's method. In an undated letter written about 1951, Tolkien explained that he found the mythical world of King Arthur artistically compromised by the fact that "it is involved in, and explicitly contains the Christian religion", a shortcoming "that seems to me fatal". This is a puzzling remark coming from a deeply religious Catholic; but then Tolkien goes on to say that he believed "myth and fairy-story" function best when they "reflect and contain in solution elements of moral and religious truth (or error), but not explicit, not in the known form of the primary 'real' world".[23]

A couple of years later, in a letter to a family friend, Father Robert Murray, S.J., Tolkien elaborated on the point with regard to *The Hobbit*'s sequel. "*The Lord of the Rings* is of course a fundamentally religious and Catholic work; unconsciously so at first, but consciously in the revision", he wrote. "That is why I have not put in, or have cut out, practically all references to anything like 'religion,' to cults or practices, in the imaginary world. For the religious element is absorbed into the story and the symbolism."[24]

This is perhaps easiest to see with something like the inspirational connection between the Virgin Mary and the Lady Galadriel, a connection Father Murray mentioned to Tolkien and that Tolkien confirmed. But as Tolkien also made plain in that exchange, the religious element isn't just to be found at this or that point in the story, or in this or that character. It's part of the warp and woof of his imaginative creation. This is why we can say without overreaching that the cluster of mores that govern and guide the most courteous figures in *The Hobbit* and *The*

Lord of the Rings, including the master of Bag End, have as their source a theological vision of man and society.[25]

The Lowly among the Lowlifes

The Hobbit isn't all bows and thank-yous and at-your-services, of course. If we require a sharp contrast to a culture of courtesy and hospitality, we aren't made to wait long. The day after the impromptu tea party, Bilbo wakes to find the dwarves departed from his home. Gandalf soon appears and scolds him for neglecting to dust his mantle and so discover the note with the 11 A.M. meeting time in the town of Bree. The master of Bag End then rushes out the door to join the company, and they are quickly on their way—through the Shire, over the river, and into the Lone-lands beyond.

Later we'll find evidence of Tolkien's admiration for honorable members of the lower class as well as evidence that Tolkien was acutely aware of how the socially powerful often exploit those beneath them. But in the early stages of Bilbo's adventures, the "lower-class" characters he meets are lowlifes, plain and simple, as inhospitable as they come.

The first of these are William, Bert, and Tom. On the surface they are rather exotic figures—giant trolls who must avoid the sun lest it turn them to stone. But under this fantastic skin lives what are basically three examples of a stock English character, the sort of ruffian who tosses around terms like "blimey", "copped", "shut yer mouth", and "lummee if I know", a highwayman who would as soon smash your nose as look at you.

William, Bert, and Tom aren't interested in an honest day's work even if one were offered them with good pay. They create nothing, build nothing, trade nothing for nothing. They are only interested in stealing, killing, eating, and—perhaps, when full enough and bored enough—stashing away the leftover spoils. Such fellows are the opposite of the conscientious Mr. Baggins or the enterprising dwarves and, to dip into the economic history of the real world for a moment, are very different from the thrifty craftsmen and merchant classes of the Middle Ages and Renaissance. These were the bourgeois who worked their way up from poverty and created the middle class Tolkien was born into (more on this historical process in the next chapter), who for all of their flaws had an almost overdeveloped commitment to the rule of law and property rights (many of them having only recently acquired property and not wishing it stolen away by robbers operating either above or beneath the law). The ruffian trolls who are on the verge of eating Bilbo and his friends are about as far from such bourgeois virtues as it's possible to be. They have only contempt for the rule of law, no interest in hard work, and are in such short supply of either trust or the spirit of cooperation that Gandalf can easily set them brawling.[26]

At the troll camp, Bilbo and his friends survive this small band of lowlifes (small in number, that is) and soon are enjoying the unmatched hospitality of Rivendell and the Last Homely House, with its high regard for both tradition and hospitality.[27] But when they make their way into the Misty Mountains, they're seized by a whole kingdom of lowlifes—the goblins—and taken underground.

Like modern industrial societies (both free and unfree), the goblins are enamored of machinery. Unfortunately, all of their mechanical creativity seems to be in the service of plundering and destroying. Goblins, we learn, "make no beautiful things", though "axes, swords, daggers, pickaxes, tongs, and also instruments of torture, they make very well, or get other people to make to their design, prisoners and slaves that have to work till they die for want of air and light."[28] Here we have the first glimpse of a theme that comes into clearer focus in *The Lord of the Rings* and elsewhere in Tolkien's Middle-Earth writings—the author's exploration of a dark, destructive artifice, a disenchanted one lacking reverence for the created order. But Tolkien, in politically incorrect fashion, bundles the mechanical villainy of the goblins with the vices you might find excoriated in late nineteenth-century boys' novels—goblins are "untidy and dirty", despising "the orderly and prosperous", delighting in "not working with their hands more than they could help."[29] It's just one more instance of Tolkien's shameless support for the opposite characteristics—hard work, cleanliness, orderliness, and the like.

Riddles and a Ring

The goblins, for all their degeneracy, have nothing on the character Bilbo meets after he is separated from the rest of the company and knocked unconscious deep underground. When he awakes in the darkness and wanders deeper into the cavern maze, he encounters a menacing creature named Gollum, a small figure who lives on the little island of an underground lake where not even the goblins dare venture. Gollum is about the size of Bilbo, but leaner and ruthless; and when he encounters the hobbit, he doesn't courteously offer to aid the poor lost traveler. Instead, he insists the two play a riddling game. If Bilbo wins, the slimy creature has to show Bilbo the way out. If Gollum wins, he gets to eat Bilbo.

What we have, then, is another contract.

For a while the riddle contest progresses smoothly. Bilbo answers several of Gollum's riddles, and poses a few hard ones himself. But soon Gollum, growing hungry and weary of the game, slides off of his little boat and comes right up to the hobbit. In this moment of danger Bilbo thrusts his hands into his pocket, feels something unfamiliar, and thinks aloud, "What have I got in my pocket?" Gollum mistakes the comment for the next riddle in the contest; and Bilbo, unable to think of anything else, sticks by the question over Gollum's protest that it isn't a proper riddle.

Bilbo isn't playing fair. But that's understandable, isn't it? After all, he's engaged in a life-or-death battle of wits, and the slimy, murderous fiend is inching toward him!

Curiously, neither the author nor the narrator ever affirms Bilbo's little trick; instead, it's treated as an embarrassment in our hero's ledger of deeds. First, Tolkien carefully constructs the scene so as to make clear that his generally honest little hero poses the "tricksy" pseudoriddle only by accident, and not as a deliberate attempt to insert an improper question into the riddle game. Then, when Bilbo has won the contest, the narrator feels the need to go on record as noting that "the riddle-game was sacred and of immense antiquity, and ... that last question had not been a genuine riddle according to the ancient laws."[30]

And that's not even the end of the matter. Later, in the prologue of *The Lord of the Rings*, the narrator is still fussing over the impropriety of Bilbo's final riddle question. He says, "The Authorities, it is true, differ whether this last question was a mere 'question' and not a 'riddle' according to the strict rules of the Game; but all agree that, after accepting it and trying to guess the answer, Gollum was bound by his promise."

What we have is a narrator so committed to custom, propriety, and honor that he cannot easily conclude that Bilbo has every right to cheat at a game in order to stop an evil enemy from literally eating him. Gollum is a lowlife, yes, and a dangerous one at that; but the suggestion is that by asking an improper riddle, Bilbo has, at least in some small measure, lowered himself to Gollum's level.

Here, then, is a conservatism that the postmodern mind, with its easy disdain for rules and *the dead hand of tradition*, finds hard to grasp. And, yes, there's surely some daylight between the punctilious narrative voice and Tolkien himself. But nothing that follows in the plot suggests that having high scruples is inherently foolish, only that it must be matured by a due regard for other moral demands and the order of grace.

Eagles, Elves, and a Bear

After Bilbo escapes from Gollum and the goblin caves, he catches up with the rest of the company. Soon Bilbo, Gandalf, and the dwarves are rushing to escape the wolves and goblins; but hurry as they might, they cannot escape their enemies. Surrounded and outnumbered, they're rescued in the very nick of time by the great eagles, who lift them out of the trees and carry them to the eyrie.

This handy bit of rescue work, the narrative makes clear, should not be taken for granted. Great eagles are not in the habit of helping dwarves. However, it seems that Gandalf once did the leader of these eagles a great favor: winning crucial allies for himself and his companions.

The next morning, when good-byes are said, Gandalf strengthens the relationship with his careful attention to customary formalities:

> "Farewell!" they cried, "wherever you fare, till your eyries receive you at the journey's end!" That is the polite thing to say among eagles.
>
> "May the wind under wings bear you where the sun sails and the moon walks," answered Gandalf, who knew the correct reply.
>
> And so they parted.[31]

Gandalf's good breeding—his ability to assist other creatures very different from himself and employ their own forms of courtesy—is crucial to the success of the company's whole interlude with the eagles.

The pattern is repeated at the house of Beorn, "a very great person" and "a skin-changer", a great bear of a man who takes the shape of an actual bear by night. He is "kind enough if humored", Gandalf warns the company as they approach the man's estate, but he is also easily angered and "appalling when he is angry".[32] Interestingly, Beorn can also spot an empty formality a mile away.

In modern parlance, we would call Beorn an introvert, and a curmudgeonly one at that. Keenly aware of this fact, Gandalf has his companions appear two or three at a time at Beorn's gate so as not to overwhelm him by showing up all at once—presumably explaining, incidentally, the piecemeal arrival of Thorin's company at Bag End at the beginning of the novel. Now Bilbo finds himself on the other end of things—and uncomfortably so, for Beorn is a good deal less polite than Bilbo and a great deal more feared by the dwarves. Happily, thanks to Gandalf's diplomatic skills, Beorn eventually does welcome the group into his home and even provides them a sumptuous feast.

After a couple of days of care and feeding, he sees them off in high style, with good advice, strong ponies, and enough food to last them weeks—"nuts, flour, sealed jars of dried fruits, and red earthenware pots of honey, and twice-baked cakes that would keep good a long time." He makes one demand: the travelers must send his ponies back when they reach the edge of Mirkwood. Four days later, however, when the company reaches the eves of Mirkwood, the dwarves are sorely tempted to take the ponies on into the forest with them. Only Gandalf's intercession saves them from such foolishness:

> Beorn is not far off as you seem to think, and you had better keep your promises anyway, for he is a bad enemy. M. Baggins' eyes are sharper than yours, if you have not seen each night after dark a great bear going along with us or sitting far off in the moon watching our camps. Not only to guard you and guide you, but to keep an eye on the ponies too. Beorn may be your friend, but he loves his animals as his children. You do not guess what kindness he has shown you in letting dwarves ride them so far and so fast, nor what would happen to you, if you tried to take them into the forest.[33]

Gandalf's argument has three main elements. One is an appeal to fear: if the dwarves don't keep their word by sending the ponies back, Beorn will exact justice from them. Another is an appeal to honor and morality: "You had better keep your promises anyway." Curiously, the wizard pivots quickly off of this *ought* argument and back to an appeal to their self-interest—"for he is a bad enemy".

The third argument emphasizes the great kindness Beorn has shown in letting the dwarves borrow his ponies in the first place. It's a moral plea like the second argument, with the emphasis on how one should behave toward a generous friend. And just as Gandalf did with the previous *ought* argument, he quickly circles back to the self-interest argument in order to cinch the case: "You do not guess ... what would happen to you, if you tried to take them into the forest."

This is significant. The fact that the ponies are Beorn's rather than theirs, and that they agreed to send them back, ought to be reason enough for them to comply, never mind their apparent need for the ponies. But Gandalf—and, we suggest, Tolkien—understood that human nature (here, dwarvish human nature) is only occasionally constrained by conscience alone. The dwarves, keep in mind, are not professional horse thieves or habitual double-crossers. They're generally law-abiding and respectable figures. But under the circumstances, it's easy for them to think about the great agricultural wealth that Beorn possesses, set that wealth against their extreme need for pack animals, and then conclude that surely a bit of impromptu wealth redistribution at the edge of Mirkwood is in order. What stops them from acting on this impulse, it seems, isn't conscience but rather the assurance of swift justice.

Beorn has already shown that he has little compunction about fulfilling government's role of bringing criminals to justice, having beheaded a goblin and skinned a warg for having tried to hunt down and slaughter Gandalf and his companions. It's unlikely such a man would have any compunction about meting out justice were his own animals wrongly endangered—animals who are not only his rightful property, Gandalf points out, but loved "as his children".

The scene, while interesting in its own right, also has winding through it a cord of themes that tie directly into the nature of thriving commercial societies, whether pre- or postindustrial. The first is that a contract (here the agreement to borrow and then send back the ponies) is more than a mere statement of current preference; it is a morally binding commitment. The second is that the arm of justice is needed to enforce contracts. The third is that property rights, while not unconditional, are sacred and not to be violated on a whim or rationalized away.

This latter point is nuanced and reinforced after the dwarves are captured by the Elvenking Thranduil deep inside Mirkwood forest, and Bilbo is forced to steal food while he searches for a way to free his companions. He is never rebuked for this theft, either by Gandalf or the author, which is in keeping with the traditional Christian teaching that property rights are not unconditional but may yield, in an emergency, to higher moral demands, such as the right to life.

That being said, later in the adventure, after the Elvenking and the dwarves have buried the hatchet, Bilbo is feeling guilty for all of the food and drink he pilfered from the king when he was trapped in his palace, so he decides to make it up by offering him a gift from some of the riches he has won in the course of his adventure. When he has to explain the proffered gift to the surprised king, he tells him that "some little return should be made for your, er, hospitality."[34] The magnanimity here is all on Bilbo's side, since what he's characterizing as hospitality was really a deep suspicion that led the elf king to toss the woebegone company into his dungeons, all but forcing Bilbo to steal food in order to avoid starvation while he searched for a means of escape for him and his friends.

Notice how punctilious Bilbo is in his view of property rights. Hardly anyone would fault Bilbo for figuring it was really Thranduil who owed Bilbo for imprisoning the hobbit's innocent companions. But our hobbit hero doesn't think like this, because we're inside a narrative with a very high view of property rights. And as if to make sure we do not miss the point by imagining that Bilbo is behaving foolishly here, Tolkien has the Elvenking sincerely praise the hobbit as "Bilbo the Magnificent!" gravely adding, "I name you elf-friend and blessed."[35]

Interestingly, of the words *property*, *proper*, and *propriety* all derive from the Latin word *proprietas*: having to do with property, ownership, propriety, appropriateness. The word reaches back still further to a Greek term carrying the sense of "one's own, special". We have in this a semantic-archeological insight into Western culture; this culture, the first to create institutions of capital accumulation open and stable enough to create a large middle class, is also one that has long seen a close connection between property and propriety.

So what is the larger connection of all this to Tolkien's vision of the free society? Just this: it might seem that nowadays every mainstream view of governance energetically supports property rights, the binding nature of contracts, and a due emphasis on the government's role in punishing the criminals who would violate them. But this isn't the case. Many on the left would prefer to erode property rights and the force of contracts, justifying these wrongs in the name of wealth redistribution.

In the twentieth century, this "progressive" view ushered in highly "progressive" income taxes (taking more than 90 percent of upper-income earnings in some cases), created central banks with the power to print money and control interest rates, expanded the jurisdiction of the state over wide swaths of civil society, dominated even the private sanctum of home loans and ownership (contributing mightily to the 2008 financial crisis[36])—and seemed to offer a political answer to every question. In both the United States and Tolkien's England, elites in both major political parties now seem to take the progressivist collusion of big government and big business for granted.

Tolkien saw much of this. During his career, the Labor Party in the United Kingdom was busy nationalizing whole industries, including, most fatefully, health care. Behind these trends was a view of property rights not as a sacred human right, but as manufactured, granted or withheld depending on the whims of those in power at any given moment. And what we have in *The Hobbit*'s controversy over whether to send the ponies back, and then later in Bilbo's insistence on compensating the Elvenking for his property, are a pair of thumbnail-sized rebukes to that whole morally slipshod vision of property and society.

And as we'll see, the issues of property and propriety, courtesy and curmudgeonliness, rights and restitution, grievances and grace, are raised to a fever pitch in the final stage of Bilbo's adventure, leading to a tragic fall but also to a moment of recognition, redemption, and reconciliation.

Chapter 3

The Lonely Mountain versus the Market

In Bilbo's adventures to this point, we have encountered a host of things that underscore Tolkien's commitment to the free society. But it's only after Bilbo has rescued his friends from the elven prison and ridden a barrel down the Forest River that we arrive at an economy reminiscent of capitalism, and the portrait is less than flattering. Although Lake-town and its trading neighbors are muddling along decently enough, there are three prominent characters in this stretch of the novel that seem to illustrate the greedy, destructive side of capitalism: Thorin Oakenshield (at his worst); the money-grubbing Master of Lake-town; and the plundering, aristocratic dragon Smaug. In all of this is illustrated an old truth affirmed by conservatives but emphasized with a drumbeat regularity by those on the left, namely, that—whether in the age of slavery, serfdom, or industrialism—members of the powerful and privileged classes regularly have exploited those beneath them. The question is this: Does *The Hobbit* go further than this truism in its critique of what we might call *capitalist man*? That is, did Tolkien, like many artists, have only disdain for business and enterprise?

All Wet

Tolkien apparently had little direct knowledge of the business world, having lost his bank manager father to rheumatic fever when he was four and having spent his own professional life in academia. Nevertheless, an attentive look at the final third of *The Hobbit* suggests he was far from adopting a simplistic view of either business or markets.

Recall that by chapter 9 of the novel, the Elvenking has locked the thirteen dwarves away in his underground prison until they agree to tell him why they were trespassing in his forest. But the dwarves' leader, Thorin, refuses to talk, figuring that if he tells about the treasure he hopes to recover from the dragon, the Elvenking will insist on a share of it as ransom for their freedom. Bilbo, for his part, realizes that Thorin is stubborn enough to hold out until they have forgotten what the sun even looks like. He takes matters into his own hands, and with the help of the invisibility ring, he finds a daring means of freeing his companions. Significantly, it depends on the fact that the woodland elves and the men of Lake-town trade with each other.[1]

Barrels arrive full at the Elvenking's palace and are often sent back downriver to Lake-town mostly empty. It is in these that Bilbo secretly stows his thirteen companions, who are then dropped one after another through a trapdoor into an underground watercourse. After the last one is pushed through the door, Bilbo grabs onto an empty barrel as it's shoved through the opening.[2]

After a night and a day of bobbing downstream, first separately and then bound together in a raft of barrels, the company is finally towed round a "high shoulder of rock into the little bay of Lake-town."[3]

A chilled and sniffling Bilbo frees his companions from their barrels, and then four of their number—Fili, Kili, Thorin, and Bilbo—enter the town and are led to a great hall, where Thorin promptly exclaims, "I am Thorin, son of Thrain son of Thror King under the mountain! I return!"[4]

At this, the men and elves at feast jump to their feet. The elves, shocked to see the prisoners standing before them free, insist that these strangers to the town are really only so many "wandering vagabond dwarves" escaped from their king's dungeon, imprisoned for sneaking through their woods. The Master of Lake-town doesn't want to get crosswise of the Elvenking, and doubts Thorin's claim of royal lineage, so he's ready to accommodate the elves' demands. But the matter is quickly taken out of his hands by the populace, who long have sung about a prophecy of a dwarf king who returns to the Lonely Mountain, routs the dragon, and ushers in a time when the rivers "golden run", the streams "in gladness", and "all sorrows fail".[5]

In the citizens and Master of Lake-town, we see a delicious orchestration of opposites.[6] On one side is the naïve and bubbleheaded populace, who accept Thorin as the fulfillment of the old prophecy without question. They quickly turn his arrival into what the Master of Lake-town fears is an interminable celebration, never mind the little matter of how a ragtag band of dwarves is going to vanquish a dragon. On the other side is the Master, shrewd but imaginatively stunted, a small-souled individual who cares only about profit and loss, about finding the smart political calculation. He's unable to even entertain the possibility that Thorin really is the grandson of the King Under the Mountain, or that this figure truly intends to reclaim his kingdom from the dragon Smaug. Ultimately, then, what we have is a town filled with people who, for either of two reasons, have a poor grasp on reality. The naïve side lacks reason and prudence. The other lacks faith and imagination, which leaves him with a stunted reason of a different kind, one operable only within the narrow range of ordinary experience, and unfit for the extraordinary.[7]

Given all this, how have the Master and the citizens managed to live in peace with their neighbors and make a decent go of things under the shadow of the dragon? The explanation is twofold. First, the citizens of Lake-town are generous and hospitable. Their gullibility is the excessive form of their virtuous capacity for trust. This capacity for trust has made it possible for them to build a cooperative trading relationship (as opposed to an estranged or warring relationship) with the elves up the Forest River and with others down the Running River.

Another reason the town has been able to muddle along is that, to echo the scoffers mentioned in the Second Letter of Peter, "things have continued as they were"[8] for time out of mind. The Master of Lake-town hasn't been forced to confront anything that transcends his everyday round of law and order, tax and trade, profit and loss. His strengths have suited such times and nicely complemented the imprudence of the populace. The Master, if you will, has kept the rafts running on time[9] in an ordinary time, ably directing into economically useful channels the often-impulsive townsfolk. Where he fails is in the extraordinary time, when the uncanny intrudes upon the realm of what supposedly can and can't happen. In such a moment, certain powers and impulses are unleashed over which he has no control—either in others or, ultimately, in himself.

The Moral Desolation of Smaug

Turn now to Bilbo and the dwarves. Having feasted and mended, the company begins the final leg of their journey. At the end of it lies the central monster of the novel, Smaug the dragon. When the company climbs the mountain and Bilbo tiptoes down the secret tunnel to confront the serpent for the first time, we quickly discover that this is a different breed of monster from the trolls and goblins who vexed Bilbo and his friends on the first half of their journey. As Shippey comments, Smaug "talks like a twentieth-century Englishman, but one very definitely from the upper class, not the bourgeoisie at all." Specifically, the dragon's manner of speech involves "a kind of elaborate politeness, even circumlocution, of course totally insincere (as is often the case with upper-class English), but insidious and hard to counter."[10] From there Shippey goes into various other ways the dragon speaks in the language of the modern English aristocracy, complete with a smothering disdain for the bourgeois hobbit, the hobbit's thirteen companions, and the ordinary folk of Lake-town. Hal Colebatch puts it succinctly: "He sounds like a testy colonel or perhaps like the Duke of Edinburgh dealing with a particularly stupid journalist."[11]

Smaug's aristocratic snobbery also calls to mind Michael Novak's historical analysis of the rise of capitalism, which he defines in terms of property rights, rule of law, stable financial institutions, and economic freedom. As Novak explains, the position of the aristocratic class was once unassailable. But in the Middle Ages bourgeois craftsmen and merchants began to challenge the aristocracy's monopoly on wealth—a process that began with the monasteries and city-states of northern Italy, progressed to England and the Netherlands, and eventually spread through much of Western Europe. The aristocracy viewed these upstart capitalists with disdain—a disdain Novak characterizes as a kind of Gnostic revulsion against the quotidian:

> A beautiful, beautiful wood work, or cutlery, or a millinery—ladies hats, and great wines, great cheeses—all of these are produced by the bourgeoisie, but the aristocrats had no respect for them and neither did the artist. Western literature is filled with putting down the bourgeoisie, and the artist tends to think of herself or himself as an aristocrat, an aristocrat of the spirit if not by birth, and they dislike the unaesthetic quality of work, and sweat, and discipline that is required to produce a really good wine, a really good cheese, a really good anything.[12]

Notice how Novak contrasts the bourgeois man of commerce with the aristocrat. Set this historical analysis alongside Shippey's description of the aristocratic Smaug, and it becomes clear that the dragon, for all his riches, is thoroughly *anti*capitalist.

Marxist literary critic Jack Zipes misses this, labeling Smaug "the picture-image of the capitalist exploiter".[13] No; the Marxist caricature of the capitalist misses the crucial historical difference between an often unproductive aristocracy and the thrifty and innovative bourgeois entrepreneurs Novak celebrates. Smaug has wealth that could be turned to capital, but he doesn't capitalize it. He sits on it, a contemptuous aristocrat with a smug belief in his own invulnerability. He is a miser rather than an entrepreneur, risking nothing, investing in nothing, clutching everything. The capitalist invests and risks in order to support a business enterprise; the miser hoards his wealth, stuffing it in a mattress, locking it away in a safe, or in Smaug's case, heaping it in a pile and sleeping on it in the dark.

Bilbo manages to steal a single cup from the vast hoard ("stolen" from a thief, keep in mind, in order to return it to its rightful owner). When Smaug awakes and discovers that part of his treasure is missing, he responds in miserly fashion, with "the sort of rage that is only seen when rich folk that have more than they can enjoy suddenly lose something that they have long had but have never before used or wanted."[14]

The cup incident marks Bilbo's first brush with the dragon—a sleeping dragon. When the hobbit returns the following day, he is confronted with a wide awake and seemingly invulnerable Smaug. In that encounter, as with the first, all of the intentional risk taking is on Bilbo's side; yet it is precisely through the dragon's delusional belief in his own invulnerability, and through the hobbit's willingness to cast his bread upon the proverbial waters—by hazarding a second trip down the tunnel—that the aristocrat ultimately will be undone.[15]

Of Bags and Sacks

Before unraveling that fateful conversation between dragon and hobbit, there's another telling contrast worth touching on—that between the relatively unpretentious Bilbo Baggins of Bag End and his next of kin, the Sackville-Bagginses. The latter are grasping in the extreme, brimming with aristocratic pretensions, and burning with a covetous desire for Bilbo's spacious home at Bag End.

Shippey shows how Tolkien, in just these few names, has given us a kind of secret map of English history. First, Shippey notes, in Tolkien's childhood his aunt Jane lived on a Worcestershire farm located on a "Bag End",[16] a more whimsical name for a street with no outlet than the usual "Dead End". A more common alternative to the funereal "dead end" is the term *cul-de-sac*, evoking the interior end of a sack. It sounds very French, but as Shippey further notes, the French actually use the word *impasse* for streets with no outlet. The term *cul-de-sac* was brought into English to give streets with no outlet a sophisticated sound.

But why do we associate French words and phrases with sophistication and class? The answer is hardly obvious if we consider just the present. Today, the English are the ones who still have royalty, not the French. To find the answer, we have to go far back in the history of the British Isles, to the invasion of 1066, the Battle of Hastings, when the Normans of France conquered England. Eventually the aristocratic descendants of these conquerors adopted English as their first language, but not before a host of Old French words came in with this new nobility and transformed English. Today, all these centuries later, we still tend to associate this class of French-derived words with sophistication over and against the class of English words that have their roots in pre-Norman Old English.

This is why it sounds right to our ears when Bilbo's cousins, with their pretensions to sophistication, Frenchify the sturdy name *Baggins* by tacking *Sackville* on the front of it. *Sackville* evokes a French *ville* (villa). It also involves a sly wink from the author at the pretentious term *cul-de-sac*, a point Tolkien punctuates by giving the more down-to-earth Bilbo the thoroughly unpretentious street address of *Bag End* (*bag* deriving from Old Norse, and *end* from Old English).[17]

Now add to all this Bilbo's Took lineage on his mother's side. Their surname is the past tense of *take*, a word (like *bag*) brought into England from the word-hoard of the rough and tumble Norse invaders of the "Dark Ages". That's certainly fitting, since it's his more unconventional Tookish side that allows Bilbo to go from an idle country gentleman to a risk-taking adventurer.

In fact, at the beginning of the novel we meet a Bilbo who is in danger of becoming like a Sackville-Baggins, the stereotypical bourgeoisie with pretensions of aristocratic class and insular to a fault.[18] Fortunately, Gandalf rescues him from such a fate, initiating the character arc we see through the course of the novel. Bilbo moves from the soft, insular, and snobbish to the dynamic, diligent, and open—recovering, in essence, the bourgeois virtues of exertion, competitiveness, and entrepreneurial daring that allowed them to join and grow the middle class in the Middle Ages.

The Bard, the Baggins, and the Vulnerable Invulnerable

Thus it is that a member of the vigorous bourgeoisie eventually confronts the miserly aristocratic villain beneath the Lonely Mountain, a powerful but unproductive dragon who uses his strength merely to exploit others while creating nothing of value for the common good, either tangible or intangible.

Fittingly, the beginning of the end for Smaug comes in the form of a bit of modest folk wisdom Bilbo's father used to repeat: "every worm has his weak spot."[19] Encouraged by the old adage, Bilbo determines to make another trip down the tunnel to see if he can discover Smaug's. This quickly entangles Bilbo in a battle of wit and will with the dragon, no mean challenge given the monster's penetrating intelligence and "overwhelming personality".

Eventually, Bilbo openly remarks that he has always heard that dragons have a vulnerable spot on their undersides. Smaug assures him that his information is antiquated and that "no blade can pierce me". Rather than argue the point, Bilbo ladles on the flattery: "What magnificence to possess a waistcoat of fine diamonds!" Smaug is "absurdly pleased" by the comment and agrees that "it is rare and wonderful indeed" to possess such a waistcoat. He then rolls onto his side so Bilbo can properly admire the glittering armor.

"Dazzlingingly marvelous! Perfect! Flawless! Staggering!" Bilbo exclaims, but to himself he thinks, "Old fool! Why, there is a large patch in the hollow of his left breast as bare as a snail out of its shell!"

But despite his vanity and arrogance, Smaug is shrewd enough to realize that Bilbo and the dwarves must have received help from the townspeople, and flies off to make his displeasure known. Meanwhile, Bilbo—unaware that Smaug is attacking the town—returns to the dwarves and tells them about the vulnerable spot on the belly of the dragon. An old thrush with the power of speech overhears their conversation and rushes to Lake-town, arriving in the midst of the dragon's merciless attack, with Bard down to his final arrow. In that last seemingly hopeless stand, the thrush alights on the bowman's shoulder and tells him to wait for the moonlight and aim "for the hollow of the left breast as he flies and turns above you!"

Up to now in the town's battle with Smaug, Bard has been the epitome of straightforward courage and physical heroism, a heroism consummated in his final desperate stand while his companions melt away in fear all around him. If Smaug is the morally debased aristocrat, Bard is the aristocrat who puts the nobility back in *the nobility*. The narrator describes him as "a descendant in the long line of Girion, Lord of Dale" and then puts the following apostrophe on Bard's lips as the dragon circles for his final descent:

> "Arrow!" said the bowman. "Black arrow! I have saved you to the last. You have never failed me and always I have recovered you. I had you from my father and he from of old. If ever you came from the forges of the true king under the Mountain, go now and speed well!"

The arrow finds it mark, plunging "barb, shaft and feather" into the dragon's belly, and he crashes "down from on high in ruin". The noble Bard's heroic act is crucial and duly celebrated.

But what is Tolkien up to in the curious point and counterpoint he has fashioned between Bilbo and Bard? We're later told that the songs celebrating the dragon's defeat focus around Bard and his black arrow speeding toward its mark; but equally necessary to the moment is the earlier heroism of Bilbo in the tunnel, the modest hobbit probing for his enemy's weakness in a battle of wits.

On the one hand we have the action-hero valor of Bard: noble, dramatic, highly public, and physically impressive. On the other hand, we have the quieter, more measured heroism of Bilbo that is, quite literally, hidden underground rather than seen and celebrated by an adoring public. This humble hero exhibits a capacity for calculated risk that is informed by patience, reason, and due regard for folk wisdom, the very qualities that helped the peasants of medieval Christendom rise from propertyless serfs to owners of their own *burhs*—Old English for "borough, town, fort, stockaded mansion",[20] and the common root from which is derived *bour-geois* and *bur-glar*.[21] In the characters of Bilbo and Bard, then, Tolkien seems to be celebrating both the bourgeois *and* the aristocratic virtues, and contrasting them with these two classes at their worst in the characters of the Sackville-Bagginses and Smaug.

Such evenhandedness is rare among artists and academics. As Novak notes, "In one of the choice ironies of intellectual history, many great scholars and artists of the first rank, themselves children of the middle class, celebrated the virtues of aristocracy in preference to those of their own class."[22] Shippey makes a related point in the specific context of Tolkien and Middle-Earth:

> Tolkien indeed had nothing against middle-class Englishmen, for he was one himself: and, unlike so many of the English-speaking writers of his time, Lawrence, Forster, Woolf, Joyce, he did not feel in any way alienated, nor have any urge to reinvent himself as working-class, non-English, in internal exile, or any other glamorous pose. It is one reason why he has never found any favour with the determinedly cosmopolitan British intelligentsia.[23]

The Dragon Called Greed

We delved into the material above to call attention to Tolkien's conservative view of the bourgeois, a class often maligned, but also to draw a distinction between the isolated, haughty, greedy, miserly aristocratic Smaug and, on the other hand, the open, enterprising, hospitable spirit characteristic of a free economy of enterprising creators. That purpose now brings us back to a virtue explored in the previous chapter and that, with the killing of Smaug, comes again to the fore as crucial to orchestrating a happy ending: the virtue of hospitality.

With the dragon gone, there remains the little matter of determining who gets what from the lavish store of treasure now sitting unguarded in the halls of the Lonely Mountain. The bulk of the treasure came from the dwarf kingdom of Thorin's forefathers. Simple enough. But then come several complicating factors. Thorin views the Arkenstone, the most precious of the treasures of the mountain, as his by inheritance, but he made no such provision when he promised Bilbo first pick in choosing his fourteenth share of the treasure. Bilbo finds the Arkenstone before anyone else and furtively pockets the gem, rationalizing it as his chosen share of the treasure even as he doubts that Thorin intended to include this most precious of family heirlooms in the agreement.

Also mingled in among the reclaimed fortune is treasure the dragon took from the human realm of Dale in the same rampage that drove the dwarves from their mountain stronghold. Still yet another complicating factor is that Smaug wouldn't have attacked and destroyed Lake-town if not for the doings of Bilbo, Thorin, and company. Now the townsmen are homeless and destitute with winter coming on.

Finally, there is the fact that the dwarves were able to recover their lost treasure only because Bard the Bowman slew the dragon with his great yew bow. It's true that a member of Thorin's company played a crucial role in this, since Bard would not have learned of the dragon's weak spot from the old thrush if Bilbo hadn't discovered it in the first place. But in the negotiations that ensue, nobody realizes this. They're operating under the assumption that Bard was alone responsible. Do Thorin and the dwarves owe Bard something for killing their mutual enemy? Is it a legally binding debt or merely a debt of gratitude to be paid out in some freewill gift of thanks after all of the dust is settled?

These are complications, to be sure, but by themselves they don't impose the stalemate that follows. The dragon was sitting on such an obscene amount of treasure that all of the major players with any claim to it could walk away laden with riches and still leave Thorin and his companions with enough treasure for a dozen lifetimes of extravagant wealth.

Then there are the practical considerations urging conciliation. With a lightly guarded mountain (thirteen dwarves and one slightly pudgy hobbit), the reasonable thing even for someone just out for his own good would be for Thorin to (a) give Bard the Bowman a significant share of the treasure as a thank-you for killing Smaug, (b) grant the townsmen who hosted him in his hour of need enough gold to rebuild their town, (c) return the treasure from the abandoned realm of Dale to Bard and his followers, and (d) make peace with the Elvenking by giving him a magnanimous gift from the hoard as compensation for their journeying through his kingdom and withholding from him their purpose there. At the moment Thorin needs allies and trading partners more than he needs a mountain of treasure.

Bard makes something like this case to Thorin, along with a plea to his sense of justice. Bilbo assumes Thorin will immediately see the sense in Bard's words, but "he did not reckon with the power that gold has upon which a dragon has long brooded, nor with dwarvish hearts." Thorin has by now spent long hours among the recovered treasure, "and the lust of it was heavy on him",[24] leading him to harden his heart against Bard, the Elvenking, and their peoples. Even if they don't come to blows, great want and tragedy await men and dwarves alike along this trajectory of greed and suspicion. The dwarves will be forced to weather a cruel winter with limited reserves, making do with whatever Thorin's kinsmen can shuttle in from the Iron Hills across the wild in the dead of winter. The people of Lake-town, their supplies and infrastructure crushed by Smaug's attack, are in dire need of gold or silver to purchase fresh provisions coming up and down the rivers. But for the friendship of the elves of Mirkwood, their situation would be hopeless.

So notice what this greed and suspicion threatens to smother—a cross-border market of creators and consumers entering into voluntary, win-win exchanges. Greed and suspicion threaten to grind trade to a halt and leave the peoples of the region fragmented and destitute.

This isn't the worst of it. Bard, for all his heroic virtues, is in no mood to patiently wait out Thorin's fit of irrational greed, and the Elvenking is already put out with the dwarves for trespassing through his woods, accosting his followers, and refusing to give any account of their doings. With the approach of Thorin's five hundred armed kinsmen from the Iron Hills, the conflict rises toward a crescendo. The tragedy of old allies slaughtering one another is averted only by a series of good deeds and greater enemies.

From a Common Enemy to the Common Good

Although loyal to his dwarf companions, Bilbo recoils from the harsh line Thorin takes with the men and elves. Realizing the conflict may soon turn violent, he slips away to the opposing camp and offers Bard the Arkenstone as a negotiating tool. He suspects that Thorin's passion for it will prod him to trade away some of his precious gold in return for the stone, giving Bard enough treasure to allow the people of Lake-town to survive the coming winter and reestablish the realm of Dale. In short, Bilbo sacrifices his share of the treasure in pursuit of the common good, and Bard and the Elvenking are duly impressed. A lately returned Gandalf is also impressed and joins the others in urging Thorin to behave sensibly.

Their efforts prove unsuccessful; but Bilbo's Arkenstone gambit, by introducing an additional layer of complexity into the negotiations, briefly delays the onset of battle, a delay of great importance because of what happens next. At the last moment, "when bows twanged" and "battle was about to be joined",[25] a sudden darkness comes over the sky. A storm, a cloud of carrion birds, and then the first wave of wargs and goblins sweep into view, intent on slaughtering men, elves, and dwarves alike. If the men, elves, and dwarves had already been deep into battle with one another when the first wave struck, they would have been an easy mark for the goblins and wargs. Instead, their sudden sense of vulnerability drives out their pride and pettiness of a moment before, and they're able to unite against a common enemy in the nick of time.

The move is thoroughly pragmatic, since there will be no dwarves, men, or elves left to squabble over the treasure if they don't unite against the goblins. But it's also an act of humility. And here we mean it in its right and theologically rooted sense rather than as a spineless readiness to grovel sycophantically in the shadow of power or conventional wisdom. Russian Orthodox bishop Anthony Bloom explains it this way:

> The word "humility" comes from the Latin word "humus" which means fertile ground. To me, humility is not what we often make of it: the sheepish way of trying to imagine that we are the worst of all and trying to convince others that our artificial ways of behaving show that we are aware of that truth. Humility is the situation of the earth. The earth is always there, always taken for granted, never remembered, always trodden on by everyone, somewhere we cast and pour out all the refuse, all we don't need. It's there, silent and accepting everything and in a miraculous way making out of all the refuse new richness in spite of corruption, transforming corruption itself into a power of life and a new possibility of creativeness, open to the sunshine, open to the rain, ready to receive any seed we sow and capable of bringing thirtyfold, sixtyfold, a hundredfold out of every seed.[26]

To invoke this deeper understanding of humility here isn't to suggest that the "good guys" in the battle are saints. It's to show that any seeming gap between pragmatism and humility is an illusion. Humility, understood aright, is the ultimate pragmatism because it is the ultimate realism, a rightly grounded sense of one's finitude. When Thorin and the others put aside their pettiness and pride, recognize their great need, and come together in a voluntary enterprise of self-defense, such humility makes them stronger, not weaker.

Also notice how Bloom's description of humility evokes hobbits at their best. Standing only about half the height of an average human, hobbits are closer to the earth. They're also earth dwellers whose feet can still feel the soil, since they go about unshod. Then, too, it's only a hobbit (Bilbo) who possesses the humility to voluntarily give up the corrupting ring of power, and later his nephew Frodo who has enough humility to carry the ring as long as he does on the quest to destroy it. The hobbit Sam also has a chance to keep the ring for himself at one point, but the humble gardener returns it to Frodo, loyal to the end. The hobbits in both novels are also a bit like Bloom's description of the soil—"always taken for granted". As Gandalf said, "Among the Wise I am the only one that goes in for hobbit-lore: an obscure branch of knowledge, but full of surprises. Soft as butter as they can be, and yet sometimes as tough as old tree-roots. I think it likely that some would resist the Rings far longer than most of the Wise would believe."[27]

This may be why Bilbo is better able to resist the dragon spell cast on the treasure than are the dwarves or the Master of Lake-town. While the proud Thorin is sick with the lust for treasure, Bilbo's rooted humility allows him to extend the negotiations and sow the seeds for a deeper reconciliation to come.

The men, elves, and dwarves win a costly battle over the invading host, and the next morning, a fatally wounded Thorin calls Bilbo to his bedside and speaks words of penance. "Since I leave now all gold and silver, and go where it is of little worth, I wish to part in friendship from you, and I would take back my words and deeds at the Gate", he says. Bilbo tells him a mountain of gold isn't worth Thorin's life, and then speaks dismissively of his own role in the adventure. Thorin's response encapsulates the novel's crucial distinction between hospitality and generosity on the one hand and miserliness and mistrust on the other. "No", Thorin said. "There is more in you of good than you know, child of the kindly West. Some courage and some wisdom, blended in measure. If more of us valued food and cheer and song above hoarded gold, it would be a merrier world."[28]

Notice it's the hospitable attitude of Bilbo that wins out here. And this shouldn't surprise us. The generous and receptive humility essential to hospitality is not a sacrifice of core convictions. You can't truly receive the other if you have lost yourself. Hagstrom touches on this when she says "hospitality reflects a radically different and compelling alternative to tolerance". Mere tolerance, she explains, "superficially entertains another's worldview, beliefs, and values", lacking as it does a "built-in telos or end that would arrive at an objective moral truth".

In contrast to mushy tolerance, "the costly, risky engagement of hospitality ... is incarnational, morally attuned, and prompted by commitments to truthfulness in word and deed."[29]

Now take her analysis of tolerance and hospitality, and think about the moral journey Bilbo undertakes in the course of *The Hobbit*. When we first meet him, he is superficially willing to entertain an old man in a pointy hat on his front porch. This quickly devolves into a diplomatic inhospitality the moment the stranger starts talking about arranging an adventure. Then the embers of Bilbo's Tookish love for the strange and wonderful are stirred and come sputtering back to life. He bravely hosts a troupe of dwarves for afternoon tea, but as yet he is still too disoriented to serve as a lodestar in the relationship. At this early stage, progress for Bilbo is merely letting himself be taken up into the adventure, but he gradually matures into a protagonist whose behavior toward dwarves, elves, and men can rightly be characterized as muscular hospitality, one at the center of so many of the good things that happen after the great battle against the goblin army is won.

This muscular hospitality is found, historically speaking, in "the burglar's" bourgeois roots. As Novak says, "The bourgeois class was, in a sense, the most open, dynamic, and expansive class. Aristocrats who chose to play by the new economic rules could join it, and so could former serfs, peasants, and the urban or rural poor."[30] And what were those "new economic rules"? A capacity for trust beyond family and clan, a capacity for innovation, an ability to see the needs and wants of other people, and a willingness to strive and risk, get one's hands dirty, in order to meet those needs.

Bilbo was nothing like this at the beginning of the novel but very much like it by the time he is commended by the dying Thorin—a hobbit with a hospitable openness to others outside his clan and people, a willingness to risk his own wealth and even his skin to serve others, and a developing capacity to think on his feet.

This vigorously bourgeois Bilbo plays a modest but significant role in the good to come. Amid the celebration and the mourning for the lost and wounded, old grievances and grasping are laid aside. Dain, the dwarf leader from the Iron Hills, honors the agreement with Bard the Bowman for a fourteenth share, along with the emeralds of Girion, which Bard then gives as a gift to the Elvenking. Bard is also generous with the people of Lake-town, while Dain gives Bilbo as much as the hobbit is willing to take, even though the hobbit had traded away his share when he gave Bard the Arkenstone. Overlooking the letter of the old agreements, Dain sends Bilbo home with a small chest of gold and one of silver, "such as one strong pony could carry".[31]

And Bilbo, as we saw, graciously compensates the Elvenking for all of the food and drink he consumed while hiding in the elven palace.

Finally, Bilbo and Gandalf make the long journey back to the Shire. Having overcome various unnamed adventures, and sorted out some bothersome difficulties involving his own relatives (which we'll discuss later), the hobbit is finally able to resume his comfortable life at Bag End.

This moment has all the markings of a natural ending, but Tolkien adds an additional beat to the story. "One autumn evening some years afterwards" Bilbo hears a knock and discovers Gandalf and Balin the dwarf on his doorstep.[32] They sit down by the fire, and Bilbo and the reader soon learn the longer-term outcome of the generosity, hospitality, and renewed trust that took root in the area around the Lonely Mountain after Bilbo's departure some years before. We learn that Lake-town's new Master is "of wiser kind" than the old Master, and that the peoples of the valley are thriving:

> Bard had rebuilt the town in Dale and men had gathered to him from the Lake and from South and West, and all the valley had become tilled again and rich, and the desolation was now filled with birds and blossoms in spring and fruit and feasting in autumn. And Lake-town was refounded and was more prosperous than ever, and much wealth went up and down the Running River; and there was friendship in those parts between elves and dwarves and men.[33]

The picture Balin sketches of wealth happily traveling up and down the river points us in a very different direction from the usual association of capitalism with unbridled avarice. While many see greed as the necessary and essential core of a market economy, the final third of *The Hobbit* undermines such a view. It suggests instead that greed, miserliness, and dishonesty are actually inimical to enterprise, since they undermine the very freedom that makes wealth creation possible.

But doesn't the old Master of Lake-town confirm the stereotype of the greedy capitalist? To be sure, he was a shrewd businessman, but notice what else he was. He was essentially the mayor or city manager.

When an economy is marked by an overly cozy relationship between politicians and capitalists, we call this cronyism. Such arrangements diminish economic freedom for the many by extending monopoly powers and special access to the privileged few. In the case of Lake-town, the chief politician and the chief "capitalist" were not merely cozy but one and the same person, and his end would be hard to top as a warning against the dangers of such concentrations of power. Bard the Bowman gives the old Master a generous portion of his reward to help rebuild a devastated Lake-town, and the Master absconds with it; eventually he starves to death "in the Waste, deserted by his companions".[34]

Fortunately, better leaders follow, and graciousness, trust, and fair dealings win out over the greed and mistrust of earlier times, and enterprise and trade actually expand in the valley. In this way, *The Hobbit* gets something right that many people on both the right and left miss—namely, that the defining characteristic of free enterprise isn't greed or lawlessness, but freedom under justice.

At the same time, the prosperity established after the dragon and the old Master are gone isn't just distinct from cronyism or a greedy, mistrustful society. It's also distinct from a communist utopia where the workers of the world unite and usher in a classless age of income equality. Bilbo learns the happy news that the citizens of Lake-town have gotten a better village where all classes have risen, but it isn't one where the managerial class has been replaced by the spontaneous organization of labor. And while there has been much generosity, it hasn't been in pursuit of some drab workers' paradise of perfect income equality. Instead the people get an age where the true robber barons have been removed from the equation (Smaug and the old Master) and replaced by such honest leaders as Dain, Bard, and the new Master of Lake-town.

Together, these prove to be skilled and generous leaders, but much wealthier than the average citizen. Tolkien makes this quite explicit, and nothing in the tone of the narrative suggests Tolkien saw any problem with such inequality. Indeed, the description of Gandalf and Balin's entrance into Bag End near the end of the novel only reinforces the sense of a perspective quite comfortable with some being dramatically more prosperous than the average person: "If Balin noticed that Mr. Baggins' waistcoat was more extensive (and had real gold buttons), Bilbo also noticed that Balin's beard was several inches longer, and his jeweled belt was of great magnificence."[35] There are no speeches excoriating the indulgent fashion choices of "the petty bourgeois" following this little announcement, just old friends passing around the tobacco jar.

Whatever one may wish to make of this economic flowering at the end of *The Hobbit*, it isn't socialism. Call it ordered liberty. That would probably please the bourgeois Mr. Baggins. He likes a house neat, bright, and spacious, with a front door freshly painted—green, round, and welcoming.

Chapter 4

The Ring of Power Corrupts Absolutely

In *The Hobbit*, the invisibility ring Bilbo finds in the goblin caves is a device mainly for elevating the bourgeois Mr. Baggins to the status of master burglar. In *The Lord of the Rings*, it is much more—a ring of extraordinary power that Tolkien employs to explore themes of domination, deception, and death, and to sound a warning against any grand political plan that depends on unchecked power *to get things done*. The novel is about many other things, of course, but it's no overstatement to say the temptation posed by the ring conveys the novel's central political theme—that, as Lord Acton put it, "Power tends to corrupt, and absolute power corrupts absolutely."[1]

One Ring to Fool Them All

This is the book's first chapter to focus on *The Lord of the Rings*, so a bit of stage setting is in order. Near the beginning of the novel, some years after the end of *The Hobbit*, Gandalf shows up at Bag End, and Bilbo complains of feeling stretched thin. It's also curious that Bilbo seems hardly to have aged in the intervening years. Gandalf senses both the unnatural youthfulness and the stretched feeling have something to do with Bilbo's long possession of the invisibility ring, and he urges him to give the ring to his beloved nephew Frodo. (The ring, as it turns out, also arrests the aging process, an aspect we explore in the final chapter of this book.) Bilbo manages with great difficulty to pass the ring on to Frodo, and Gandalf departs to see what else he can learn about the mysterious device. When he returns years later, he asks Frodo for permission to perform a test on it. Frodo reluctantly permits it, and a script in a strange tongue appears on the ring. Gandalf translates it into the common tongue: "One Ring to rule them all, One Ring to find them, One Ring to bring them all and in the Darkness bind them."[2]

The script confirms Gandalf's suspicion. Frodo's ring is the master ring, forged long ago by the evil Lord Sauron as a tool of dark magic to dominate the free peoples of Middle-Earth. The ring is a device of surpassing power that allowed Sauron to ensnare nine kings of men, seducing them with the promise of power and immortality and eventually reducing them to frightening wraiths that do his bidding. But Sauron lost the ring in battle three thousand years before, and then the ring was lost altogether soon thereafter, passing into legend. Since then Sauron has lurked as a disembodied spirit, slowly regaining strength but always searching for his lost ring. And now, through the creature Gollum, he has likely learned of hobbits and will soon come searching.

Frodo suggests they simply destroy the ring then and there, but Gandalf explains that the ring is virtually indestructible and that even most dragon fire isn't hot enough. Next, Frodo offers the ring to Gandalf, since surely a wizard as powerful as Gandalf could use the ring to defeat Sauron and do tremendous good. The wizard's reply stands in stark contrast to the spirit of the age with its worship of raw power: " 'No!' cried Gandalf, springing to his feet. 'With that power I should have power too great and terrible. And over me the Ring would gain a power still greater and more deadly.... I do not wish to become like the Dark Lord himself. Yet the way of the Ring to my heart is by pity, pity for weakness and the desire of strength to do good. Do not tempt me!' "[3]

The One Ring, to be sure, is a work of dark magic and contains some part of the evil Sauron, so it corrupts actively as well as by its promise of seemingly unconstrained power. That being said, the second of these means is far from inconsequential. As Tolkien himself put it in one of his letters, "It was part of the essential deceit of the ring to fill minds with imaginations of supreme power."[4]

In any case, Gandalf—having convinced Frodo of the pernicious effects of the ring, and of the folly of trying to destroy it by any ordinary and convenient means—urges the hobbit to take the ring and make for the elven realm of Rivendell. When Frodo and his companions arrive after many adventures, the lord of Rivendell, Elrond, calls together a Council to determine what is to be done about the ring and the growing threat of Sauron. The free peoples of the West could use the ring to enhance their power for the coming clash, but—like Gandalf—they fear the ring's corrupting power. So instead a most counterintuitive plan is hatched. A fellowship of dwarf, elf, men, wizard, and hobbits—Frodo and eight companions—are to set out from Rivendell with a single purpose: sneak the ring deep into Sauron's realm of Mordor—slipping past all of his soldiers, spies, and watchtowers—and throw it into the one fire hot enough to destroy it, the fires of Mount Doom.

Thus does Tolkien turn the quest genre on its head. The fellowship will pursue a quest not to obtain something precious and status enhancing, but to destroy the very object that whispers most seductively of glorious power without limit.

It's a desperate gambit, of course, but the united wisdom of the noblest leaders at the Council stand behind it. Among these is the millennia-old Elrond, who tells the Council how the king of Gondor cut the ring from Sauron's finger in battle long ago, and how Elrond urged him to destroy it in the fires of Mount Doom. Isildur refused this counsel and "soon he was betrayed by [the ring] to his death". The point of the story runs deeper than an untimely death. As Elrond says, "Death maybe was better than what else might have befallen him."[5] Isildur's early death, in other words, spared him from being slowly corrupted by the Ring of Power.

Later Aragorn, the mysterious ranger who met up with Frodo and his companions in Bree and saw them safely to Rivendell, refuses to take the ring when he has the opportunity, even though as Isildur's heir he has a natural claim to it, both as a family possession and for the good he might do with it as a strong king in the line of the powerful Númenóreans. Then, in the elven realm of Lothlórien late in *The Fellowship of the Ring*, another wise and noble character faces a similar test. There Frodo is befriended by the wisest, fairest, and most powerful of the elves of Middle-Earth, the Lady Galadriel. Frodo, feeling inadequate to the quest, offers Galadriel the ring, believing that surely here is one pure and wise and strong enough to use the Ring for good alone. Galadriel's response is perhaps the novel's most memorable exclamation against the cult of political power.

"And now at last it comes", she responds. "You will give me the Ring freely! In place of the Dark Lord you will set up a Queen. And I shall not be dark, but beautiful and terrible as the Morning and the Night! Fair as the Sea and the Sun and the Snow upon the Mountain! Dreadful as the Storm and the Lightning! Stronger than the foundations of the earth. All shall love me and despair!" It is a vision of total political power in the service of the common good, but it ends in despair. The narrative continues: "She lifted up her hand and from the ring that she wore there issued a great light that illumined her alone and left all else dark. She stood before Frodo seeming now tall beyond measurement, and beautiful beyond enduring, terrible and worshipful."[6]

She, like Gandalf, finds the ring extremely tempting, but in the end the good Galadriel resists the temptation: "Then she let her hand fall, and the light faded, and suddenly she laughed again, and lo! she was shrunken: a slender elf-woman, clad in simple white, whose gentle voice was soft and sad. 'I pass the test,' she said. 'I will diminish, and go into the West, and remain Galadriel.' "

Sam Gamgee, Frodo's gardener and faithful companion on the quest, somehow misses the force of Galadriel's warning and again proposes she take the ring: " 'But if you'll pardon my speaking out, I think my master was right. I wish you'd take his Ring. You'd put things to rights. You'd stop them digging up the Gaffer and turning him adrift. You'd make some folk pay for their dirty work.' 'I would,' she said. 'That is how it would begin. But it would not stop with that, alas!' "

The logic of the good and humble Sam is eerily similar to Saruman's, who earlier tells Gandalf, "We must have power, power to order all things as we will, for that good which only the Wise can see."[7] When Gandalf refuses, Saruman imprisons him and gets back to the work of hacking down trees and growing an army of mutant Uruk-hai.

Then we have Boromir, the heir of the Steward of Gondor and the most sympathetic of those who succumb to the ring's siren call. At the Council in Rivendell he urges them to use the ring for good. Later, as a member of the fellowship, he finds Frodo alone in the woods and vents his frustration over their decision to destroy the ring. He calls it "mad" not to use the ring's power against Sauron, and says that the "fearless" and "ruthless" can alone achieve victory over Mordor. Boromir then limns an image of himself as the heroic ring wielder:

> "The Ring would give me power of Command. How I would drive the hosts of Mordor, and all men would flock to my banner!" Boromir strode up and down, speaking ever more loudly. Almost he seemed to have forgotten Frodo, while his talk dwelt on walls and weapons, and the mustering of men; and he drew plans for great alliances and glorious victories to be; and he cast down Mordor, and became himself a mighty king, benevolent and wise.[8]

The corrupting effects of this ring are by now obvious, but Tolkien puts an exclamation point on the theme by allowing Boromir's narrative thread to run out to its logical (and tragic) end. Frodo begins inching away from his unbalanced companion. Boromir, sensing he's losing his audience, urges Frodo to unburden himself of the ring, telling him he could even blame Boromir if he would like. And here the scene comes to a head: "'You can say that I was too strong and took it by force. For I am too strong for you, halfling,' he cried; and suddenly he sprang over the stone and leaped at Frodo. His fair and pleasant face was hideously changed; a raging fire was in his eyes."

Frodo eludes him by slipping on the ring. "Miserable trickster!" Boromir screams, by now completely unhinged. "Curse you and all halflings to death and darkness!" And so a moral dissolution that under normal circumstances might stretch over several years of a leader's power-aggrandizing career is through the mode of the fantastic telescoped into mere weeks. The lesson is old and oft forgotten: even well-intentioned leaders are tempted to annex to themselves more and more power in their efforts to fight evil and improve the lot of their people. In such cases, the potential for good lies in plain sight, while the danger of unchecked power seems distant, abstract, and quite manageable. What distinguishes the wise leaders of *The Lord of the Rings* is their ability to see past this illusion.

Domination versus Inspiration

Tolkien further critiques unchecked power by contrasting the "one ring to rule them all" with the three elven rings possessed by Elrond, Galadriel, and Gandalf. When it's suggested that these three rings be used to overthrow Sauron, Elrond explains that "they were not made as weapons of war or conquest: that is not their power. Those who made them did not desire strength or domination or hoarded wealth, but understanding, making, and healing, to preserve all things unstained."[9] It's the difference between communion and coercion, creating and controlling, authority and authoritarianism.

The contrast is perhaps most striking in the case of the elven ring held by Gandalf. Late in *The Silmarillion* we learn that Círdan, a great elven lord and shipwright, first possessed it and freely lends it to Gandalf. "Take now this Ring," he tells Gandalf, "for thy labours and thy cares will be heavy, but in all it will support thee and defend thee from weariness. For this is the Ring of Fire, and herewith, maybe, thou shalt rekindle hearts to the valour of old in a world that grows chill."[10] Círdan's counsel is in keeping with the proper vocation of the wizards, whose purpose, according to Tolkien, was to "train, advise, instruct, arouse the hearts and minds of those threatened by Sauron to a resistance with their own strengths; and not just to do the job for them."[11]

Mason Harris summarizes the difference when she comments that "Gandalf's self-conscious restraint in his use of magic provides the opposite pole to Sauron's attempt to seduce or overawe the sense of self in others."[12] Sauron maims, tortures, and kills to repossess a ring taken from him by force in battle, a ring he designed in order to terrorize and dominate. Gandalf obtains his ring as a gift freely proffered from another lover of freedom, and it serves the wizard in his vocation of inspiring and ennobling those around him to rise up freely and conquer tyranny.

Thus does the telescoping power of the fantasy genre foreground the essential differences between the totalitarian and the free society, differences elaborated as we encounter the various societies—free and unfree—in the course of the adventures. One is a landscape of fear and domination; the other is a place where exchanges and mutual endeavors are pursued freely and where needs not filled by markets are typically met through voluntary gift giving and receiving. In a letter about *The Lord of the Rings*, Tolkien wrote that "the supremely bad motive is (for this tale, since it is specifically about it) domination of other 'free' wills."[13] Sauron and his ring exemplify this supremely bad motive—Gandalf and the ring of fire, the opposition.

The Ring, the Eye, and the Panopticon

There is something revealing, too, in the One Ring's power to turn its wearer invisible. Enhancing one's capacity to skulk about unseen, pick pockets, deftly slit an enemy's throat, perhaps play the peeping Tom—this isn't the sort of power usually associated with the heroic. H. G. Wells makes essentially this point through the title character of his 1897 science-fiction novel *The Invisible Man*. The character invents a way to make himself invisible and, when he belatedly discovers the effect is irreversible, gradually degenerates from a citizen scientist in good standing to a social pariah bent on vengeance and a "reign of terror".[14]

It's hard to say to what degree the novel influenced Tolkien, since the invisibility trope has an ancient and recurring place in literature. But we do know Tolkien was familiar with Wells' fiction, and the parallels to Sméagol/Gollum are striking. As with the title character of Wells' novel, Smeagol deteriorates into a social pariah, thanks to his habit of using the invisibility ring to spy on his fellow villagers and putting what he learns "to crooked and malicious uses". Constantly on the alert for "all that was hurtful", he naturally becomes very unpopular and eventually is "shunned (when visible) by all his relations".[15] Ostracized, he takes up a furtive life in the shadows and spends his final days as a tortured and isolated soul obsessed with reclaiming his precious ring and getting revenge on one and all. "We shall get it, the Precious", he reassures himself as he plots to get the better of the giant spider Shelob. "O yes, then we'll pay Her back, my precious. Then we'll pay everyone back!"[16]

In both cases, the power to see others while remaining unseen is a power that "corrupts absolutely", or at least contributes mightily to the process of moral degradation. Tolkien and Wells may have both been taking a cue from a passage in Plato's *Republic*, where the character of Glaucon relates the story of a shepherd who comes into possession of a magic ring that can turn its wearer invisible. The shepherd uses the newfound power to infiltrate the royal palace of Lydia, seduce the queen, kill the king, and seize his throne. It isn't clear whether Glaucon holds a cynical view or is merely playing the devil's advocate, but he draws from the story the moral that man without the threat of consequences is certain to become most immoral:

> No man would keep his hands off what was not his own when he could safely take what he liked out of the market, or go into houses and lie with any one at his pleasure, or kill or release from prison whom he would, and in all respects be like a God among men.... And this we may truly affirm to be a great proof that a man is just, not willingly or because he thinks that justice is any good to him individually, but of necessity, for wherever any one thinks that he can safely be unjust, there he is unjust.[17]

While Plato himself apparently rejected such a view through the figure and arguments of Socrates, it's possible that H. G. Wells embraced the cynicism conveyed in Glaucon's parable. Tolkien's view is surely complex, but his well-documented Christian orthodoxy lent him the means to balance a low view of fallen, unfettered man with the biblical truth that "fear of the LORD is the beginning of wisdom".[18] If you have faith in a just, holy, and omnipotent God who will bring "every deed into judgment",[19] you're less likely to imagine you could ever "safely be unjust" or "in all respects be like a God". Sauron, originally a good and powerful angel, loses this faith and eventually comes to see himself as "a God among men". Remember that at this stage in the history of Middle-Earth, he manifests himself as "the Eye"—not, of course, the "all-seeing eye" that the early twentieth-century Southern gospel hymn warns is "watching you", but certainly a sort of diabolical imitation of divine omniscience.[20]

At Rivendell, Bilbo tells Frodo he missed the ring and that, at times, "I have felt it was like an eye looking at me." Later the narrator describes the Eye of Sauron as "rimmed with fire". Then, very late in the quest, Frodo says the ring now appears to him as a "wheel of fire" that he sees "even with my waking eyes, and all else fades".[21] Peter Jackson's *Lord of the Rings* film trilogy suggestively uses this hellish rim of fire to evoke the One Ring, constantly reminding viewers that Sauron's goal is to meld his ability to see with the ring's power. The diabolical ideal of this Eye possessing the invisibility ring suggests, in turn, an idea of nineteenth-century utilitarian philosopher Jeremy Bentham: a watchtower with an all-seeing watcher unseen by those being watched. Bentham envisioned a prison—what he termed a Panopticon—in which the watchtower is designed so the overseer can view all of his prisoners, while simultaneously obscuring whether the overseer is present or absent. He thus has the freedom to come and go, while his prisoners are never free of the possibility they're being observed.

French philosopher Michel Foucault explored the notion of modern society as a Panopticon writ large, and we could say that Tolkien was already exploring the idea decades before in the figure of Sauron, who seeks to engineer a Panopticon Middle-Earth with his Eye and his many spies on land and in air. Were Sauron to repossess the ring that grants invisibility and magnified power, his goal of overseeing all while remaining unseen would be complete—the Panopticon observer perfected.

In Lothlórien, gazing into the Mirror of Galadriel, Frodo experiences this possibility in the extreme: "In the black abyss there appeared a single Eye that slowly grew, until it filled nearly all the Mirror. So terrible was it that Frodo stood rooted, unable to cry out or to withdraw his gaze. The Eye was rimmed with fire, but was itself glazed, yellow as a cat's, watchful and intent, and the black slit of its pupil opened on a pit, a window into nothing."[22]

The feeling of helplessness before Sauron's gaze is redoubled later when Frodo is near the Seeing Seat of Amon Hen. Slipping the ring on his finger to escape Boromir, "suddenly he felt the Eye" of the Dark Tower, a "fierce eager will" that "leaped towards him" and "soon it would nail him down".[23] Later, as he nears the Black Gate, Frodo imagines the Eye of Sauron striving "to pierce all shadows of cloud, and earth, and flesh, and to see: to pin you under its deadly gaze, naked, immovable".[24]

We come to a similar image later when the chief Ringwraith threatens the maiden Eowyn on the field of battle, telling her he will bear her away "to the houses of lamentation, beyond all darkness, where thy flesh shall be devoured, and thy shrivelled mind left naked to the Lidless Eye."[25] Then, late in the quest, when Frodo is nearing Mount Doom and the evil of the ring is weighing heavily on him, Sam tries to encourage him by asking if he remembers some pleasant moment from earlier in their journey. Frodo's answer marks one of the tale's darkest moments: "No, I am afraid not, Sam.... At least, I know that such things happened, but I cannot see them. No taste of food, no feel of water, no sound of wind, no memory of tree or grass or flower, no image of moon or star are left to me. I am naked in the dark, Sam, and there is no veil between me and the wheel of fire. I begin to see it even with my waking eyes, and all else fades."[26]

If the kind of gazing Frodo is suffering under had to be distilled into a word, it might be the word *gloating*. One can hardly imagine Galadriel or Gandalf or Aragorn fixing someone with a gaze and *gloating* over him, but the corrupted characters in the novel seem to do it almost every chance they can get. When Sauron fixes Pippin's gaze in the palantír, Pippin feels as if he's "being stabbed with knives". Afterward, Pippin tells Gandalf, "Then he gloated over me. I felt I was falling to pieces."[27] Elsewhere the "monstrous and abominable" spider Shelob gets in on the fun, her many eyes "bestial and yet filled with purpose and with hideous delight, gloating over their prey trapped beyond all hope of escape."[28] Orcs are also champion gloaters, described as "gloating" and "fingering their knives"[29] while they stand over a captured Frodo.

Notice the way gloating in all three instances is equated with violence—the first with being torn to pieces, the second with the imminent threat of Shelob's bite, and the third through the descriptive coupling of gloating and knives eagerly fingered. So gloating, far from an act of understanding and communion, is more a gesture of violent domination.[30]

Another way to get at the essence of gloating is to contrast it with some very different examples of powerful gazing in the novel. Allison Harl summarizes the point when she likens "Galadriel's omniscient, powerful gaze" to that of the Eye, and her mirror to Sauron's palantír, but notes that "the Lady of Light's intentions are the inverse of the Dark Lord's".[31] Galadriel employs her power of seeing into people only for good, and uses it only very cautiously, warning Frodo that "seeing is both good and perilous".[32] Galadriel's positive example suggests—again in the words of Harl—that "the visual act of 'seeing' only becomes evil when its function results in domination, possession, and control."[33]

At the same time, Tolkien did communicate a clear preference for the verbal over the visual, for the experience of hearing an imaginative story over seeing it. In "On Fairy-Stories", he explains his preference in terms immediately relevant to the question of political control. As he said, "The radical distinction between all art (including drama) that offers a *visible* presentation and true literature is that it imposes one visible form." He then elaborates:

> Literature works from mind to mind and is thus more progenitive. It is at once more universal and more poignantly particular. If it speaks of *bread* or *wine* or *stone* or *tree*, it appeals to the whole of these things, to their ideas, yet each hearer will give to them a peculiar personal embodiment in his imagination. Should the story say "he ate bread," the dramatic producer or painter can only show "a piece of bread" according to his taste or fancy, but the hearer of the story will think of bread in general and picture it in some form of his own.[34]

How often have you read a book and then, upon seeing the movie, mourned that the protagonist didn't look at all like you had imagined? With film, which offers "a *visible* presentation", the filmmaker chooses, whereas in the literary arts each reader participates in creation. Notice in Tolkien's preference for the verbal over the visual mode his abiding interest in "abolition of control",[35] as he put it in describing his small-government political views.

It also calls to mind the battle of wills between Sauron and Denethor, Steward of Gondor. Sauron cunningly uses the palantír possessed by Denethor to place images before the Steward that warp his outlook and eventually lead him into despair. By isolating and carefully selecting the images Denethor sees, the Dark Lord gradually reshapes Denethor's outlook. So, whereas the Council of Elrond takes strength and wisdom from reasoning together in community, building courage and consensus through story and civil debate, Denethor leans heavily on the images in the palantír and, in his pride and isolation, is drawn into despair. In this way, Sauron used a sham Panopticon—an orb that seems to grant Denethor the power to see all—as a means to disempower the steward.

Big Eye, Big Brother

Lord Sauron's Panopticon society also calls to mind the surveillance society of George Orwell's dystopian work *Nineteen Eighty-Four.* Orwell's novel was published in 1948, after the main elements of *The Lord of the Rings* were long established and most of it written, so whatever similarity exists between the two works is apparently a case of two authors wrestling with a common concern of their times rather than one author influencing the other. Although Orwell was an English socialist and Tolkien an English conservative, they both understood that totalitarian political power was rarely pursued in the interest of the common good. Late in *Nineteen Eighty-Four,* the villain O'Brien frankly reveals the Party's interest in power for its own sake, a power that demands the control and domination of other people's wills. As he explains to Winston, the novel's protagonist, such power necessarily involves making the subservient person suffer; otherwise, how do you know if it's your will that's directing the other person's rather than simply the two wills coinciding? As Mason Harris notes in his comparison of *Nineteen Eighty-Four* and *The Lord of the Rings,* the English poet and Tolkien contemporary W. H. Auden identified a similar impulse in the Dark Lord.[36] As Auden put it in his enthusiastic review of *The Lord of the Rings,* "The kind of Evil which Sauron embodies, the lust for domination, will always be irrationally cruel since it is not satisfied if another does what it wants; he must be made to do it against his will."[37]

In both Orwell and Tolkien, the power of evil eventually overwhelms the protagonist. Winston is tortured until, in one of literature's most disturbing instances of Stockholm syndrome, he declares with great sincerity, "I love Big Brother." Frodo is also undone in the final moment above the fires of Mount Doom. His will and energy spent, he yields to the ring's seductive power and insists on keeping it, even though this is the surest way for it to land back in Sauron's hands. But here the differences end. Orwell's novel ends in hopelessness and despair, while in Tolkien's novel the good guys win out over tyranny, freedom is restored, and a process of healing is begun. In *The Lord of the Rings*, the One Ring is powerful, but in the end it proves not absolutely powerful. Aided by a higher providential power (more on this in the next chapter), the free peoples of the West are able to destroy the ring and restore freedom to the West.

Wagner versus Tolkien

We have brought in everything from Plato and the Panopticon to Orwell and Wells to situate Tolkien's exploration of totalitarian power, but a chapter on the ring wouldn't be complete without looking at what many consider the most striking parallel to Tolkien's ring of power: the magical ring at the center of Richard Wagner's magisterial nineteenth-century opera cycle, *Der Ring des Nibelungen*.

Since both artists were influenced by the Norse sagas and the Middle High German epic poem the *Nibelungenlied*, you might suppose Tolkien had a fondness for Wagner's Ring Cycle, but you would suppose wrong. Tolkien apparently loathed the Ring Cycle,[38] so much so that he downplayed the obvious similarities, insisting at one point, "Both rings were round, and there the resemblance ceased."[39]

The family resemblance remains, however. Edward R. Haymes ably summarized the points of overlap in a speech to the Wagner Society of New York:

> I'd like to begin by telling a little story.
>
> A greedy, smaller-than-human creature finds a treasure in the depths of a river. He carries it to his underground retreat where he retains it until it is stolen by a visitor from the upper world. He swears eternal hate to the thief. The treasure is, of course, a ring of great power. The ring exerts strange influences on its owners including giving them the ability to disappear. The ring becomes the object of a fatal struggle between close friends or brothers, in fact it seems always to bring danger or death

to its owners. A hero enters the fray armed with a reforged sword that had been broken. Various races of humanoid beings attempt to gain control of the ring by magic and by heroism until it is finally brought at great cost and sacrifice back to its origin where it is purified by fire. The last pursuer perishes along with the ring.

Is this the retelling of Richard Wagner's four-part cycle *Der Ring des Nibelungen* or is it a summary of Tolkien's prose epic *The Lord of the Rings*? Actually it's both.[40]

Haymes, as he concedes, has deftly worded things to magnify the similarities and downplay the differences. For example, Wagner's ring finder is a dwarf rather than a hobbit, and the dwarf actually forges the ring, whereas Gollum merely finds the ring used for evil purposes that the evil and larger-than-life Sauron forged long ago. Haymes also doesn't mention other ancient, medieval, and modern sources that may have influenced Tolkien (as well as Wagner in the case of the premodern instances). These include an invisibility ring used for evil purposes in Plato's *Republic*, the invisibility ring in Chrétien de Troyes' medieval Arthurian romance "The Knight with the Lion", and various magical rings that grant protection or invulnerability in other medieval romances (for example, the rings in *Sir Perceval of Galles*, *Sir Eglamour of Artois*, *Le Morte d'Arthur*, and arguably the ring offered to, and declined by, the hero in *Sir Gawain and the Green Knight*[41]). Besides these, a couple of early twentieth-century novels also may have influenced the "one ring to rule them all". These include English author E. Nesbit's *The Enchanted Castle* (1907), which features a magic ring that bears whatever magical properties its owner declares it to have (and that turns characters invisible), and the 1931 novel *Many Dimensions* by Tolkien's friend and fellow Inkling Charles Williams. At the center of Williams' novel is a magical stone that grants extraordinary powers, powers that tend to corrupt and spin out of control, threatening the world. Another element of the novel that anticipates *The Lord of the Rings* is talk of casting the dangerous object into the ocean, an idea that in both novels is rejected as failing to provide a permanent solution.

Clearly, then, Tolkien, had a rich mine of sources for the Ring of Power at the center of *The Lord of the Rings*, some of those sources older than Wagner and some much closer to Tolkien. The interesting question isn't whether Wagner's Ring Cycle asserted some influence on Tolkien. It almost certainly did, at least at an unconscious level. The more interesting line of inquiry is why Tolkien disliked Wagner's Ring Cycle and in what meaningful ways their treatments differed. The answer to the second may also answer the first, since the main differences involve the two things most likely to get a person in trouble at a party—religion and politics.

Wagner hovered between atheism and pantheism, an outlook embodied in the opera cycle's older and wiser earth goddess. In the cycle, she stands over and against the other gods who are doomed to perish in order to make way for an age without religion, or at least for an age free of everything but nature religion. Haymes suggests that in Wagner the good characters are at their best when following nature, while in Tolkien the heroic characters are often at their best when exerting their wills against the ring and against the inclination to do the easy or *natural thing*. Actually, it's a bit more complex than this, since some of Wagner's characters resist keeping the ring, a good Tolkien character errs by ignoring what we might think of as instinct,[42] and Sauron and Saruman's contempt for the natural world contrasts negatively with the appreciation for nature and the natural world epitomized in the good elves and hobbits. All the same, Haymes' suggested contrast is an illuminating one—the pantheistic follow-your-bliss Wagner versus the Catholic Tolkien with a high regard for humility, moral discipline, and transcendent morality, and a well-developed suspicion of fallen human impulses.[43]

An essay by Alex Ross in *The New Yorker* highlights other differences between Tolkien and Wagner, charging Tolkien with discarding "the most significant property" of Wagner's ring, "that it can be forged only by one who has forsworn love." He then characterizes Tolkien's novel as sexually opaque and suggests the treatment of the ring's allure is psychologically impoverished:

> It is the little ring that brings out the lust in men and in hobbits. And what, honestly, do people want in it? Are they envious of Sauron's bling-bling life style up on top of Barad-dûr? Tolkien mutes the romance of medieval stories and puts us out in self-abnegating, Anglican-modernist, T. S. Eliot territory. The ring is a never-ending nightmare to which people are drawn for no obvious reason. It generates lust and yet gives no satisfaction.[44]

Undoubtedly the Catholic Tolkien would have been surprised to learn that a psychological landscape of self-abnegation and self-destructive, irrational desire is uniquely a feature of Anglican-modernist literature. *Crime and Punishment*, by the Russian Orthodox novelist Fyodor Dostoyevsky, and *The Inferno*, by the Italian Catholic poet Dante Alighieri, come to mind as counterexamples. But the more pertinent point is that Ross finds the allure of power for power's sake baffling and uninteresting, preferring instead Wagner's use of the ring "to shine a light on various intense, confused, all-too-human relationships".[45] The implication is that the allure of power for power's sake is foreign to human experience, or at least relatively insignificant.

Ross much prefers Wagner's theme: "Alberich forges the ring only after the Rhine maidens turn away his advances. Wotan becomes obsessed with it as a consequence of his loveless marriage; he buries himself in his work."[46] Ah, so Tolkien's sin is that *The Lord of the Rings* isn't a soap opera centered around the star-crossed love lives of men, elves, dwarves, hobbits, wizards, orcs, ents, and whatnot.[47] It's not that the common grist of sexually charged afternoon soap operas can't also be the grist for great art. It can. But is this really the only proper focus of great art? Those with an idolatrous view of human sexuality may feel so, but it's an impoverished outlook Tolkien didn't share.

Ross moves from here into a summary and gloss of the Ring Cycle's denouement: "The apparatus of myth itself—the belief in higher and lower powers, hierarchies, orders—crumbles with the walls of Valhalla. Perhaps what angered Tolkien most was that Wagner wrote a sixteen-hour mythic opera and then, at the end, blew up the foundations of myth."[48]

True, the aesthetic incoherence of such a project may have bothered Tolkien—not specifically that Wagner "blew up the foundations of myth" but that Wagner's sublimity was an ersatz sublimity, emptied as it was of the transcendent. Tolkien, through faith in the transcendent God, understood the source of true sublimity as well as the source of the thirst for power for power's sake: the desire to make of oneself a god in the place of God.

Chapter 5

The Free Peoples and the Master of Middle-Earth

Near the end of *The Fellowship of the Ring*, Frodo is fleeing from Boromir, who wants to seize the ring from the ring bearer. As a last resort, Frodo slips the ring on his finger and climbs the stairs to the lookout of Amon Hen. From there, Frodo can see east over the River Anduin and into Mordor. Unfortunately, his exposure alerts Sauron, who begins to search Frodo out. Suddenly Frodo finds himself transfixed by the Eye of Sauron. As it draws Frodo in, however, Frodo hears a countervoice in his mind, encouraging him to pull away and to take off the ring. We later learn that this is Gandalf, whom Frodo believes is dead. Frodo is like a fraying rope in the mother of all tugs-of-war. Tolkien describes the hobbit at this moment as "perfectly balanced" between two competing wills that seem to fill all the space in his conscious mind. But then Frodo suddenly becomes "aware of himself again. Frodo, neither the Voice nor the Eye: free to choose, and with one remaining instant in which to do so."[1] Here we see in essence a theme that appears throughout the Middle-Earth writings: the encounter with our own freedom and responsibility.

Frodo is at risk of losing himself in the battle between the Voice and the Eye. But amid that battle, Frodo becomes aware of himself—the third person in the conflict—and once he is again self-aware, he can choose without being compelled to do so. The narrator informs us that if he had kept the ring on his finger "one remaining instant longer", he would have lost his ability to remove it. He would have lost his freedom.

We all know the experience: we have felt pulled between what we think we ought to do, and what we're tempted to do. If we give in to temptation habitually, we can eventually lose the freedom we first had.

That's the essence of addiction, which may begin with a free act of the will, but ends in bondage and the loss of freedom. This is the effect of the One Ring. Frodo chooses the right course just in time.

Here and throughout the Middle-Earth literature, Tolkien flouted the intellectual fashion of the day, which increasingly denied the existence of such freedom.

The Dark Side

In Frodo's struggle at Amon Hen, we also encounter the complexity of evil. An object can only be a temptation if you, or at least part of you, wants it. When you give in to an evil temptation, you haven't quite been compelled. *You* are giving in. This is the subjective side of evil. At the same time, we experience evil as an objective reality, coming at us either from the natural world, from other people, or, again, as an addiction that was fed until it exercises control over us.

Tom Shippey analyzes Tolkien's double-faceted view of evil, which he describes as a tension between the more orthodox "Boethian" view and the heterodox Manichaean view.[2] Boethius was a Roman senator and philosopher of the fourth and fifth centuries who wrote *The Consolation of Philosophy*, a book widely read in the Middle Ages and discussed by theologians such as Thomas Aquinas. Boethius as well as his near contemporary, Saint Augustine, proposed a now classic solution to the problem of evil. That problem is essentially this: if God is all-powerful and wholly good, and created everything other than himself, whence came evil? If evil exists, then God must have created it. But that contradicts the claim that God is all-good. If evil exists because God couldn't prevent it from coming into existence, then God is not all-powerful.

One shallow way to resolve this trilemma is to conclude that evil is an illusion. Unfortunately, this contradicts our universal human experience.

Boethius and Augustine's solution was based on an analysis of being. God is the very ground of being, and so everything that has being is good insofar as it exists. God is wholly good, and so too is anything he creates. What about evil? It does not exist in the same way that good exists, but that doesn't mean it's unreal. Evil is a privation of being. An evil act is a movement from being and its source toward nonbeing. In this way, even evil depends, so to speak, on the prior existence of being—of good. It's like a shadow. A shadow can have a shape and size.

It can cool your house and cause you to stumble if your eyes don't adjust to it quickly. But no shadow has its own independent existence. It is rather a privation of light. If there is no light, there can be no shadow.

This idea may seem pretty abstract, but it does resolve some of the perplexity of the problem of evil. By itself, however, it seems incomplete, since we surely experience evil as an active, objective reality. Is Nazism really just a privation of good?

This is where Manichaeism comes in. On this view, good and evil are two forces, equally real, equally powerful, but eternally opposed to each other. Evil, in other words, exists in just the same way as good. Manichaeism has the virtues of not explaining evil away and of resolving the apparent paradox of how evil can exist if God is good and all-powerful. Unfortunately, it resolves the paradox by dissolving it. Manichaeism clearly contradicts the Christian (as well as the Jewish and Muslim) belief that there is only one, all-powerful, wholly good God, not two gods in opposition to each other. It also seems to undermine our conviction that good is, well, good, and evil a deviation from that. If evil is as much part of ultimate reality as good is, then the idea of a happy ending, a eucatastrophe—to use Tolkien's choice word—in which good is superior to evil and triumphs over it, doesn't make much sense. If Manichaeism is right, there will always be good, and always be evil, and that's all there is to it.

Shippey argues that a "good way to understand *The Lord of the Rings* in its full complexity is to see it as an attempt to reconcile two views of evil, both old, both authoritative, both living, each seemingly contradicted by the other."[3] It is easy to find elements of both these threads in *The Hobbit* and especially *The Lord of the Rings*. The Nazgûl, for instance, are wraiths—shadows of former men. During the initial siege of Gondor, Gandalf tells the Lord of the Nazgûl: "Go back to the abyss prepared for you! Go back! Fall into the nothingness that awaits you and your master." At this, the Witch-king of Angmar defiantly flings back his hood, revealing "a kingly crown; and yet upon no head visible was it set."[4] This seems to confirm Gandalf's point, however. The Nazgûl is no longer a man, no longer a king, but is an ephemeral shadow of his former self.

Frodo also voices this conviction that evil has no independent existence or creative power. Even after he enters Mordor, he can say that "the Shadow ... can only mock, it cannot make: not real new things of its own."[5] Or as Treebeard says of the trolls, they "are only counterfeits, made by the Enemy in the Great Dark."[6]

What of the originals? At the Council in Rivendell, Elrond explains that "nothing is evil in the beginning. Even Sauron was not so."[7] The trolls were made from innocent stone, and even Melkor, the ultimate master of Sauron, was initially a noble being, an Ainur, created by Ilúvatar. He is much like Satan, who was created as the angel Lucifer, to reflect the light of God.

If Tolkien's portrayal of evil only depicted evil as privation, as something shadowy, it would seem anemic. But it's not the full picture. The forces of evil in Middle-Earth are, well, forces. Even more than forces, they are active agents. The Nazgûl, wraiths though they are, wield sword and mace and ride horses. The wound one of them inflicts on Frodo at Weathertop never really heals, and Éowyn and Merry suffer strange and unnatural wounds from their fight with the Lord of the Nazgûl, even though they manage to slay him. Sauron unleashes armies comprised of Nazgûl, orcs, trolls, and men—agents all.

Shippey argues that "Tolkien's way of presenting this philosophical duality was through the ring."[8] On the one hand, the ring is a temptation, its evil manifest when its bearer succumbs to the temptation to use it or wear it, and it eventually becomes an addiction. Here the evil is subjective and located in the person being tempted. On the other hand, the ring seems to have a will of its own. It "betrays" Isildur, "abandons" Gollum, even tries to be found and return to its master. It's also more actively enticing than a nonmagical ring that tempts only passively through its beauty and great worth. The One Ring is not just a temptation but also a tempter. Both of these aspects of the ring "are kept up throughout the three volumes: sentient creature or psychic amplifier", as Shippey puts it, which "correspond respectively to the 'heroic' view of evil as something external to be resisted and the Boethian opinion that evil is essentially internal, psychological, negative."[9]

Freedom and Evil

Can these two insights—what Shippey dubs the Boethian and Manichaean—be reconciled? Not in their stark forms. A single, all-powerful, and wholly good God cannot, by definition, be opposed by another equally powerful countervailing force of evil. But Tolkien shows that their combined explanatory power can be had if one has recourse to the Judeo-Christian idea of free creatures created good but who chose evil. On this view, evil is not independent of the one, ultimate reality of good, but evil still manifests itself in the world actively—through the actions of intelligent creatures who have chosen evil. The ring can only illustrate this duality of evil because Tolkien invests it with the powers of agency—choices, intentions, purposes.

Simply put, the objective and subjective aspects of evil are united in the choices of free creatures. This is as true in Middle-Earth as in the biblical story—which locates the origin of evil in the free choices of Lucifer, Adam, and Eve. Shippey notes that the duality is present even in the Lord's Prayer, which concludes with both "lead us not into temptation", and "deliver us from evil." That's why he concludes that "Tolkien's double or ambiguous view of evil is not a flirtation with heresy after all, but expresses a truth about the nature of the universe."[10]

Part of that truth is this: evil cannot be ruled out for any world in which God chooses to make creatures who are genuinely free to reject him, the source of all being and goodness. Even God accepts a trade-off. Indeed, without the contrast between good and evil choices, and between greater and lesser goods, our freedom would be insignificant. Presumably God deems a world with free, sinful creatures greater than one populated only by atoms, animals, and automata. Anyone who has been drawn into a creepy movie where characters are turned into zombies or Stepford wives intuits the superiority of the free world over the other. In a subtler way, the characters that populate Middle-Earth bring home to us the fitness of the divine choice to create free creatures. Tolkien's handling of these elements also offers insights into the kinds of political and economic arrangements that best accord with the nature of such free creatures, a vein we'll mine after we explore Tolkien's vision of human freedom a bit further.

Free to Choose

In the same way that we have direct awareness of our own individual existence—that's the point of Descartes' *cogito, ergo sum*—we all have immediate experience of our freedom, of our responsibility to do the right thing and resist the evil paths that tempt us.

Imagine for a moment that you're stepping up to a quickly growing line to buy a drink on a hot day. Suddenly you see a small child wandering toward fast-moving traffic. No one else seems to have noticed the danger, and you could easily rush over and save the child, but you'll lose your place in line. Even most hardened criminals would know the right thing to do in this situation, and wouldn't believe that a hankering for a Dr. Pepper robs them of their freedom to choose the right thing. They wouldn't have any illusion about what they ought to do, and can do, even if they were caffeine addicts coming off a bad night's sleep.

This simple scenario illustrates something profound: we experience—we know of—our freedom and responsibility more directly and more certainly than any truth of history or natural science. And the complexity of our moral nature makes the reality of it more, not less, obtrusive. We *know* the strange paradox that we can both want and want not to want the same thing (for example, to eat that second or third donut at work). Yet, when we are free, we can choose to do what we do not want to do and choose not to do what we want to do.

For Frodo on Amon Hen, stuck between the power of Sauron and Gandalf, his awareness of himself and of his freedom and responsibility are all a single act. "It is his awareness of himself that makes him aware of his freedom to choose", Matthew Dickerson writes. "Why? Because the freedom to choose is fundamental to what it means to be a self."[11] If we were automata who could not experience choice, temptation, and responsibility, it's not clear that we could even be self-aware.

Freedom must be more than merely doing what we want to do. After all, if you have been determined by either physics, your upbringing, or an evil scientist to desire cleaning army latrines twelve hours a day, it's hardly a consolation that you're doing what you want to do. You're clearly not free.

Frodo and the principal characters in *The Hobbit* and *The Lord of the Rings* exercise what philosophers call "libertarian freedom"—the ability to choose between alternatives. If we are not merely shaped but determined by nature, nurture, or manipulation to choose one course of action, there is no "I" that remains.

It's hard to exaggerate how unfashionable this commitment to freedom was when Tolkien was writing *The Lord of the Rings*. Scientific materialism and logical positivism were all the rage, and neither had any room in its procrustean bed for agents that can make free choices. Atheist philosopher Bertrand Russell simply deduced from his materialist philosophy that freedom couldn't exist and, by extension, that men and women can't be responsible for their actions. In his book *Why I Am*

Not a Christian, he wrote, "When a man acts in ways that annoy us we wish to think him wicked, and we refuse to face the fact that his annoying behavior is the result of antecedent causes which, if you follow them long enough, will take you beyond the moment of his birth and therefore to events for which he cannot be held responsible by any stretch of the imagination."[12]

While Tolkien was doing pioneering work in philology and creating Middle-Earth on the side, B. F. Skinner and the "behaviorists" who followed him were busy reducing human persons to mere feedback mechanisms for external stimuli. This was psychology under the rubric of positivism, the belief that only "sense data" is real or knowable. Accordingly, Skinner viewed freedom as just so much nonsense. In his tellingly titled book *Beyond Freedom and Dignity*, he called the "abolition" of "autonomous man" long overdue. He continued:

> Autonomous man is a device used to explain what we cannot explain in any other way. He has been constructed from our ignorance, and as our understanding increases, the very stuff of which he is composed vanishes.... To man qua man we readily say good riddance. Only by dispossessing him can we turn to the real causes of human behavior. Only then can we turn from the inferred to the observed, from the miraculous to the natural, from the inaccessible to the manipulable.[13]

This train of thought, fashionable as it was in Skinner's time, is rationally perverse. After all, we know from direct introspection both our freedom and the limits of our freedom. We know them far more directly than we can know an abstract postulate of positivism or materialist philosophy. Russell and Skinner inverted that basic priority in our knowledge and used what they merely assumed to overturn what everyone, including Russell and Skinner, knows as well as he knows anything. The more rational course would be to seek out an account of reality that accommodates, rather than excludes, our direct experience of freedom and our knowledge of ourselves.

The Doom of Freedom

For Tolkien, human freedom is both an opportunity and a burden. Presumably a hydrogen atom never encounters a dilemma. It simply does whatever the laws of physics require. But to be in a position to *choose* between two or more competing possibilities, with no infallible foreknowledge of the outcome, is a heavy burden.

We see this at the end of *The Fellowship of the Ring*, where Aragorn tells Frodo that the "burden" of choosing his future course lies upon the hobbit alone. Aragorn soon laments his own choices. "Alas," he cries at the beginning of *The Two Towers*, "an ill fate is on me this day, and all that I do goes amiss." With Gandalf gone, he struggles with whether to go to Minas Tirith, which his "heart desires", or go after Merry and Pippin. Either choice would mean abandoning the ring bearer. After lamenting his predicament, Aragorn finally chooses. He, along with Gimli and Legolas, chase Merry and Pippin, with the hope of rescuing them from their captors.

When he encounters Éomer while pursuing Merry and Pippin, a horseman of Rohan asks him, "What doom do you bring from the North?" Aragorn does not recount his many struggles since leaving Bree. He answers simply, "The doom of choice." The answer reflects Tolkien's knowledge of the history of words. *Doom* is one of the sources of our word *freedom*. Aragorn refers to a choice that he has already made for himself and that now confronts Éomer's king. "You may say this to Théoden, son of Thengel: open war lies before him, with Sauron or against him. None may now live as they have lived, and few shall keep what they call their own."[14]

This is Théoden's predicament. He cannot avoid the necessity of choice. To do nothing is itself to choose a likely outcome: defeat. He is not free to avoid war. His freedom consists in being able to choose between the live alternatives, namely, to fight or to surrender to death or enslavement. And the choice to fight will not put an end to choice, but rather open up another branching tree of options. Such is the nature of freedom.

No Freedom, No Heroism

Intimately linked with freedom are responsibility and virtue. You can't have the latter two without the former. We can only be responsible for our actions if we have some measure of control over them. The heroism exhibited by Aragorn, Gandalf, Bilbo, Frodo, and the other heroic characters only makes sense if they have some measure of freedom and so bear responsibility for their actions. Without freedom there is no heroism or courage. We praise Gandalf, Elrond, and Galadriel because they resist the temptation to take the ring. We fault Saruman because he does not resist its allure when he could have. We praise Sam and Frodo for pursuing the right course even though they believe it will lead to their deaths.

Implicit in these judgments is our sense that there is freedom of choice as well as a moral structure to things. It's both good and generally possible to resist the temptation to wickedly dominate others, and wrong to freely give into that temptation. Conversely, it's praiseworthy to risk and even sacrifice your life for a good cause. "Greater love has no man than this, that a man lay down his life for his friends", said Jesus.[15] The coherence of the Middle-Earth narratives requires that the reader constantly make these moral distinctions, and most readers do just that.

This moral vision of Tolkien's is, once again, completely out of keeping with the materialistic assumptions in elite twentieth-century culture, which are increasingly trickling down to twenty-first-century pop culture. Moral distinctions have no place in a materialistic mindset. Of course, your atheist friend knows that murder is wrong, and he will be morally outraged if someone steals his car. But a consistent materialist must be committed to explaining away all such moral judgments, including his own.

Darwinian materialists Michael Ruse and E. O. Wilson summed up the inevitable attitude when they said, "Morality, or more strictly our belief in morality, is merely an adaptation put in place to further our reproductive ends.... Ethics as we understand it is an illusion fobbed off on us by our genes to get us to cooperate."[16] In other words, those of our ancestors who acted in certain ways tended to enhance their survival prospects, and the same logic holds for entire societies. At some point in our evolutionary past, our ancestors came to believe that certain actions were right (caring for children, protecting the elderly, encouraging monogamy) and other things were wrong (eating siblings, sacrificing children, and so forth). But the important point, for Ruse, Wilson, and others who share this view, is the survival-enhancing behavior that correlates with our moral judgments, not the truth of the moral judgments themselves. In fact, in Ruse's view, those moral judgments are but useful illusions. To put it bluntly, it's not that it's really wrong to eat one's siblings out of spite or jealousy, but simply that any society that habitually tolerated such behavior would tend to be selected out of the gene pool.

Of course, Ruse and Wilson, like B. F. Skinner and Bertrand Russell above, do not know that materialism is true. Rather, they're taking a philosophical speculation about reality and using it to trump what they know directly. This is not a rational posture. Rationally, we should seek an understanding of reality that accommodates what we already know.

The Road to Heroism

A father praises his daughter for finishing her algebra homework, because he knows she could have frittered away the afternoon watching *Cake Boss*. And if instead she has frittered away the afternoon, he can justly discipline her, because she was under no necessity to do so. He does so hoping that through this system of praise and discipline his daughter will develop proper study habits, and that those habits will eventually shape her so that she will make virtuous choices even without the prospects of praise or punishment from her father. If she continues to exercise virtue, she may be able to do so even if the path of virtue becomes the path of suffering and death. That is the mark of the hero.

We see this process of developing the heroic capacity in the character of Bilbo. He begins as a decidedly unheroic hobbit, but that gradually changes in the course of his adventures. Having been hired to burgle by Thorin and Company, he screws up his courage and tries to burgle the evil trolls, despite the danger of being eaten. A bit later he pursues his captured dwarf companions even though it means dealing with goblins. And later still he saves his friends from giant spiders in Mirkwood. Each of these acts of bravery is one step up the summit that marks true heroism.

When the companions finally arrive at the Lonely Mountain, Bilbo has built up heroic capital he didn't have before he left the Shire. This is a good thing, since he soon finds himself descending the tunnel to the inner part of the mountain fortress, where he knows the dragon Smaug lies in wait. The tunnel reminds him of Bag End. "If only I could wake up and find this beastly tunnel was my own front-hall at home", he wishes, even as he continues down the tunnel, possibly to his own death. "Going on from there was the bravest thing he ever did", the narrator tells us. "He fought the real battle in the tunnel alone, before he ever saw the vast danger that lay in wait."[17] His heroism consisted not in his military exploits, but in his moral courage, his willingness to do what he ought, even if, as seemed likely, his own death be the result.

This is especially clear when he takes the precious Arkenstone to the camp of the men and elves and offers it to them in hopes of averting a tragic war. He reaches this point by having chosen the courageous path at several earlier points along the way. He reached it, in other words, by practicing the virtues of selflessness and courage.

Here we see that freedom is more than simply making a choice. We do not praise anyone for exercising his freedom, but for what he does with it. Bilbo made all sorts of decisions on the way to the Battle of the Five Armies. But his consistent choices, like the disciplined practice of a great athlete, allowed him the freedom to exercise heroic courage he lacked at the beginning. This is what is referred to as freedom for excellence, which goes far beyond mere freedom of choice. To become a hero, one must be what Nassim Nicholas Taleb calls "antifragile", which means you benefit from a certain, limited but unpredictable adversity.[18]

As a political aside, an unintended effect of a nanny state that backstops all risk can be to stifle the development of freedom for excellence, as when it bails out banks that ought to experience costs as well as benefits so that those leading them can develop the virtue of taking prudent risks. At the individual level, an overly intrusive welfare state that undercuts initiative can blunt the pedagogical value of experience. Sometimes the best improver is to face the consequences of our actions, and to be allowed to strive in the school of hard knocks on the path to achievement. We see this principle at work in "The Scouring of the Shire". Gandalf and Aragorn could have taken care of Saruman and his thugs in short order, but the Shire would never have developed its own capacity for courage, resolve, and independence if they had treated the hobbits as helpless children.

A Theology of Middle-Earth

There are subtle hints of religion in the Middle-Earth novels: the men of Gondor turn to the west before they eat, and at the bridge of Khazad-dûm, Gandalf challenges the Balrog by declaring, "I am a Servant of the Secret Fire, wielder of the flame of Udûn.... Go back to the Shadow! You cannot pass."[19] For Tolkien, this Secret Fire was the Holy Spirit.[20] But the implicit religious elements in *The Hobbit* and *The Lord of the Rings* are explicit in *The Silmarillion*. One is justified in reading the hobbit novels in light of this work—first, because Tolkien was working on *The Silmarillion* before, during, and after his work on *The Hobbit* and *The Lord of the Rings*; second, because it explicitly connects to characters and events in those two novels; and finally, because he was still niggling away at this Middle-Earth legendarium in the last years of his life. The fact that it was only released to the public in 1977 (as edited by Christopher Tolkien, four years after Tolkien's death) is due to the scope of the project and the vicissitudes of publishing, not to the importance of the work in his own thinking.

The beginning of *The Silmarillion*, called *Ainulindalë*, is similar to the first chapter of Genesis. It describes Ilúvatar, which means "father of all", bringing everything else into existence. (He is also called Eru, which means "the One".) In the Bible, God speaks the world into existence. Ilúvatar creates the world with music. In the Middle-Earth creation story, Ilúvatar first creates the Ainur, the "offspring of his thought". To these he presents a theme and then instructs them to make from it beautiful harmonious music. Unfortunately, the greatest of the Ainur, Melkor, wants to make his own music, so he rebels and takes some other Ainur with him. This gives rise to cosmic disharmony that Ilúvatar must reform again and again. Eventually, Ilúvatar gives the Ainur a vision of his great work Arda—the Earth—and invites them to enter into it, and to help him continue the work of creation.

Transfixed by the vision, some of them enter Arda. The more powerful of these Ainur become the Valar. The less powerful take on physical forms and become the Maiar. Among the Maiar are Sauron, the Balrogs, and all the wizards—Saruman, Gandalf, and the rest. It is the Valar who then fashion the world for men and elves.

There are subtle differences and striking parallels with the biblical Creation narratives. Both are clearly theistic. In the Genesis account God directly creates Adam and Eve, just as Ilúvatar directly creates men (and elves). But Ilúvatar, seemingly in contrast to the biblical account, delegates some of the nitty-gritty duties of creating to the Valar. Even here, however, there is a subtle biblical precedent. In his Creation week before the creation of mankind, God simply declares, "Let there be". This differs from when he creates his image bearers. Then he seems to speak to himself: "Let us make man in our image, after our likeness."[21] This text, with the plural "us", has confounded interpreters for millennia. Is God speaking to himself or to the unnamed heavenly host in his midst? If the latter, did they play some role in Creation? It's not easy to say, although the Church Fathers tended to interpret it as an early hint of the doctrine of the Trinity. The divine delegation is certainly much more explicit in *The Silmarillion*. Still, there is a clear sense in which, by making creatures to "have dominion" over the rest of creation, God has delegated some portion of his plans to his creatures.

Middle-Earth, then, is part of a larger, monotheistic reality, even if most of this is off stage within the pages of *The Hobbit* and *The Lord of the Rings*, and even though religion itself makes few appearances in the story.

Theists, not Pagans

Superficially, Tolkien's heroic figures appear simply to be noble pre-Christian pagans. Certainly the somewhat less cultured warriors of Rohan have a great deal in common with the noble pagans that appear in some early Medieval works such as *Beowulf*, which were at the core of Tolkien's work as Oxford's Rawlinson and Bosworth Professor of Anglo-Saxon.[22] The link to these noble pagans is unarguable, but why do the nobler human cultures of Middle-Earth lack the worst vices common to actual pre-Christian pagans, such as raping, killing, or permanently enslaving the women and children of conquered villages?[23] At their best, Tolkien's pre-Christian pagans are nobler—more Christian we might say—even than the pagans found in the Norse sagas he admired (and, indeed, nobler than Christian warriors behaving wickedly).

This has to do with the fact that in Tolkien's fantasy world, they are the beneficiaries of special revelation from the Creator. Gandalf is an emissary from an almighty and transcendent Creator—a notion that is not at home in pre-Christian paganism. Moreover, the Dúnedain—of whom Aragorn is the chief—remain connected to and committed to faith in this deity through their friendship with the high elves, from whom they learn many culturally important things, not least of them being the absolute goodness of the Creator and his moral precepts. (The Dúnedain, in turn, pass some or all of these cultural treasures on to their eventual allies—such as Rohan and the Shire.) So, like the pagan heroes in the Norse sagas, they possess a stern allegiance to the good, but unlike the virtuous pagans of those sagas, they also are privy to a bit of special revelation about the omnipotence, holiness, and will of the Creator.

And through this, they possess an abiding faith in he who is the ground of all good, the One, the Creator of the world.

The Creator of Freedom

Tolkien's Middle-Earth writings give us culture undergirded by a belief in the Creator, but they go even further to suggest that we could never have free will to begin with, if it weren't for the prior existence of a free and powerful Creator. In *The Silmarillion*, the power to create other beings with free will, such as men and elves, is reserved to Ilúvatar alone. When Aulë, one of the Valar, decides to make dwarves, they are simply automata that do what he wants. As an act of repentance, he plans to destroy them. But Ilúvatar is moved to compassion and, rather than destroying the dwarves, gives them the free will that Aulë could not.[24]

The suggestion here is that, without a supremely free, powerful, and self-existent Creator, it's not likely—it might not even be possible—that there would be creatures with freedom in the world in the first place.[25] An eternal and personal Creator, however, would have it within his power to create other agents. The fact that we enjoy freedom, then, is itself a sign of the existence of God.

Now, it's true that some atheists defend freedom, and even human dignity. Ayn Rand, for instance, rightly insisted that "every man is an end in himself, not a mere means to the ends of others."[26] But if we're just matter in motion, how could we be an end rather than merely a link in a mindless causal chain? And why would freedom, even if it existed, be good? Whence comes our intrinsic dignity? Why should men be treated as ends in themselves, rather than mere means to the ends of those more powerful and intelligent? Agency, freedom, human dignity—these are ideas at home in a theistic context, but not at all in the cramped quarters of materialism.

Freedom, Providence, and the Meaning of Life

Some atheist libertarians have claimed that individual freedom is possible only if God doesn't exist. God in their view could only be a divine dictator, predetermining every action of every creature, so that no alternative—no choice—would be possible. But they have it backward.

The opposite thesis—that freedom is only possible if God *does* exist—is much nearer the mark. To see this, we need a proper understanding of God and of ourselves.

To take the second point first, as we have seen, real human freedom consists not in having unlimited choices (we are not omnipotent), but in having real, even if limited, choices, which, if we pursue rightly, will allow us to develop virtues—a freedom for excellence. If we habitually choose wrongly, we will not find greater freedom, but bondage.

Although there have been some extreme outliers in Christian history, the broad, well-attested view of God in the Christian tradition is not of a Cosmic Tyrant, but of a loving Creator who has given "even to creatures the dignity of causality",[27] as Thomas Aquinas put it. And to human creatures, he has given us not just causality but creativity. The mind, searching for simple images, is quick to imagine that the only choices are either theological determinism—in which God predetermines everything and so makes no room for freedom—or "open theism", in which God allows freedom and must therefore simply let us make our choices, which he learns about after the fact.

The traditional view of providence, however, is subtler. God creates and oversees the world, but he is also intimately involved in it. He can act directly in the world—to turn water into wine or raise Jesus from the dead—or he can work through so-called secondary causes, whether they be inanimate objects or our own actions. Through his providential care, he can even take our evil choices—as Joseph told his brothers who had sold him into slavery—and turn them to good.

This is basic Christian theology. It is also Tolkien's theology. Some Tolkien interpreters miss this because the theology is so thoroughly baked into the pudding—dissolved fully into the stories.

Even apart from their rich backstory, the hobbit novels buzz with what can only be called providence, not least because the sagest figures—Tom Bombadil, Gandalf, Elrond, and Galadriel—all emphasize that there is a purposeful order behind events, even if that order is often obscure in daily life.

It's so common in the novels that a complete survey would require a chapter unto itself, but consider an especially clear example in a conversation between Frodo and Gandalf. Frodo is lamenting that the ring has come to him. Gandalf tells Frodo that, despite appearances, Gollum did not merely lose the ring. The ring *wanted* to be found, and so it "left him". Why would the evil ring want to be found by Bilbo, a character not loyal to Sauron? It seems that there was another "power at work", Gandalf explains to Frodo. "I can put it no plainer than by saying that Bilbo was *meant* to find the Ring, and *not* by its maker. In which case you also were meant to have it. And that may be an encouraging thought."[28]

The subtle nature of Tolkien's art is evident in this passage. Note the passive tense of the verbs—"was meant" and "were meant". This allows the reader to infer the existence of the agent behind mundane events without the divine agent being named. If an event was "meant" to happen, then it happened as the result of purposive design rather than happenstance. And design requires a designer. With Tolkien's construction, readers can make that inference, even though the cosmic stage director remains hidden behind the curtain.

Gandalf's immediate point to Frodo is that the presence of design is encouraging. Indeed it is. If the greatest designs of evil, even the One Ring of the evil Sauron, can be orchestrated toward good, then not only our mundane acts, but the darkest episodes in history might just be scenes in a vast cosmic comedy that will come to fulfillment in a "eucatastrophe"—like Christ's Crucifixion resolving in his Resurrection —in which the seemingly tragic threads of a story are surprisingly resolved for the good of the protagonist.

If you're accustomed to thinking of God's providence in a deterministic way, you may be surprised that Tolkien believed that providence doesn't destroy our freedom but rather guarantees it. Providence, in both our world and the world of Middle-Earth, not only grounds our freedom. It takes our isolated choices and weaves them into a vast tapestry of purposeful meaning.[29] Without providence, history would be just "one damn thing after another", as one historian put it.[30] What's the point of free will in a universe like that?

The Fates of Greek mythology seem to embody such a notion. In the modern context, several of Tolkien's literary contemporaries were pioneering an absurdist theater that insisted we live in such a universe—one without purpose. Tolkien wasn't among them. In Middle-Earth, "fate" isn't a meaningless determinism. Our fate, rather, is our destiny, our calling, the *purpose* for which we have been born. As Elrond tells the Council gathered at Rivendell in *The Fellowship of the Ring*, they have been "called hither" for a specific purpose—to decide what to do with the ring. "You have come and are here met, in this very nick of time, by chance as it may seem. Yet it is not so. Believe rather that it is so ordered that we, who sit here, and none others, must now find counsel for the peril of the world."[31]

As the quest unfolds, the characters sometimes become aware that they're in a story that's still being told, with an ending that is just out of sight. In *The Two Towers*, Sam reflects on how even misguided choices can somehow turn out right in the end. "We shouldn't be here at all," Sam says to Frodo, "if we'd known more about it before we started." He continues:

> But I suppose it's often that way. The brave things in the old tales and songs, Mr. Frodo.... I used to think that they were things the wonderful folk of the stories went out and looked for.... But that's not the way of it with the tales that really mattered.... Folk seem to have been just landed in them, usually—their paths were laid that way, as you put it. But I expect they had lots of chances, like us, of turning back, only they didn't.... I wonder what sort of a tale we've fallen into?[32]

As we learn near the end of the story, it's a tale in which simple acts of kindness, mercy, and courage shape the history of the world for good rather than evil. So, for example, the seemingly trivial mercy shown to Gollum by Bilbo, Frodo, and others makes it possible to destroy the One Ring in the fires of Mount Doom after Frodo has lost the ability to part with the ring freely. But for Gollum, and but for the acts of kindness that kept him in the story to the very end, the quest to destroy the ring would have failed. More astonishingly, the story resolves even individual acts of evil, such as Gollum's own lust to acquire the ring, into an overarching good.

The characters in the story, just as the actors in history, don't know the ending ahead of time. Fortunately, freedom does not require omniscience. Most of the protagonists in the Middle-Earth novels are confined, much as we are, within this earthly vale. They don't know the outcome of their choices ahead of time. At least some elves, such as Galadriel and Elrond, as well as the Maiar Gandalf, Saruman, and Sauron, have glimmers of clairvoyance and telepathy. But none of them can predict the future infallibly, and most can see only a few trees and rarely even the outlines of a forest. Occasionally, however, the characters get a glimpse, such as the references to fulfilled prophecies in *The Hobbit* and

The Lord of the Rings, and they learn enough through song and history and conversation to have faith that there is an overarching pattern to events.

For Tolkien, then, *fate*, *luck*, or *destiny* isn't blind; it's the path along the ever-reticulating network of free choices that ultimately are taken up into a much grander and purposeful story, one orchestrated by the Author who transcends but remains fully involved in it.

Free to Create

Finally, Tolkien ties freedom and creativity together because real creativity requires freedom. To create in the fullest sense belongs only to God,[33] who can create from nothing. Nevertheless, Tolkien described certain creatures as "sub-creators" because they can produce things that are genuinely new, even if they rely on what God has already created. We are made in the image of the creative God to be sub-creators. We can produce things that never would emerge naturally from mere physics or chemistry. God created clay and straw, but left it to us to make bricks. God created sand, but left it to us to use sand to fashion integrated circuits and fiber optics.

We would not even be sub-creators of these things if we were merely links in an ironclad causal chain, any more than a golf club creates a hole in one off a perfect drive. But we can be sub-creators because, to use Saint Thomas' language again, we have been given "the dignity of causality"—a causality so robust that we can make free choices on the way to fashioning new things from the stuff of God's Creation. We touched on what this means for the free society in chapter 1, and we will explore it further in chapters 7 and 8. Here, suffice to say, societies such as the Shire and Rivendell flourish by protecting the space for creativity while the arch-villain Sauron crushes that freedom, and the resulting picture isn't pretty.

The Conditions for Freedom

A free society for Tolkien isn't merely something that's nice if you can get it; it's worth laboring, fighting, and dying for. The reason the free peoples of the West fight Mordor is to preserve their freedom, which requires that they resist the slavery and subjugation he offers them at the point of a sword. It's true that we are free by nature, but Tolkien and his heroic characters understand the breadth and depth of our freedom varies depending on when and where we live. Some places are friendly to freedom, others are not.

The phrase "free society" is easy to toss around but less easy to use in conversation without talking past one another. Let's lay out a clear description of the term, and then look briefly at some examples of these qualities among the free peoples of Middle-Earth. A society is "free" insofar as it allows widespread freedom for individuals and communities. A society that allows a Sauron to enslave the others isn't free—neither is a society in which everyone can do whatever he wants to, since that society would quickly degenerate into one in which the strong and ruthless prey on the weak. A free society will be one in which the rule of law is generally respected and enforced, both by the state and the citizenry, for the strong and the weak.

A free and therefore lawful society, at a minimum, will never force a person to choose among alternatives all of which commit him to some intrinsic evil, such as violating the rights and dignity of himself or another. To give an extreme example, a couple won't be forced either to get an abortion or send the baby they insist on keeping to a religion-inoculation camp.

People in a free society also will have broad freedoms in the market. You won't be compelled to work in a car factory if you'd really like to try to become a doctor. At the same time, you won't be able to force your neighbor with impunity to let you remove her appendix so you can learn how to be a doctor. If you want to succeed as a physician, you have to do what is necessary—education, hard work, hospital residency, licensing—in order for people to freely choose you as their doctor. In this way, a lawful, free society encourages its citizens to make voluntary exchanges, that is, exchanges that are freely chosen on both sides. The only way this will happen with any regularity in a free economy, since no one is being forced to buy anything, is for participants to offer things that fulfill a need or desire.

There's no place in Tolkien's Middle-Earth writing where such an extended definition of political and economic freedom is given, of course. He was writing novels rather than tracts. But what he gives us are societies that contain these dimensions of freedom, the Shire being the most articulated.

There is another dimension of freedom we find cultivated by the wise and good leaders in Middle-Earth: a richly free society allows its people to pursue freedom for excellence; it encourages rather than discourages them to pursue their own calling and passion.

This purpose or end includes this earthly life but also eternal life with God and the saints. Our ultimate purpose—to combine the claims of the Catholic catechism and Westminster confession—is to love, seek, know, glorify, and enjoy God forever. Such a message is only latent in *The Lord of the Rings*, but we are offered glimpses of it, as with Gandalf's fervent service to the "Secret Fire", and in Frodo's realizing he can find ultimate healing only by leaving Middle-Earth and sailing to the Undying Lands.

Jesus said the greatest commandment is to love God, and the second is like it, to love our neighbor as ourselves. Love that is coerced is not love. Jesus said that if you love him, you will obey his commandments. But to obey him, we must be free to fulfill our other God-given purposes as beings made in the image of God—to love our families and fellow man and to exercise the virtues required to do that. Recognizing this, a free society allows and encourages its members to be creative and fruitful as they exercise dominion as God's stewards over his Creation.

We know empirically that a free economy, of all the options, best coordinates the gifts and needs of a diverse population. And we should not be surprised that economists have found that countries that enjoy the most economic and political freedom prosper more than those that don't.[34]

There is no unique form of government that will ensure such freedom. Absolute dictatorship obviously won't qualify, but certain forms of democracy, where the majority can run roughshod over the basic rights of the minority, can be just as oppressive. Tolkien can be challenging for American readers since his books portray hereditary monarchies, and an exceedingly benevolent king. Aragorn, unlike the American stereotype of King George III, recognizes and protects the rights and dignity of his subjects. The distant peoples under his authority expect him to remain limited in his use of his authority, and he doesn't disappoint. Even though the Shire lies within the jurisdiction of Gondor and enjoys the king's protection from hostile, outside forces, the government itself is so remote that hobbits largely govern themselves. After Aragorn becomes king, we learn in the appendix to *The Return of the King* that he comes near to visit old friends but never enters the Shire, as a sign of respect for their freedom.

The king has a crucial role to play in this picture of ordered liberty, but Tolkien emphasizes the indispensable role of the citizens as well. For generations leading up to the action of *The Lord of the Rings*, the hobbits maintain deep respect for the authority of the long absent king, to whom they attributed the laws known by reason:

> [F]or nearly a thousand years, and even the ruins of Kings' Norbury were covered with grass. Yet the Hobbits still said of wild folk and wicked things (such as trolls) that they had not heard of the king. For they attributed to the king of old all their essential laws; and usually they kept the laws of free will, because they were The Rules (as they said), both ancient and just.

This virtuous commitment to the "essential laws" allowed them to have a minimalist set of rules for daily life—to have, in other words, "hardly any 'government' ".[35]

As one delves into Tolkien's legendarium, one finds examples of oppressive human kings, as with the Númenórean kings corrupted by Sauron in *The Silmarillion*. So, clearly Tolkien didn't see monarchy as a cure-all. For Tolkien, there were no cure-all political systems. Still, he viewed widespread respect for freedom and human dignity and widespread suspicion of concentrated political power as indispensable ingredients to a free society, without which even the wisest of political arrangements were to no avail.

Here we come to the great similarities between Tolkien's outlook and that of the American founders. The founders, like Tolkien, emphasized the need for a moral culture to maintain freedom.[36] Both were adamantly committed to limiting the power of government as well. The American Experiment and Tolkien's greatest literary experiment, *The Lord of the Rings*, are quite different in the means—a republic of checks and balances versus a modest, benevolent monarchy—but the ideal is the same: limited government and a free society.

Tolkien and the American founders also both understood the paradox that many earlier political experimenters had failed to appreciate: sin is the main reason we need government and also the main reason to limit government. They knew about the failed republics in ancient Greece and Rome, where the line between majority and mob rule was thin and fragile. They had studied biblical history and the history of Europe. And they took sin seriously. "If men were angels," said founder James

Madison, "no government would be necessary. If angels were to govern men, neither external nor internal controls on government would be necessary. In framing a government which is to be administered by men over men, the great difficulty lies in this: you must first enable the government to control the governed; and in the next place oblige it to control itself."[37]

The nineteenth-century British statesman Lord Acton spoke of absolute power corrupting absolutely. We saw in the previous chapter how Tolkien explored the corrupting effects of power through the One Ring of power. Tolkien's depiction of freedom also exemplifies another axiom of Lord Acton, that "liberty is the delicate fruit of a mature civilization."[38] Those societies in Middle-Earth committed to ordered liberty, limited government, and freedom for excellence—such as the Shire, Rivendell, and Gondor under Aragorn—tend toward personal and cultural flourishing, but clearly their freedom must be won and guarded with great vigilance. Tolkien, it seems, is trying to tell us something: the free peoples of the world would do well to guard and cultivate their freedom.

Chapter 6

The Just War of the Ring

After Frodo and his companions barely make it from the Shire to Rivendell, the Council of Elrond decides to destroy the ring rather than wield it. This central strategy to defeat the forces of Sauron requires a voluntary rejection of power on their part, and their resolve is tested again and again. Only by resisting the temptation for as long as they possibly can, only by destroying this most powerful of weapons, are they finally able to restore peace and freedom to Middle-Earth.

Thus is *The Lord of the Rings* ultimately about the noble rejection of the power to dominate. Given this, it might seem paradoxical that the book is punctuated by fighting and violence on both sides of the conflict. Anyone familiar with *The Lord of the Rings*, however, knows that the Council's decision is not a wholesale rejection of the methods of war in pursuit of a just cause. None of the Council nurses illusions about Sauron's intentions, and none of them believes the free peoples of the West should lay down their weapons and urge Sauron to join hands and sing, "Give peace a chance." They know war is coming. The question is whether to ignore that knowledge or meet the threat with all of the strength and wisdom they can muster. They choose the latter. In this is encapsulated Tolkien's complex moral vision of war—neither pacifism nor unbridled pragmatism, but a view older, richer, and, as we'll argue, more realistic.

Blood, Guts, and Glory

One occasionally hears complaints that Tolkien glorifies war.[1] If true, this would be particularly troubling since Christian theology teaches the value of human life and warns that we carry Adam and Eve's fallen tendency toward evil and misuse of power. It would be incongruous, in other words, if the Christian Tolkien extolled militarism, a pagan glorification of war, or an embrace of raw power.

So, what about all the war and killing? What about the bodies of orcs piled high on Pelennor Field and consumed by the trees after the battle at Helm's Deep? A superficial reading might suggest that all this warfare amounts to militarism, or to a glorification of war. But a closer reading of the books leads to a very different conclusion.

Tolkien scholar Matthew Dickerson shows how carefully Tolkien crafts key passages to make clear that he had no illusions about the horrors of war. Tolkien never loses sight of the personal and individual experience of war, even in the midst of great conflict. Take the two ultimate battles in his best-known books, the War of the Five Armies in *The Hobbit*, and the Battle at the Black Gate in *Return of the King*. Tolkien's description of these conflicts is, Dickerson observes, "so closely parallel ... that I can only imagine the parallel is intentional."[2] Both are described as "terrible". Both "involve several different armies coming together to fight a common foe, both involve a single Hobbit (as an unimportant character), and both end with the unexpected coming of the Eagles presaging an unlooked-for hope and victory. Both battles also involved Gandalf as a critical agent in bringing the allied forces together to fight the common enemy."[3] Though the accounts give some details about the battle, both narratives suddenly shift in the midst of the fighting "from a distant omniscient view to the perspective of the unimportant Hobbit".[4] We learn the feelings of Bilbo and Pippin. We see their subjective experience of fear and smallness. In this way, Tolkien personalizes these cataclysmic events and thus prevents the reader from losing sight of the individual in the sweeping theater of battle.

Dickerson ably defends Tolkien from the glib assertion that he "glorified" war. However, he comes close to explaining away the warfare as a literary convention that Tolkien devised to make various points about responsibility and moral courage. This also leads him to spiritualize key elements of the narrative. When the captain of the Nazgûl throws back his hood, for instance, no face appears but only a crown on top of an invisible head. As a result, Dickerson observes, "We might well conclude that since the only foe we see close up on the Pelennor Fields is a wraith, the real enemy that must be faced in Middle-earth is a spiritual enemy."[5]

But this sets up an "either/or" where Tolkien clearly presented a "both/and". Tolkien's view of reality was overwhelmingly sacramental. He never implied that the physical world is unreal, or a mere stand-in for the spiritual realm. He believed rather that events in the physical world are integrally tied to a much wider spiritual realm. Both are real; both are important.

Dickerson's subordination of the reality of war to spiritual lessons leads him to some implausible interpretations. Take Gandalf himself. Dickerson quotes a 1954 letter in which Tolkien describes Gandalf as an incarnate "'angel' ... an emissary from the Lords of the West, sent to Middle-earth, as the great crisis of Sauron loomed on the horizon." Such "Powers", Tolkien wrote, were "primarily sent" to "train, advise, instruct, arouse the hearts and minds of those threatened by Sauron to a resistance with their own strengths: and not just to do the job for them."[6] This helps explain why Tolkien is careful to remove Gandalf from the action at certain points in both *The Hobbit* and *The Lord of the Rings*. Otherwise, his power would swamp the efforts of the others. From this Dickerson concludes that "Gandalf was sent for reasons having to do with the spiritual rather than the physical plane."[7] But Gandalf isn't always away at crucial moments, and when he is present, he's often doing more than just advising and encouraging. Think, for instance, of both the major battles noted above, not to mention numerous other skirmishes. And even when he is away, he is typically aiding in ways both spiritual and physical, as when he rounds up more soldiers for the Battle of Helm's Deep and then shows up to fight alongside them. It's notable that Tolkien said that Gandalf, unlike ordinary angels, is an *incarnate* angel. He is *enfleshed* and contributes in very fleshly ways at many points in the stories. Nothing in his character or the narrative suggests that the physical details of Tolkien's story should be assimilated to the spiritual.

Since Gandalf is arguably the wisest of many wise figures in the novels, what are we to surmise from how he aids the free peoples of the West? Gandalf fights over and over again in *The Hobbit* and *The Lord of the Rings*, and he badgers men who are inclined not to fight against a wicked enemy. Throughout *The Lord of the Rings*, Gandalf's job is to rouse the forces of the West to resist the ambitions of Sauron with swords, arrows, and other tools of war. Given the way both the narrator, the other wise characters, and the fruits of Gandalf's advice all point toward him being a seat of great wisdom, the lesson seems clear: to prematurely beat swords into plowshares is not just foolish but immoral when the swords are needed to protect the innocent. One may not like the fact that the wisest character in *The Lord of the Rings* has no qualms about fighting and killing under certain conditions, but that's how the text is given to us.

One more example: What to do with the scene in the battle at Helm's Deep when Legolas and Gimli compete while killing orcs? The passage is "certainly disturbing", Dickerson comments, since it makes a "sport" of "war and killing".[8] Dickerson tries to minimize the incident by noting that despite the contest, "we witness very few of the actual tallies. We are with Gimli for numbers one, two, and twenty-one (of forty-two), and that is all.... As for Legolas, we see only number thirty-nine (of forty-one), and that from a distance."[9] The obvious response is, so what? The text would be boring and burdensome if it contained a blow-by-blow account of every killing. The fact is that the contest between the dwarf and the elf is in the story, and there's no hint that Tolkien disapproves of it. Our interpretation of Tolkien should accommodate that fact.

Just War

Because of the inherent horrors of war, many conclude that morality and war can't go together, that the only options are an unconstrained embrace of military power or its wholesale renunciation. More sophisticated contemporary thinkers try to resolve this dilemma by accepting the necessary evil of war, at least in principle, as Dickerson does. Many go much further and try to "balance" this acceptance by shrouding it with ironic posturing and by treating the moral claims of the warring parties as necessarily equivalent and suspect. In the extreme, this can lead to the position that the only just wars are those for which we have no national interest.

Tolkien took none of these views. Instead, he took a view with deep roots in the Christian tradition. Called the Just War tradition, it stretches back to the Church Fathers and is rooted in Scripture and natural-law reasoning. The Old Testament, for instance, distinguished between killing in war on the one hand and outright murder on the other, and identified instances of unjust war, as when King Saul waged war against David and his men. In Romans 13, Paul says the government "does not bear the sword in vain" (vs. 4) but uses it to fulfill its primary purpose—punishing evildoers (a point Peter seconds in 1 Peter 2). This includes maintaining justice at home and protecting citizens from foreign aggressors.

Just War is a common view in Christian history, though it also has secular proponents.[10] As a formal set of principles, it started with theologians such as Saint Augustine, and its proponents appeal to the fact that, both intuitively and legally, we distinguish different types of killing. Premeditated murder, for instance, is much worse morally than killing someone who dashes in front of your car on a dark highway. We even distinguish between different forms of murder. We punish murder during the commission of a robbery more severely than murder committed in the heat of passion. And of course, if a man tackles a knife-wielding maniac who had been killing people in a department store and fights the murderer to the death, we don't condemn the man but commend him.

At the same time, the Just War tradition applies specifically to warfare rather than to ordinary civilian life. It is a defense of war as morally right, even imperative, under certain conditions, and according to certain rules of engagement. Under these conditions, waging war is *just*, and not merely a necessary evil. The moral good and the military good sometimes converge.

This perspective differs from so-called realism on the one hand and pacifism on the other. Realists argue that trying to apply moral rules when we are defending ourselves against hostile enemies is to tie our hands behind our backs. If we try to avoid enemy civilians, our enemy will just use them as a shield. If we use our resources to care for prisoners of war, our enemies will get ahead by working their prisoners—our compatriots—to death. It's not that realists don't care about right and wrong. They just believe it's better to do what needs to be done to win quickly, even if it means setting aside justice. The scruples can always be picked up again after the victory is secured.

Among realists, the primary question is whether one's cause is the moral one. Once that's answered in the affirmative, the details of method fade into the background. "Realism" thus tends to reduce defense and foreign policy to national self-interest, without regard to questions of what constitutes moral and just behavior in war. Virtually any means is justified so long as it serves that end.

In *The Lord of the Rings*, Saruman speaks like a modern "realist". He urges Gandalf to allow him to use the One Ring and battle Sauron, even though, as Gandalf explains, the ring inevitably corrupts its possessor. Soon it becomes clear that Saruman has chosen the side of might rather than right, and so chosen to ally with Sauron rather than fight against him. But even then, he is not loyal to the Dark Lord. The alliance between Isengard and Barad-dûr, in Saruman's mind, is a temporary expedient.

Just War supporters agree that a nation has a duty to defend its legitimate interests, but, unlike "realists", they argue that we can, and should, use moral judgment when dealing with the details of war and its aftermath. And as Tolkien's Middle-Earth stories suggest, Just War proponents are actually more realistic and prudent, in a far-reaching way, than the realists, since they look ahead to the long-range consequences of morally dubious strategies, strategies that may serve well in the short term but contain within them the seeds of their own destruction. This insight is dramatized in the tragic spiritual and physical demise of Denethor and Saruman, two "realists" undone by a reality beyond their reckoning.

Just War proponents also disagree with pacifists who treat warfare as wrong no matter the reason. Pacifism levels the jagged moral landscape of reality into the parking lot of moral equivalence. There's a popular bumper sticker that boils this confusion down to three words: "War is terrorism." This ignores obvious distinctions. Going to war to stop, for instance, Nazi Germany from taking over half the planet and wiping out the Jews may be painful, wrenching, and filled with human tragedies, but it's not terrorism. If you hold a precept that blurs the distinction between allied soldiers liberating a Nazi concentration camp and hijackers flying civilian planes into the World Trade Center in 2001, you should discard the precept.

Or take some examples closer to home. If, as pacifists hold, all forms of violence are wrong, then police work, parents protecting their children from intruders, and self-defense against rape are all wrong. Short of the consummation of God's kingdom, such a pacifist policy would lead to a world where thieves, rapists, and murderers feared nothing but other wicked people.

The theoretical details are complicated, but the Just War criteria fit on a short list:

(1) Just cause
(2) Right intention
(3) Proper authority and a public declaration

(4) Last resort
(5) Probability of success
(6) Proportionality[11]

A just war, very simply, is one that is pursued publicly, as a last resort but with a realistic chance for success, by the proper authority for the right reasons to accomplish a just cause without using far more force than is needed to win. These principles also provide guidance on how to treat an enemy after it is vanquished. Just warriors will not exterminate a hostile military or civilian population, or enslave them, after hostilities have ceased.

Tolkien was a combat veteran, a scholar, and a solidly orthodox Catholic, so we can be sure that he was familiar with the Just War tradition. And, thus, we shouldn't be surprised to find the noblest characters in his novels adhering to Just War principles. In fact, much of *The Lord of the Rings* could be read as an extended interpretation of them, and one that rebukes some of the more fashionable ways of interpreting them.

A War Book

The picture Tolkien presents in *The Lord of the Rings* includes both a renunciation of the power to dominate and enslave others—the central function of the One Ring[12]—and vigorous support for the use of power to rightly resist the destructive forces of evil.[13] Thus, while Frodo takes the long journey to Mount Doom to destroy the One Ring in the caldron of Orodruin (Mount Doom), the fellowship fight and kill orcs, wargs, Uruk-hai, and Ringwraiths. On Weathertop, Strider and the four hobbits had rebuffed the attacks of the Ringwraiths, with one nearly fatal casualty: Frodo is stabbed with a Morgul blade. His use of the ring is partly to blame, but there is never the faintest indication that Aragorn was wrong to fight. Later, when the fellowship passes through the Mines of Moria, they must fight an assortment of orcs, as well as a giant cave troll, and, finally, a Balrog.

Tolkien scholar Tom Shippey rightly says *The Lord of the Rings* is "a war-book, also a post-war book, framed by and responding to the crisis of Western civilization, 1914–1945 (and beyond)."[14] It isn't an allegory of those wars, but the light it sheds on Just War principles gives them applicability to questions of war generally.

It's true that a first reader could get through *The Fellowship of the Ring* without quite realizing he's in a "war-book", since many of these incidents look like isolated skirmishes in which the protagonists merely defend themselves from attack. But as one reads deeper into *The Lord of the Rings*, skirmishes give way to larger and larger battles.

Orcs and wild men, incited by Saruman, descend upon the villages of Rohan, raping and pillaging as they go. Gandalf, now resurrected as Gandalf the White, encourages King Théoden to attack these hordes outright, lest they establish a foothold in the lands of men. Théoden agrees, but takes what might seem to be the safer route: he leaves Rohan's capital, Edoras, and moves to the hardened mountain fortress of the Hornburg at Helm's Deep. Saruman sends forth his ten-thousand strong army of Uruk-hai, bred solely to destroy the world of men, and reinforced by wild men from the hills, as well as great siege-works and an explosive device invented by Saruman. Despite the overwhelming odds and the nearness of defeat, the Rohirrim emerge victorious with last-minute help from Gandalf and the cavalry led by Erkenbrand (in the Peter Jackson movie, Erkenbrand's character is merged with Éomer's). The wild trees of the forest, apparently led by the Ents, attack and destroy the fleeing Uruk-hai. Meanwhile, Merry and Pippin successfully enlist Treebeard and the other Ents in a parallel battle at Isengard.

By this point, the reader has already been well-prepared with hints of a greater and even more malevolent danger. When marching to Helm's Deep, for instance, Legolas tells Gandalf that he can make out in the distance some ominous "darkness" and "shapes moving with it". It is the Uruk-hai army marching south from Isengard to Helm's Deep. "And behind us comes a very storm of Mordor", replies Gandalf. "It will be a black night."[15] The combined forces of Rohan and Gondor meet the leading edge of that great storm at the Battle of Pelennor Fields. There the men of the West, plus the odd hobbit, dwarf, elf, and wizard, must battle a terrifying array of exotic enemies—everything from orcs and men of the south to trolls, oliphaunts, and Nazgûl on flying reptiles. Initially, it looks as if the great city of Minas Tirith will be overrun until the cavalry of the Rohirrim arrive.

But even then the combined forces are too slight to withstand Sauron's army. They are only saved when Aragorn arrives in the nick of time. In a parallel storyline, he has summoned an army of undead soldiers—perhaps a commentary on the necessity of unsavory allies in war—who help him defeat the Corsairs of Umbar allied with Mordor. Aragorn then liberates the slaves aboard the ships, who rally to him as he hurries upriver in the black-sailed ships to join the great battle. With the heir of the last king of Gondor raising the sword of the king in battle once again, the free peoples of the West rally and win a great victory.

But the war has still not reached its climax. Sauron has used only a fraction of his military might in this battle, retaining vast forces in Mordor; so the War of the Ring rages on. It is in this final battle that Gandalf puts into play his most desperate, seemingly imprudent, gambit: distract Sauron by marching out to meet his vastly superior forces in battle before the gates of Mordor so that Frodo and Sam can slip deeper into enemy territory, climb Mount Doom, destroy the One Ring in the Cracks of Doom, and so destroy Sauron (its maker) and all his evil works. Gandalf concedes that it is a desperate strategy but the only one with any hope of success, since Sauron's army is far too large to defeat in battle, and the ring far too evil and corrupting for any good leader to wield without himself becoming another Sauron. It's for these reasons that Gandalf and the other heroes pursue a combination of conventional and unconventional warfare—some of which could only seem folly to the unwise.

Conduct in War

We have seen that the cause of Gandalf and his companions is just and executed along the only lines that give it a real, if small, hope of success. And even a cursory reading of the novel shows that Gandalf, Aragorn, and their companions are also just in the way they treat their defeated enemies. Perhaps we should say that this is clear from "even a cursory reading of the novel *by someone who hasn't been eating psychedelic mushrooms*", because the phrasing needs to accommodate an early and bizarre review of the book by Alfred Duggan. In the *Times Literary Supplement* he complained that the heroes and villains in *The Lord of the Rings* were indistinguishable: each side simply kills the other.[16] But this reading misses crucial and obvious differences, even setting aside the fact that the villains of the novel are trying to enslave and kill while the heroes are trying to protect the freedom of free people.

The poet W. H. Auden gave the classic response to Duggan's complaint, arguing that the difference between the two is central to the plot and to the Council's choice to destroy the ring. "Evil", Auden observed in his review essay from 1956, "has every advantage but one—it is inferior in imagination. Good can imagine the possibility of becoming evil—hence the refusal of Gandalf and Aragorn to use the Ring—but Evil, defiantly chosen, can no longer imagine anything but itself."[17] Because Sauron can only imagine the desire for brute, top-down domination, he never dreams that any masterful hero among his enemies will choose to destroy the ring rather than seize it and try to set himself up as a tyrant.

That blind spot is his undoing, but it's more than this. The empathetic imagination of the heroes doesn't just allow them to outwit Sauron. It also speaks to crucial moral differences in the way the two sides wage war. A few examples will suffice to expose the emptiness of Duggan's complaint.

When Sauron captures Gollum he has the creature tortured until he reveals to them the ring's location.[18] Later, after Gollum escapes from Mordor, Aragorn, Gandalf, the wood elves, and later Sam and Frodo all coerce, interrogate, threaten,[19] and hold Gollum captive at various times; but they still treat him with relative if sometimes harsh dignity. The wood elves so dislike keeping the creature in captivity that they take him for walks in the forest, thus inadvertently giving him a means of escape.

Similarly, when the men of Rohan capture the hillmen aligned with Saruman, the hillmen are forced to hand over their weapons and work to repair the damage, but they receive forgiveness and the opportunity to start again. "Help now to repair the evil in which you have joined," they are told, "and afterward you shall take an oath never to attain to pass the Fords of Isen in arms, nor to march with the enemies of Men; and then you shall go free back to your land. For you have been deluded by Saruman."[20] There are similar acts of mercy after the Battle of Pelennor Fields, and before the Black Gate. Surely Tolkien intended a lesson here. Victors in war, while enjoying the fruits of victory, should offer reconciliation and forgiveness to the vanquished, rather than annihilation, slavery, or punitive reparations—as had been imposed on Germany after World War I to disastrous effect.

The protagonists also respect the right of others to maintain neutrality. When the Rohirrim march to Minas Tirith, the Woses, wild men of the woods, do not join them; but they offer their services to the Rohirrim by guiding them through the forest and out of the sight of watchful orcs. Théoden accepts their aid, but does not try to compel them to join the fight.[21]

Tolkien was also careful to preserve the humanity of the protagonists' human enemies. When Sam and Frodo first come upon Faramir and his men, Faramir is leading an ambush against the Haradrim—men from the south—who are marching north and east to join the forces of Sauron. In the ensuing fight, one of the Haradrim falls through the trees to his death, just where Sam and Frodo are hiding. Sam, we're told, "wondered what the man's name was and where he came from; and if he was really evil of heart, or what lies or threats had led him on the long march from his home; and if he would not really rather have stayed there in peace."[22] In the Peter Jackson movie adaptation, the sentiment is transferred, plausibly, to Faramir. As he tells Sam (in the book): "I do not slay man or beast needlessly, and not gladly even when it is needed."[23]

We see this, too, in Gandalf's counseling mercy. Early in *The Fellowship of the Ring*, when Frodo says that it was a pity that Bilbo didn't kill Gollum when he had the chance, Gandalf insists that it was rather "pity that stayed his hand". Frodo admits that he feels no pity for Gollum; "He deserves death", he says. And Gandalf replies, "Deserves it! I daresay he does. Many that live deserve death. And some that die deserve life. Can you give it to them? Then do not be too eager to deal out death in judgement. For even the very wise cannot see all ends."[24] Frodo heeds Gandalf's advice, and when Gollum falls in with Frodo and Sam for a time, Frodo's mercy ultimately saves the day. If he hadn't spared Gollum, Gollum wouldn't have been there to seize the ring from a spiritually and physically exhausted Frodo and, in a moment of hysterical glee, stumble over the edge and into the Cracks of Doom with the Ring of Power.

Finally, there is the stark difference between what Brian Rosebury calls "the diversity of good and the sameness of evil".[25] There is widespread and mostly tolerated diversity among the free peoples of Middle-Earth, which extends to what doesn't happen. For instance, Aragorn's Rangers could have despoiled the Shire, but they didn't. Compare this to the homogenizing slavery and oppression of those who bow the knee to Mordor. Only a willfully blind reader could miss the contrast.

"Leave Your Trowels and Sharpen Your Swords!"

One rule of thumb in determining whether a war is just is whether it is, in some sense, defensive. A war to take land or property from one's neighbor is simply theft writ large, but entering a war to help an ally who has been wrongly attacked would qualify as defensive in the Just War tradition. Thus, we might say that Treebeard the Ent initially employs a narrow view of defense, believing the Ents should only fight when directly attacked and not worry about injustices in the wider world. Fortunately for the other free peoples of the West, Gandalf, Merry, and Pippin persuade the Ents to interpret the defensive principle more broadly and go on the attack both at Isengard and at Helm's Deep. That decision proves crucial to the later victory over Sauron, and thus crucial to the Ents themselves, since Sauron and his minions of orcs would hardly have left them alone had they successfully conquered the other free peoples of the West.

The danger is to misread the moment and assume a narrowly defensive posture. When Gandalf and Pippin later make their mad sprint on Shadowfax from Helm's Deep to the capital of Gondor, they encounter soldiers repairing Rammas Echor, the outer protective wall, northwest of the capitol, on the side "least open to attack".[26] "I would say that you are overlate in repairing the wall of the Pelennor", Gandalf tells them. "Courage will now be your best defence against the storm that is at hand—that and such hope as I bring. But leave your trowels and sharpen your swords!"[27] It's not a stretch to think of similar acts of futility in Tolkien's own experience, such as the ineffectual Maginot Line that the French imagined would repel a German invasion in World War II.[28]

Sometimes the best defense is a good offense.

Of course, even though at times it is right to go to war to defend others, it doesn't follow that a powerful nation must play the role of indiscriminate global policeman, defending every worthy group against every unjust attacker.[29] Drawing the line between a prudent and imprudent intervention involves a host of tough judgment calls. This is why even proponents of the Just War tradition may disagree on whether a particular military conflict is good and wise to enter. Still, the debate is likely to be far more thoughtful and illuminating if the parties in the conversation first embrace the wisdom of the Just War tradition. Doing so allows them to avoid the blanket cynicism of the misnamed realist perspective on the one hand and the moral leveling of pacifism on the other. Instead, Tolkien models a group of thoughtful leaders who all implicitly employ Just War reasoning, and who come together at the Council of Elrond and fruitfully debate their way to the right decision about when and how to go to war.

Just War Enriched

Matthew Dickerson is right to highlight the importance in Tolkien's stories of moral victory, rather than mere military victory. But in doing so, Dickerson seems to trivialize the latter. Yet Tolkien is at pains throughout the battle scenes to emphasize the importance of both. If Rohan or Gondor had employed disastrous battlefield strategy, if Aragorn had not persuaded the dead to fight, if the combined forces had not marched to the Black Gate, the outcome would have been entirely different. It distorts the narrative to imply that it's the moral victory alone that matters.

Certainly Tolkien hated war. He had witnessed it firsthand and at its most unglamorous in the trenches of World War I. And yet in his novels and letters he clearly held to the twin truths that war is not to be sought, but neither can it be wished away with peace slogans and sentimental talk of the brotherhood of man. He dramatized the painful truth that sometimes it's morally obligatory to go to war.

In fact, contrary to Dickerson, one might think that Tolkien actually departed even from Just War by abandoning one of its principles: probability of success. Again and again, the noble characters in *The Lord of the Rings* seem to profess despair and count their situation as hopeless, with little or no chance of victory.

Just before the Battle of the Pelennor Field commences, Pippin and Gandalf are reflecting on the perils that they imagine Frodo and Sam are enduring. "Tell me," asks Pippin, "is there any hope?"

"There never has been much hope", replies Gandalf, putting his hand on Pippin's head. "Just a fool's hope, as I have been told."[30] Yet Gandalf still believes that the errand of Frodo and Sam is proper.

As Tom Shippey has discussed at length, Tolkien desired to recover the ideal of steely heroism—indeed, moral courage in the face of almost certain defeat. It is this sort of courage that Tolkien saw in Old Norse mythology and Norse-inspired stories such as *Beowulf.* It was this "theory of courage" that Tolkien argued in 1936 was the "great contribution to humanity" of the northern, pre-Christian culture.[31] In Norse mythology, the final day of doom (called Ragnorök) was not, as in Christianity, the day when good finally triumphs over evil, but rather when the forces of evil will enjoy their ultimate victory. Yet there's no hint that the prudent or just course is to admit ultimate defeat and ally oneself with evil. On the contrary, it's better to be in the right and suffer total defeat than to make a deal with the devil.

For this reason, Shippey argues, "in a sense this Northern mythology asks more of people than Christianity does, for it offers them no heaven, no salvation, no reward for virtue except the somber satisfaction of having done right."[32]

Such moral courage is one of the virtues most portrayed in *The Hobbit* and *The Lord of the Rings*, from Bilbo approaching Smaug by himself, to Sam and Frodo, who continue their trek to Mount Doom though they doubt their prospects for success. Indeed, even after the quest succeeds, they are not filled with hope but assume their own demise. "I am glad you are here with me. Here at the end of all things, Sam", Frodo says, just before he and Sam are rescued by the eagles.[33] The Norse ideal of courage commends the warrior who fights to the death for a just cause, even if he is certain of ultimate defeat.

Fighting when there is no hope for success seems to conflict with the Just War principle that a war should only be fought if there is a reasonable chance of success. Perhaps in its original pagan form there's a conflict; but Tolkien matures the pre-Christian virtue of courage and thus creates a consistent unity between a pagan virtue and the Christian view of a just war. The element of this Norse virtue most in need of tweaking is its tendency to encourage rash and impetuous actions. No one in *The Lord of the Rings* is commended for rushing foolishly and prematurely into battle. When Denethor sends Faramir on a suicide mission to protect the eastern defenses, Gandalf implores Faramir, "Do not throw your life away rashly or in bitterness.... You will be needed here, for other things than war."[34]

More subtly, Tolkien's description of infantry attitude and strategy often reflected modern rather than Norse battle techniques. In defending Lake-town, for instance, Bard acts much like a twentieth-century British infantryman. "He exercises not merely heroism as displayed in ancient saga", notes Shippey, "but discipline, the virtue prized in nineteenth-century British imperial life."[35] Discipline, rather than mere headlong courage, turns out to be crucial to ultimate victory in that battle and the happy peace that follows.

Today, Just War reasoning needs such a modified theory of courage. Without it, the rule of probability of success could easily devolve into an excuse factory for weak resolve, risk aversion, and easy surrender. This is a misreading of the tradition, but a misreading quite common among twentieth-century academics and churchmen, who often have used Just War criteria as a cover for de facto pacifism. War is treated as a necessary evil that is almost never necessary.

The poverty of this tendency is well-illustrated in a historical example of its dramatic opposite. In 480 B.C. three hundred Spartans, along with four hundred Thespians and three hundred Thebians, held back the invading Persian hordes at the battle of Thermopylae. Near the end, some of them retreated, but three hundred Spartans, led by King Leonidas, held strong and were annihilated. Was this foolish pagan defiance?

A Spartan with a knack for math and an aversion to risk would no doubt have calculated the Greek's prospects for success as virtually nil. The Spartans were outnumbered at least a hundred to one. Would it not have been better for them to surrender and ally themselves with Persia? If Leonidas had calculated his probability of success, Sparta would have become part of the vast Persian forces. As it was, the standoff at Thermopylae delayed the Persians and fortified and inspired the other Greek peoples, allowing them to go on to defeat the Persians at the Battle of Salamis in late 480 B.C. The history of the world might have been different, and the West never have emerged as it did, but for the heroic self-sacrifice of several hundred men. None of this was known to Leonidas. He had to act courageously in the present with a veil over the future.

Similarly, the protagonists in *The Lord of the Rings* often find that their live options are to fight to the death and hope that it will redound to victory for their cause, or simply be annihilated. In such stark and clarifying light, with no knowledge of the future, probabilities are poor guides and can counsel only despair. When Gandalf defends the strategy of sending a group to Mordor to destroy the ring, he recognizes that it may look foolish. "Despair, or folly?" said Gandalf. "It is not despair; for despair is only for those who see the end beyond all doubt. We do not. It is wisdom to recognize necessity, when all other courses have been weighed, though as folly it may appear to those who cling to false hope. Well, let folly be our cloak, a veil before the eyes of the Enemy!"[36]

The stand at Helm's Deep looks until the very end as if the forces of Saruman will annihilate Rohan. And when King Théoden and the Rohirrim march to Minas Tirith in the "gathering gloom",[37] they do not expect to be victorious or return to their homes. Meanwhile, Aragorn, Legolas, Gimli, and some of the Dúnedain have taken the Paths of the Dead, which seems akin to suicide to Éomer and the others.

As the malevolent forces of Mordor lay siege to the White City, what odds would a scribe holed up behind its stone walls have given Gondor? Yet only Denethor truly gives in to despair. With his enemies gathering in the Pelennor Fields, Denethor looks into the palantir, is deceived by Sauron, and believes that all hope is lost. He chooses suicide and death for himself and his one surviving son rather than defeat. "Better to burn sooner than late, for burn we must", he tells the messengers who are seeking orders from their leader. "No tomb for Denethor and Faramir.... We will burn like heathen kings before ever a ship sailed hither from the West. The West has failed. Go back and burn!"[38] Tolkien registers his disapproval of Denethor, who alone succumbed to despair, by including the anachronistic word *heathen*.

That contemporary strain of thought that rarely ever sees war as prudent or necessary doesn't, of course, advocate suicide by flame when faced with looming defeat. But it does stand in contrast to the desperate courage of the most valorous figures in *The Lord of the Rings*. These heroes can point us away from that misuse of the Just War tradition, and inspire us to courage even in the face of desperate odds.

Pacifism

Tolkien had more reason to hate war than many of us do. From June to October 1916, he served with the Lancashire Fusiliers on the front lines at the River Somme in France. He languished in cramped and disease-ridden trenches where months of bombardment by mortar and machine-gun fire resulted in prodigal death and destruction, but little military progress. The no-man's land between Allied and German trenches was so forbidding that the bodies of fallen men could remain strewn for months without burial—no doubt a source for the dead faces that Frodo, Sam, and Gollum encounter in the Dead Marshes. When the Battle of the Somme ended on November 18, 1916, the Allies had lost 615,000 and cost the Germans 500,000, for an advance of less than eight miles.[39]

By the end of the "War to End All Wars", many millions of Europeans had died from injuries in battle, and millions more—both military and civilian—had died from disease and hunger. Two of Tolkien's three closest friends were killed in the same year, with one of them, Rob Gilson, dying on the very first day of the Battle of the Somme. Tolkien contracted trench fever, a disease born by body lice, and spent the last two years of his service convalescing and, for a time, manning the sea wall in southern England.[40]

The Allies won the war, but Britain was never the same. "Until August 1914," A.J.P. Taylor wrote, in his *English History, 1914–45*, "a sensible, law-abiding Englishman could pass through life and hardly notice the existence of the state, beyond the post office and the policeman. He could live where he liked and as he liked. He had no official number or identity card. He could travel abroad or leave his country for ever without a passport or any sort of official permission.... All this was changed by the impact of the Great War."[41]

Americans entered the war very late, lost about 120,000 troops, and never fought on home soil, so it is hard for contemporary Americans to fathom the traumatizing effect of heavy industrialized warfare on the psyche of Europeans born in the nineteenth century.[42] On August 3, 1914, even before the horrors had begun, British statesman Edward Grey told his friends: "The lamps are going out all over Europe; we shall not see them lit again in our life-time."[43] And indeed, rather than solving anything, World War I, a war ignited by little more than happenstance and rash judgment, laid the foundations for the even more global Second World War.

Tolkien, in other words, experienced war in a particularly ugly and nearly futile form, an experience that undoubtedly lent him a great sympathy for pacifists of the brave and sincere sort. While he never advocated pacifism, he does create a respectful space for it in *The Lord of the Rings* while simultaneously suggesting its limits. After Frodo and Sam are rescued from Mount Doom and the free peoples celebrate in military dress, Frodo swears off such attire, having no desire to carry a sword. He retains the stance to the very end of the novel, in what one might describe as a calling or charism to nonviolence. During the scouring of the Shire, Frodo, weary of violence, urges restraint on the hobbits as they take up arms to regain their liberty from Sharkey (Saruman) and his toadies. His is a courageous stance; he has already endured the greatest danger in the journey to Mount Doom, and he remains close to the danger in the battle for the Shire, if anything in greater danger for going unarmed. It would be hard to imagine a more respectful presentation of a more beloved character's decision to lay down arms forever.

Nevertheless, Tolkien gives the combative Merry the more pointed line in the scene: "'But if there are many of these ruffians,' said Merry, 'it will certainly mean fighting. You won't rescue Lotho, or the Shire, just by being shocked and sad, my dear Frodo.'"[44] The outcome isn't a verbal feud between the two old friends. Instead, Merry and Frodo enrich each other as iron sharpens iron. The war-weary Frodo's almost paralyzing revulsion to killing and Merry's military pragmatism both inform the conduct of the hobbit soldiers so that they successfully expel Saruman's minions from the Shire, but in a way that is merciful in victory to the surviving invaders and hobbit traitors.

In his portrayal of war, Tolkien wove the themes of power and its renunciation together into a complex and satisfying whole. Might certainly does not make right. But might does not necessarily make wrong either. There are times to reject the allure of power, especially when it involves dominating others, and there are times when the right and just course is to take up arms and fight unreservedly against the forces of darkness. Indeed, Tolkien suggests, there are times when one must do both.

Chapter 7

The Scouring of the Shire

To read the works of Tolkien and miss his love and concern for the natural world is to miss Tolkien. Consider the beauty of the Shire, or the lovingly rendered depictions of the natural environment that color the hobbits' wanderings, or the poignant descriptions of wanton environmental destruction wrought by Sauron, Saruman, and their tree-hacking minions. In Middle-Earth, good cultures employ and develop technologies in elegant harmony with the natural surroundings they cherish, while the arch-villains care only for the industrial and the artificial and how it can augment their power. As the ancient Treebeard says of the wicked Saruman, "He is plotting to become a Power. He has a mind of metal and wheels; and he does not care for growing things, except as far as they serve him for the moment."[1] Taken together, these and various other environmental threads running through Tolkien's sub-creation suggest an author with a deep and abiding love for "green and growing things".

This concern is perhaps most poignantly conveyed in a late chapter of *The Lord of the Rings*, "The Scouring of the Shire", where a destructive industrialism threatens the peace, health, and beauty of the Shire. Tolkien once commented that the chapter had its roots in the fact that "the country in which I lived in childhood was being shabbily destroyed before I was ten".[2] The extent of that ongoing disfigurement was brought home to him in 1933, when he decided to show his wife and kids the countryside where he had spent four of his most cherished years as a boy, a place called Sarehole Mill, the inspiration for the village of Hobbiton.[3] His diary entry on the unsettling experience distills and explains as well as anything the conservationist zeal so evident in his work:

> I pass over the pangs to me of passing through Hall Green—become a huge tram-ridden meaningless suburb, where I actually lost my way—and

> eventually down what is left of beloved lanes of childhood, and past the very gate of our cottage, now in the midst of a sea of new red-brick. The old mill still stands, and Mrs Hunt's still sticks out into the road as it turns uphill; but the crossing beyond the now fenced-in pool, where the bluebell lane ran down into the mill lane, is now a dangerous crossing alive with motors and red lights. The White Ogre's house (which the children were excited to see) is become a petrol station, and most of Short Avenue and the elms between it and the crossing have gone. How I envy those whose precious early scenery has not been exposed to such violent and peculiarly hideous change.[4]

The experience probably was doubly painful for Tolkien because he associated the once idyllic setting with the all-too few years he had with his beloved mother, and because he had been made to leave a similarly pleasant rural setting and move to crowded Birmingham immediately after her death. "Ronald, still numb from the shock of his mother's death, hated the view of almost unbroken rooftops with the factory chimneys beyond", biographer Humphrey Carpenter writes. "The green countryside was just visible in the distance, but it now belonged to a remote past that could not be regained.... And because it was the loss of his mother that had taken him away from all these things, he came to associate them with her."[5] In a single stroke, the boy was stripped of the pastoral and the maternal.

Tolkien found his way back to that remote past, or rather to a Faerie version of it, through his creation of Middle-Earth. He once commented, "If you really want to know what Middle-Earth is based on, it's my wonder and delight in the Earth as it is, particularly the natural earth."[6] Many contemporary environmentalists have discovered this wonder and delight and taken the author for one of their own. For all they share in common, however, a deep gulf separates Tolkien from many of them, and their failure to acknowledge that gulf has led to various distorted readings of the world and maker of Middle-Earth. These distortions are so common that we need to distinguish them clearly from Tolkien's actual views.

Beyond Rousseau

One mistake that Tolkien-appreciating contemporary environmentalists seem prone to is seeing Tolkien as a kissing cousin of eighteenth-century

French philosopher Jean Jacques Rousseau. Now, it's true that—like Tolkien—Rousseau was a Catholic, at least nominally and for a time. (He realigned himself with Calvinism when he moved back to Geneva.) And also like Tolkien, Rousseau professed belief in a good and loving Creator whose goodness is imbued throughout nature. But unlike Tolkien, Rousseau's orthodoxy more or less peters out beyond this. He rejected the idea of the Trinity, the deity of Christ, and miracles, and his animus against the doctrine of the Fall decisively shaped his political philosophy.

Near the beginning of his career as a public philosopher, he suddenly felt very strongly "that man is naturally good", and that it was only from the institutions of civilization "that men become wicked".[7] The English writer and psychiatrist Theodore Dalrymple summarizes Rousseau's view as "the complete opposite of the idea that man is born with original sin", and suggests that it spread quickly through Western culture "because it means all you have to do to be good is to be your true self, and since your true self is really determined, you know what your true self is by doing exactly what you like." The idea does more than excuse bad behavior, Dalrymple emphasizes. On Rousseau's telling, "doing what you like, exactly what you like, becomes virtue, which is one of the reasons, for example, why in this country now, people who get very drunk in public believe that they're acting virtuously.... It's spontaneous; it's not artificial."

Dalrymple goes on to limn the mindset of a subculture shaped by Rousseau's philosophy of natural man, a subculture Dalrymple came to know firsthand serving as a hospital and prison psychiatrist in inner city Birmingham and London's East End. "Because they've come to believe, via intellectuals, that the natural man is the good man, the real me should come out, and all harm stems from suppressing the real me, then behaving in that fashion is good in itself", he says. "And so the idea that there could be any sort of authority outside oneself, outside one's impulses, outside one's desires, was destroyed, or at least much reduced."[8]

Like Rousseau, Tolkien loved nature and was deeply concerned about where our civilization was headed, so it might be easy to suppose that the two were of one mind on this matter, that the natural man—uncorrupted by the ugly pull of civilization and all its trappings—is the good man. Did Tolkien weave such a view into the fabric of his Middle-Earth novels? Chris Baratta seems to think so, though in his view, the particular evil in Tolkien's world is industrial civilization. In "'No Name, No Business, No Precious, Nothing. Only Empty. Only Hungry': Gollum as Industrial Casualty", Baratta describes Gollum/Sméagol as a naturally good figure spiritually poisoned by the industrial, a tortured figure "struggling internally between his natural self and the corruption of industry, symbolized by the One Ring, an entity that breeds an obsession with material goods and an abandonment of nature."[9]

There are a couple of problems with this reading. First, Gollum spends almost five hundred years about as far from industry as he can get, living on a tiny island in an underground lake far beneath a mountain. If the ring symbolizes the temptations of industry, why when Gollum possesses it is he so nonindustrious, in both the positive and negative senses of the term? It's true he ends up cut off from grass, woods, and sunshine; but is it "the corruption of industry" that drives Gollum deep underground? Rousseau might like that interpretation, but Tolkien offers a very different explanation by way of Gandalf.

As the wizard explains to Frodo in an early chapter of *The Lord of the Rings*, before Sméagol had ever laid eyes on the One Ring, the creature ceased "to look up at the hill-tops, or the leaves on trees, or the flowers opening in the air; his head and his eyes were downward."[10] Then, when Gollum gets his first glimpse of the ring, before he's even in possession of it, he immediately murders his friend Déagol in order to gain the ring. Savage, yes, but not the noble savage Baratta implies with his suggestion of an innocent natural self.

This tendency to read Rousseau's thought into Middle-Earth is surprisingly pervasive, so much so that it crops up in a generally illuminating work on Tolkien and the environment by a pair of Christian scholars, Matthew Dickerson and Jonathan Evans. Their book, *Ents, Elves and Eriador: The Environmental Vision of J. R. R. Tolkien*,[11] helpfully situates Tolkien's views within the novelist's Christological understanding of creation and human nature; and it ably rebuts Lynn White's 1969 essay arguing that Christianity is principally to blame for what White labeled "the Ecological Crisis".[12] White claimed that "to a Christian a tree can be no more than a physical fact." Dickerson and Evans point out that this would only be true if Christianity were based on philosophical materialism, where humans were merely animals without a maker, regarding trees as a metaphysically unreflective squirrel might, as merely a resource. Instead, Christianity teaches that trees are a gift and work of art by the divine artist, and that he is the ultimate owner of the trees.[13] As the psalmist says, "The earth is the LORD's and the fulness thereof".[14] Especially helpful is Dickerson and Evans' nuanced description of four views of stewardship, identifying Tolkien with the view that humans are best seen as both managers and servants, gardening a natural order that is useful but also valuable in its own right.[15]

However, in a late section that borders on the surreal, the writers scold Tolkien for portraying some animals as dangerous and evil. We say *surreal* because Dickerson and Evans are writing explicitly as Christians, and Tolkien is on pretty firm ground in terms of precedent, what with the first book of Scripture featuring an evil serpent in the garden, the final book of the Bible talking about an evil beast "rising out of the sea",[16] and the Gospels throwing in a herd of demon-possessed swine.[17] Undeterred by biblical precedent, Dickerson and Evans scold Tolkien for portraying so many wild animals as forces of evil. In Tolkien's fictional world, they complain, "except for eagles, the wild creatures that do appear are almost always associated with the sources of evil in Middle-earth".[18] If the depiction of wild animals were really all that one-sided, Dickerson and Evans might be on to something, but Tolkien's depiction of wild animals is far from all nasty all the time. There are good birds besides the eagles (a thrush and a raven) who play a pivotal role in the death of Smaug. There are various woodland creatures Gandalf urges his fellow wizard Radagast the Brown to communicate with in their common battle against the forces of darkness. There's the innocent deer that bounds across the path of Bilbo and the dwarves in Mirkwood, as well as the wild rabbits and fish Gollum captures and kills for food, none of which is depicted as evil. Even the daunting oliphaunts used by the armies of Mordor are essentially beasts of burden conscripted for war, not symbols of evil.

Dickerson and Evans are especially incensed on behalf of wolves, creatures routinely made to play the villains in Tolkien's imaginative world. "In the real world," Dickerson and Evans insist, "there have been no verifiable, documented reports of healthy adult wolves killing human beings."[19] Well, Tolkien was writing fantasy and might be excused for rendering some animal species nastier and some nobler than in our world (wolves and eagles, for instance). Even so, is it true that there are no documented reports of healthy adult wolves killing humans? Ever? Wolves are generally shy of humans, particularly of men, but cases of healthy wolves attacking men, women, and children are widespread and well-documented.[20] Dickerson and Evans censure Tolkien for vilifying wolves not only in his hobbit-centered novels but also in his legendarium, most prominently in the figure of Carcharoth the wolf, a chief servant of Morgoth. But a crucial detail is that the evil Morgoth and later his chief servant Sauron have taken, twisted, and corrupted wolves for their evil purposes (reminiscent of the Gospel story of the legion of demons possessing and driving into madness the herd of swine). There's a clue of this even in *The Fellowship of the Ring*. It's just after the fellowship has survived a strangely brazen attack by a pack of wolves:

> When the full light of the morning came no signs of the wolves were to be found, and they looked in vain for the bodies of the dead. No trace of the fight remained but the charred trees and the arrows of Legolas lying on the hill-top. All were undamaged save one of which only the point was left. "It is as I feared," said Gandalf. "These were no ordinary wolves hunting for food in the wilderness. Let us eat quickly and go!"[21]

So, there are a few wild creatures aligned with, or enslaved by, Sauron and the forces of darkness; a few aligned with the forces of good; and, we can assume, the great mass of unaligned animals in Middle-Earth that never come into the tale of the ring because, like wild creatures are wont to do, they have successfully gotten clear of all the people tramping about. The question then becomes, does Tolkien's multifaceted picture of the wild illuminate reality in some important way, or is the complexity just so much complicated machinery for a complex fantasy novel plot? We suggest that it's both.

There are More Things in Heaven and Middle-Earth, Horatio

Tolkien's complex depiction of wild animals serves his plot at various points (for example, evil birds spying, noble eagles rescuing, wolves attacking), but that complex depiction is also rooted in his nuanced understanding of reality, one that corresponds to reality far more than does Rousseau's idea of an unfallen nature over and against evil civilization.

On the one hand, Tolkien's vision of the natural world isn't the dark and meaningless landscape of a Hume or a Darwinian materialist, "nature red and tooth and claw"[22] and "only this and nothing more".[23] On the other hand, it's also not that of the carefree child of nature frolicking in the harmless woods, or even the vision of one who recognizes the bloody and ferocious side of nature but registers no hint of the evil work of "the prince of this world",[24] that being who fell before the Fall of man. Instead, in Tolkien's vision, the wild is full of beauty, goodness, and the sublime, but it also has in it the trees of the Old Forest, full of cunning and malice; the mysterious giants of the mountains smashing boulders about in a destructive frenzy; and animals both wild and tame who fight on the side of evil.

The rebuke to Rousseau runs deeper still. We don't find Rousseau's noble savage a common feature of Middle-Earth, or much support for the idea that civilization corrupts. The one major character who has turned his back on society and civilization is the twisted and hideous Gollum; some of the least civilized human groups fight on the side of the wicked Sauron; and the most technologically advanced human realm, the kingdom of Gondor, fights on the side of the good. Both the free peoples and those aligned with Sauron appear to run the gamut from technologically primitive to highly sophisticated, suggesting that the moral differentiator lies somewhere other than where Rousseau attempted to place it. Rather, Tolkien would have us understand Creation to be the good work of a good Creator, but a Creation that is in some palpable but mysterious sense fallen, with the mystery of both good and evil too complex for some overly tidy binary of devil and sinful man versus pristine nature.

Evil Beyond Greed

This more nuanced picture is especially obscured in Baratta's reading of Tolkien. Baratta's critique seems to have as its bogeyman not *industrialism* simpliciter but *industrial capitalism*, particularly in its buy-buy-buy consumerist guise. The ring "breeds an obsession with material goods", Baratta asserts. But Gollum was from a well-to-do family, and after he came into possession of the ring, he left that life behind and took up an underground existence so austere as to give a medieval hermit an inferiority complex. When Baratta talks of an obsession with material goods, does he have in mind Gollum's love for raw fish? However you slice it, there's a clear difference between Baratta's description of the ring's effect and its effects on the character of Gollum.

Now, Baratta's reading does have a grain of truth in it: the ring does wither one's love for wholesome things like flowers, sunshine, and a good meal with friends. But we don't see the ring replacing this withered affection with an obsession for material riches. Sauron doesn't seem to be obsessed with amassing gold and fine jewels in the way that, for example, the dwarf lord Thorin Oakenshield and the Elvenking of Mirkwood were in *The Hobbit*. Instead, all the indications are that Sauron's obsession is with power for the sake of power, power to dominate other wills and to avenge whatever grievances he nurses against Ilúvatar, the supreme Creator described in *The Silmarillion*.

Think, too, of Frodo as he nears Mount Doom. You don't find him growing more and more obsessed with jewels and finery or with the idea of dining expensively every day. Instead, the psychological landscape that the ring pulls him toward is a diabolically Gnostic turn away from the Creation. At one point Sam reminds Frodo of a pleasant campfire meal they enjoyed only a few days before in the beautiful woods of Ithilien. Frodo responds by describing the walking nightmare that his existence has become as they near Mount Doom and as the debasing effects of the ring grows stronger. "No taste of food, no feel of water, no sound of wind, no memory of tree or grass or flower, no image of moon or star are left to me", he tells Sam. "I am naked in the dark, Sam, and there is no veil between me and the wheel of fire. I begin to see it with my waking eyes, and all else fades."[25]

This is significant. The primary evil of the ring isn't to lure one into making idols of secondary goods, to value good material things—like beautiful houses, jewels, well-made clothing, even golden rings—above higher goods. The ring's evil, rather, is an extension of Sauron's driving ambition, to rebel against the Creator and make of himself a demi-god in Middle-Earth. It is the fundamental evil of fleeing from the ground of being in pursuit of the insubstantial mirage that is self-idolatry. This is the particular evil of the ring, steadily eroding Frodo's capacity for self-sacrifice.

How could Baratta be so off base in his interpretation of the ring? Maybe it's the company he keeps. He quotes approvingly from the Marxist journal *Historical Materialism*, where "Ishay Landa sees the Ring as the 'historical dilemma of capitalism' and suggests that Tolkien is able to compress into the Ring 'all the contradictions of the capitalist system: the enormous productivity with the annihilating destructiveness, the unlimited power of the few with the utter impotence of the many, the extravagant luxury and the epidemic poverty, the sanguine promise with the horrible betrayal.' "[26] Here we have left Middle-Earth and entered the topsy-turvy world of Marxist revisionism.

Notice, too, how neatly (if inadvertently) Landa's description maps not onto capitalist societies but onto the Marxist experiments of the twentieth century. Okay, the part about "the enormous productivity" doesn't quite fit, but Communism did manifest an "annihilating destructiveness", with millions killed in the purges of Soviet Russia and Red China, and with a dismal record of environmental devastation.

As for Landa's talk of "extravagant luxury" and "epidemic poverty", this also characterizes the Marxist experiments of the twentieth century with eerie precision, since these command-and-control economies inevitably devolved into a few government insiders living very well while the rest of society found themselves trapped in dreary poverty. The freer economies of the West have enjoyed extravagant luxury, but they've also raised the standard of living of the average poor person, with the official poverty line in the United States today marking an economic standard of living far above the middle class of a century ago, or even of the middle class in China of a generation ago.[27] Landa is correct that a "sanguine promise" was made and broken, but it was the promise of a new man and a worker's paradise, and that promise was betrayed by leaders corrupted by totalitarian power and by an economic theory out of touch with human nature. The betrayal, in other words, was the betrayal of Communism.

By misunderstanding the clear lessons of twentieth-century economic history, Baratta and Landa lend aid and comfort to the very system that was hardest on both the poor and the environment.[28] And by misunderstanding the evil of the One Ring—misinterpreting it as a symbol of industrial capitalism—they miss the deeper insights that Tolkien has to offer to those who seek to live well and in harmony with the natural world.

Nature and the Rational Numinous

Baratta and Landa use the One Ring and the theme of environmental destruction to present Tolkien as, if not a card-carrying academic Marxist, at least a fellow traveler. Chris Brawley puts Tolkien's environmental concerns to a different, if equally, radical end. He claims that Tolkien sought to transcend rationality and the dichotomy of good and evil.

Brawley suggests Tolkien used the tools of the fantastic mode of literature to shift our perspective from the human to the ecocentric, as when Treebeard helps us see things as trees might if they were sentient. From this Brawley concludes that such techniques "allow readers to experience what is not covered by our rational modes of knowledge."[29] But Brawley's interpretation involves a misunderstanding of Tolkien's view of reason. This becomes clear when Brawley goes on to argue that the sensitivity and reverence for the natural world communicated in *The Lord of the Rings* "has its expression in the non-rational experience of the numinous as outlined by [Rudolf] Otto in *The Idea of the Holy*", and that Tolkien's work has a religious quality about it "because it is infused with the emotive, non-rational dimension which is the core of religious thought."

This is all very high-sounding, but there's no evidence that Tolkien believed the core of religious thought to be emotive and nonrational. Catholicism, along with some prominent branches of Protestant thought, holds that religious experience is robustly reasonable, even if there is also a powerful emotional component as well as divine mysteries we cannot exhaustively describe in rational, analytic terms (such as the doctrine of the Trinity). The reason of God, in other words, is immanent in his Creation while also transcending that Creation. In the beginning wasn't *the fuzzy feeling* or *the nonrational ecstasy*. In the beginning was *the Word*, the *Logos*.

Christianity is a historical religion that has always made appeals to reason and evidence as part of its evangelistic mission in the world. When Tolkien was instrumental in converting C. S. Lewis from agnosticism to theism and eventually Christianity, he didn't do so by inviting Lewis to abandon reason. Instead, he urged him to leave the irrational flatland of materialism for the deeper and wider reason of theism, and to understand myth as offering glimpses into that deeper reality.[30] Tolkien's aim wasn't to leave behind the rational but to propose an understanding of reason richer than the arid materialism of his day would allow.

By mischaracterizing the core of Christian religious experience as emotional and nonrational, and by characterizing Tolkien's narrative communion with the natural world in *The Lord of the Rings* as religious in this confused sense, Brawley fundamentally mischaracterizes the environmental vision communicated by Tolkien's Middle-Earth fiction.

A scene early in the final chapter of *The Lord of the Rings* nicely distills Tolkien's true environmental vision. In his seemingly hopeless task of restoring a Shire ravaged by Saruman, Sam remembers the box of Lothlórien soil the Lady Galadriel gave him. He's trying to decide how best to use the gift, and the advice Frodo gives isn't to let go and feel his way toward some ecstatic sylvan dance under the moonlight, flinging the soil hither and yon at random. Instead, Frodo urges Sam toward a high but reasonable faith in the power of the soil received from Galadriel (reasonable because they have witnessed the power and the wisdom of Galadriel as a steward of Lothlórien) and to use Sam's powers of reason as he goes about his restorative work. "Use all the wits and knowledge you have of your own, Sam," Frodo says, "and then use the gift to help your work and better it." Sam takes Frodo's advice, and the result of the gardener's carefully reasoned environmental stewardship is a renewal of the Shire more rapid than any the hobbits had hoped for or imagined.

Brawley did have a basis for his reading of Tolkien that we haven't mentioned yet, a passage from a letter Tolkien wrote in 1954, where he explains that Tom Bombadil "represents something that I feel very important, though I would not be prepared to analyze the feeling precisely".[31] From this Brawley concludes that "Tolkien's comments are reminiscent of the non-rational, emotive core of the numinous which Otto describes in *The Idea of the Holy*, that Bombadil embodies, in the words of Otto, 'the feeling which remains where the concept fails' (Otto, Foreword)."[32] It's an important point that the artist often communicates truths that cannot be rationally reconstructed or exhaustively captured in language. Even in science, argued philosopher of science Michael Polanyi, "we know more than we can tell".[33] However, Brawley goes beyond this insight to say that "Tom represents the experience of the numinous which defies language's ability to express it."[34] Perhaps. But everything we learn about Tom Bombadil, and everything he has to teach us about nature and our proper relationship and behavior toward it, is communicated precisely through words. Tom Bombadil is a character in a novel, after all.

Undeterred, Brawley adds that "Tolkien's view of the God-man relationship was personal, in which no proper names are required."[35] How strange that Brawley would conclude this of an artist and philologist who dedicated his professional life to words, showered his major characters with multiple proper names, and even had the woodsiest of all his nature-loving characters, the wise and ancient Treebeard, speak of the need for longer, fuller names in order to fully and intimately communicate the nature of a person. Tolkien, after all, is of the same faith as the apostle John, whose God reassures him and his readers in the book of Revelation that to the faithful follower he will give "a white stone, with a new name written on the stone which no one knows except him who receives it".[36] Here the bestowing of a new name strengthens and renders more intimate the personal relationship between God and the faithful follower. This is the God Tolkien served.

Certainly Brawley is helpful in calling attention to the numinous in Tolkien, and certainly there is a time, all too often neglected in our plugged-in society, to "[b]e still, and know that I am God."[37] But to set the numinous in opposition to *Logos*, to language, and to rationality conflates Tolkien's vision with a contemporary environmental vision that often sees the constructive, rational, and compositional aspects of human civilization as necessarily at odds with the natural environment. It wrongly implies that the creative drive toward human civilization is necessarily at odds with the good of nature.

Brawley's confusion extends to the moral order. "The fact that Treebeard does not care for sides shows that, like Tom Bombadil, his applicability resides in the fact that he symbolizes something which is beyond the rational, beyond the mere duality of good or evil", he writes. "This unaligned quality has its origin in the numinous, that sense of awe which is feeling-oriented rather than part of a rational, Manichean universe."[38] In asserting this, Brawley seems (but surely isn't) unaware that Treebeard eventually does take sides with the good and against the evil, and that everything about Tolkien's unfolding plot stands in approval of that decision, with Ents, elves, dwarves, hobbits, and men all benefiting.

More fundamentally, Tolkien clearly did see good opposed to evil, and his doing so doesn't imply Manichaeism. Recall that the Manichaean mistake isn't to see good and evil as opposed; it's to see them as *equal* and opposed. Christianity insists that only good has existed eternally, in Yahweh, the Maker of all things.

Brawley's talk of the numinous transcending "the mere duality of good or evil" has about it the frisson of the Gnostic initiation, but it actually obscures Tolkien's more encompassing theology of environmental stewardship. It's true that Treebeard says few even among the good seem to be on the side of the Ents, but the lesson isn't that there's some numinous realm of enlightenment beyond good and evil. The Ents remind us, instead, that the fellowship of the good should never forget the goodness that persists in God's Creation, or our call to be good inhabitants and stewards of that Creation.

Ownership Cultures Good and Bad

Brawley's confused analysis of nature, rationality, and the moral order bleeds over into his view of property and ownership. "The attitude of environmental owning is precisely what keeps one from acquiring the sacramental vision", he writes. "We cannot experience the sense of awe to which Otto refers unless we divorce ourselves from a possessive, utilitarian worldview."[39] Tolkien did use his fiction to critique "a possessive, utilitarian worldview" drained of the sacramental, but Brawley's language blurs the line between such utilitarianism and a humble ownership of property leavened by a sense of wonder.

Think of the beautiful Shire. It isn't some communal utopia where everything is held in common. Far from it. People own property, and the rich own more property than the poor. For that matter, the minimal government that does exist, represented by the peripatetic Shirriffs, is focused on protecting the property rights of its citizens by keeping stray animals from one person's property from grazing the grass on another's.[40] It's when this healthy ownership culture is upended late in *The Lord of the Rings* that the positive environmental effects it had on the Shire are brought home to hobbits and readers alike:

> The travelers trotted on, and as the sun began to sink towards the White Downs far away on the western horizon they came to Bywater by its wide pool; and there they had their first really painful shock. This was Frodo and Sam's own country, and they found out now that they cared about it more than any other place in the world. Many of the houses they had known were missing. Some seemed to have been burned down. The pleasant row of old hobbit-holes in the bank on the north side of the Pool were deserted, and their little gardens that used to run down right to the water's edge were rank with weeds.[41]

Before, when the hobbit families of the Shire were secure in their sense of property ownership, the landscape was beautifully gardened right down to the water's edge. To Sam and Frodo's dismay, that's all gone now, thanks to Saruman and his band of "gatherers and sharers".

There's a curious parallel here between this return to the Shire and the one described near the end of *The Hobbit*. In each novel, the victory has been won and the curtain is surely about to fall when another beat in the plot intervenes. Each occurs when the hero returns to the Shire, and each involves an aggressive attempt to commandeer and redistribute private property—one that in each case is passed off by the nasty characters as above board.

In *The Hobbit* it's a relatively small affair: Bilbo's next of kin, the Sackville-Bagginses, race to declare Bilbo dead during his long and unexplained absence so they can inherit his property. The result is that when Bilbo arrives home, he finds a large notice announcing an auction to sell "the effects of the late Bilbo Baggins Esquire, of Bag-End, Underhill, Hobbiton". Bilbo arrives home in the middle of the auction. Many of the local hobbits had been only too happy to cooperate in the scheme, since Bilbo was well-to-do and the Sackville-Baggins are selling Bilbo's belongings at fire-sale prices to clear the way for their furniture. When he announces himself, not everybody is pleased to see that Bilbo is very much alive. "The legal bother, indeed, lasted for years", the narrator says. "It was quite a long time before Mr. Baggins was in fact admitted to be alive again. The people who had got specially good bargains at the Sale took a deal of convincing; and in the end to save time Bilbo had to buy back quite a lot of his own furniture."[42]

The parallel event near the end of *The Lord of the Rings* is more serious in tone and encompasses not just Bag End but the whole of the Shire. It involves a group of "gatherers and sharers ... going around counting and measuring and taking off to storage", supposedly "for fair distribution"; but what becomes of most of the bounty is any hobbit's guess. Robert Plank describes the change this way:

> The essential political innovation is the rise of an unprecedented police force, headed by the Chief Shirriff. The character of government is totally altered while its forms are not markedly changed. Whereas before the Shire enjoyed an easy-going laissez faire regime, with maximum freedom and a minimum of government interference, the new regime operates through monstrously expanded restrictive rules, enforced by equally monstrously expanded military and para-military forces ... : the purpose of government is plainly to maintain, consolidate, and expand its own power.[43]

The matter culminates in a battle between the hobbits on one side and a diminished Saruman and his lackeys on the other, ending with dead and wounded on both sides but with the cause of freedom and the Shire triumphant.

The crisis is extraneous enough to the main plot that Peter Jackson was able to excise it gracefully from his film trilogy of *The Lord of the Rings*, alluding to it only as a dark possibility glimpsed by Frodo in the Mirror of Galadriel when the fellowship is in Lothlórien. That Tolkien would tack onto his majestic epic an anticlimactic and seemingly extraneous side conflict is curious in its own right. It's doubly curious since the conflict recapitulates on a larger, darker stage *The Hobbit*'s eleventh-hour conflict at Bag End, with each episode involving a descent into social disorder and theft masquerading as punctilious social order.

So, what are we to make of "The Scouring of the Shire"? As we saw above, it was first inspired by Tolkien's experience of urban sprawl beginning to damage the beauty of Sarehole Mill when he was a boy.[44] At the same time, conservatives and progressives alike have recognized this final portion of *The Lord of the Rings* as a pointed critique of modern socialism. Hal Colebatch argues that Saruman's joyless regime of bureaucratic rules and suffocating redistribution "owed much to the drabness, bleakness and bureaucratic regulation of postwar Britain under the Attlee labour Government."[45] Robert Plank notes several parallels between Saruman's Shire and two varieties of Fascist socialism that rose to prominence between the world wars—Hitler's National Socialist German Workers' Party (the Nazi Party) and the Italian Fascism headed by Benito Mussolini, a longtime member of the Italian Socialist Party before breaking with it over the question of neutrality in World War I.[46]

Are these readings too specific? "The Scouring of the Shire" is about much more than this or that variety of socialism, of course. It's about the ugliness of a vengeful heart (Saruman's), the will to ugliness of so much modern urban and suburban development, the love and good stewardship of one's homeland, the value of a people defending its own freedom rather than depending on others to do so, the danger of mindlessly following "the rules"—on and on we could go. At the same time, Tolkien's dim view of socialism is well-attested in his collected letters, and it's hard to imagine a defter way to satirize socialism's pose of moral superiority than with Saruman's "gatherers and sharers" using the coercive powers of government to take away the fruits of labor for "fair distribution".

Brawley, having presented Tolkien as a fellow traveler of the environmental left, approvingly quotes Tom Shippey's observation that "the Sarumans of the real world rule by deluding their followers with images of a technological Paradise in the future, a modernist Utopia; but what one often gets ... are the blasted landscapes of Eastern Europe, strip-mined, polluted, and even radioactive."[47] True, but Brawley misses the irony here: the Eastern Europe that Shippey offers as an example of environmental Sarumanism was made up of socialist countries that sought to obliterate private property. They were dedicated, in other words, to the regime of the "gatherers and sharers". The result of that experiment wasn't a thousand small-is-beautiful Shires blossoming on a thousand hills; it was centralization of power for its own sake and the brutal, shortsighted abuse of environmental resources.

Humanophobia

Brawley completes his misreading of Tolkien by portraying humanity as the enemy of the Ents, offering an unintended glimpse at what may be the most disturbing thread of contemporary environmentalism. "The ultimate fate of the Ents seems bleak, and although these characters are Tolkien's closest embodiment of the necessity of recovering a new relationship with nature through the sacramental vision, the message seems to be that, with the dominion of Men, all will be lost", Brawley writes. "As Treebeard states, 'for the world is changing: I feel it in the water, I feel it in the earth, and I smell it in the air.'... The sacramental vision must give way to the machine-loving enemy."[48]

But the enemy Treebeard speaks of is Saruman and Sauron; and later in the novel both are destroyed. Is Brawley saying the humans of Middle-Earth—all humans—are necessarily the enemy, and that's why the Ents eventually disappeared? Tolkien could easily have suggested this; instead he went out of his way to emphasize the friendship among Ents and men that follows Aragorn's ascension to the throne, and to give a different explanation for the later disappearance of the Ents—the split between the Ents and the Entwives. This, as Treebeard explains, is why there are no more Entlings.

This poignant side story of the Ents and Entwives is just one instance of a little-noticed theme in *The Lord of the Rings*—that a culture's lack of fertility is the effect and cause of cultural decline, a theme of particular relevance today because the environmental movement has become aggressively committed to minimizing human fertility. To give an extreme example, in 2006 the Texas Academy of Science gave Eric Pianka its Distinguished Texas Scientist Award. In his speech, Pianka reportedly fantasized about a mutant Ebola virus unburdening the natural environment by wiping out 90 percent of the human population. He was given a standing ovation.[49]

Neither this twisted vision nor any kinder, gentler version of it represents anything close to Tolkien's environmental vision. Evidence for this is in plain view in *The Lord of the Rings*. When Gandalf and Pippin ride into Minas Tirith on Shadowfax, the narrator paints an unsettling picture of the great city's decline, noting that "it was in truth falling year by year into decay; and already it lacked half the men that could have dwelt at ease there." Many houses of great families now "were silent, and no footsteps range on their wide pavements, nor voice was heard in their halls, nor any face looked out from door or empty window."[50]

A bit later in the same chapter, as the battle with Sauron's army approaches, the guardsman Beregond describes to Pippin a road in the distance and "the wains that bear away to refuge" the women, the aged, and the children. "It is a sad necessity", he adds; "there were always too few children in this city." Later, in the chapter called "The Last Debate", the good Prince Imrahil worries that the gate of Minas Tirith has been destroyed. Aragorn responds by saying that "men are better than gates, and no gate will endure against our Enemy if men desert it." Both passages hint at the connection between Gondor's cultural health and its fertility, between its vigor and its willingness to reproduce.

The appendix to the novel makes the connection explicit. "For more than a thousand years the Dúnedain of the South grew in wealth and power. Yet the signs of decay had then already appeared; for the high men of the South married late, and their children were few."[51] These kings, Faramir tells Frodo in Ithilien, "made tombs more splendid than houses of the living, and counted old names in the rolls of their descent dearer than the names of sons. Childless lords sat in aged halls musing on heraldry.... And the last king of the line of Anárion had no heir."[52] When Gondor embraced a decline in fertility, it almost became extinct.

Then, too, there are the passages offering positive support for a robust birth rate and a growing population. When the dwarf Gimli bemoans the tendency of humans to begin projects of great promise and then to flag, the elf Legolas responds, "Yet seldom do they fail of their seed.... The deeds of Men will outlast us, Gimli."[53]

Later, after Sauron has been defeated and Gandalf, Frodo, Sam, Merry, and Pippin pass through Bree on the way back to the Shire, Gandalf and Barliman the innkeeper fall into a conversation about some of the worrisome happenings around Bree and the prospect for better times. Gandalf, remember, has been a voice of wisdom throughout *The Hobbit* and *The Lord of the Rings*. And now he tells Barliman that "better times are coming" and that under Aragorn's happy rule, "the Greenway will be opened again, and his messengers will come north, and there will be comings and goings, and the evil things will be driven out of the wastelands. Indeed the waste in time will be waste no longer, and there will be people and fields where once there was wilderness."

When Barliman voices his concern about outside government interference and the threat to the wild of a growing population, Gandalf reassures him that Aragorn won't be a meddlesome ruler and that there will be plenty of green space left to enjoy, but he never retracts his upbeat depiction of "people and fields where once there was wilderness".[54]

Think about this scene for a moment. Tolkien, the loather of aesthetically parched suburban sprawl, puts the hand-wringing comments about population growth and encroaching development in the mouth of the parochial and relatively uncultured Barliman; and he puts the case for vigorous, thoughtful population growth and development in the mouth of what is arguably the central voice of wisdom in the novel, Gandalf the White.

And as if all this weren't enough, Tolkien puts a punctuation mark on the brave, wonderful life that is Sam Gamgee's by having him not only marry the pretty Rose Cotton but have thirteen (!) children with her—Elanor, Frodo, Rose, Merry, Pippin, Goldilocks, Hamfast, Daisy, Primrose, Bilbo, Ruby, Robin, and Tom. It's hard to imagine a clearer or more winsome way for Tolkien to punctuate the novel's pro-fertility theme.

So how could an author who detested ugly suburban sprawl think and write this way? Tolkien the orthodox Catholic, father of four, and lover of trees and untrammeled nature, living in a time and place of rapid population growth and suburban sprawl, surely registered the tension. Was he simply incoherent, or did he see a resolution to the tension that many others have overlooked? How are Christians to balance our call to be fruitful, multiply, and fill the earth with our call to be good stewards of Creation?

Two facts that often go overlooked render the tension less tense than it appears at a glance. First, as Tolkien well understood, mankind is not just a consumer of resources but also consists of creators, a truth easily missed if one has absorbed the fixed-pie assumptions of the secular left through untold information channels of educational and popular media. Such fixed-pie thinking has led doomsayers since Thomas Malthus to predict that looming overpopulation is about to destroy civilization. Each of these dire predictions has proven false as mankind has found new and better ways to provide for ourselves,[55] so much so that countries at advanced stages of development tend to take better care of their forests, lakes, and rivers than impoverished nations, who lack the technology and economic margin that would allow them to energetically pursue conservation.[56]

Also, as nations become economically more developed, they tend to trade the growing pains of rapid population growth for the problem of a looming demographic winter. An eye-opening book on this growing and little-heeded threat is David Goldman's *How Civilizations Die*.[57] Whether it's Japan, Poland, South Korea, Iran, or various other contemporary societies, as soon as education, technology, mass media, and secularism become widespread in the culture, people tend to opt for small families—or for no children at all. In this way, their cultures cease to reproduce at replacement levels, meaning that more and more countries will soon face the prospects of declining and aging populations, leaving a smaller and smaller number of workers to provide goods and services for a bulging wave of retirees.

Goldman does point to a silver lining. The people in developed countries who are more religious, particularly Jews and Christians who attend religious services often, have resisted the siren call of sub-replacement fertility. This pattern offers some hope for the future, since a disproportionate number of children in the next generation will be from families committed to the idea of larger families. At the same time, the pattern of precipitous fertility decline in developed societies is sufficiently widespread—with even the United States recently dropping below replacement-level fertility. Jews and Christians no longer have any rational basis for allowing talk of runaway global population to convince them we've reached the expiration date on the biblical teachings that children are a blessing from the Lord and to be fruitful and multiply.[58] With fertility rates crashing around the globe, the concern today should be just the opposite—namely, that there are so few couples willing to accept God's command to be fruitful and multiply that the planet appears poised to enter into a demographic winter where the ratio of old to young, of retiree to worker, will create a powerful new source of scarcity, poverty, and intergenerational strain.

The canary in the coal mine is the growing challenges facing government-sponsored pension and retirement programs in Europe, Japan, and the United States. Programs that worked beautifully when there were thirty or forty workers for every retiree are now being squeezed to the breaking point as the ratio drops to four-to-one, three-to-one, and even two-to-one. The problem is sufficiently dire that one techno-utopian, Peter Diamandias, has fantasized about the development of personal robotic nurses to take care of the old people when the ratio becomes unsustainable.[59] Oh brave new world that has such lonely creatures in it!

If the thought of such a future is properly disturbing, then for the love of God and his highest creation, humanity, let's leave off the dated hand-wringing about global overpopulation and join Sam Gamgee, Gandalf, and Tolkien in celebrating human fertility and the value of human and cultural flourishing.

It's Gandalf, after all, rather than Radagast, who emerges as the great hero of the Maiar. Certainly Radagast is one of the good guys, described as "a worthy wizard, a master of shapes and changes of hue; and he has much lore of herbs and beasts"[60] and is "the friend of all beasts and birds".[61] But as Bradley Birzer notes in a brief, indispensible discussion of the environmentalist response to Middle-Earth, Tolkien's own writing underscores what should already be apparent from the novel itself: Tolkien has given us something more than a univocally positive portrait of the *green* wizard.[62] Specifically, in a passage in *Unfinished Tales*, Tolkien explains that Radagast's marginal role in the battle against evil stems from his having become so enamored of nature that he drifts from his primary calling of helping the peoples of Middle-Earth. In Tolkien's 1954 essay on the wizards (the "Istari"), before describing Saruman's betrayal, he singles out Gandalf, the last of the Istari to come to Middle-Earth, and Radagast: "Indeed, of all the Istari, one only remained faithful, and he was the last comer. For Radagast, the fourth, became enamoured of the many beasts and birds that dwelt in Middle-earth, and forsook Elves and Men, and spent his days among the wild creatures."[63] Like many environmentalists today, Radagast seems to be in danger of making an idol of untrammeled nature. Gandalf avoids this error. He loves and appreciates nature, but the flourishing of the free peoples of Middle-Earth is always his higher priority.

Civilizations Green and Growing

Tolkien's life and writings point to a gaping ideological chasm between him and the humanophobic environmentalism of today. Tolkien did not see every additional human as necessarily a burden on the planet. Instead, he saw people as fallen, yes, but also as stewards over Creation, called to be fruitful and multiply both in their roles as spouses and as sub-creators with a capacity for conservation and innovation. Tolkien, after all, understood that humans are made in the image of God.

Dorothy Sayers puts the matter beautifully in *The Mind of the Maker*. Imagine you are coming to the Bible for the first time. You open to the first page of the first book of the Bible, and you begin reading, "In the beginning God created the heavens and the earth." You read on down the page and find this divine being creating this and creating that, and soon you come to a passage that reads, "So God created man in his own image, in the image of God he created him; male and female he created them."[64] What is the primary thing the book of Genesis has told you about God up to this point? That he is a creator, a maker. And now you learn that we humans are made in his image. The implication is inescapable: we, too, are "creators", made in the image of *the* Creator.[65] Of course, we don't create *ex nihilo* (out of nothing) as God does, which is why Tolkien refers to us as "sub-creators".[66] But as creatures made in his image we have a capacity to reason, imagine, and design, a capacity to make new things and envision new solutions, a capacity beyond anything else in the animal kingdom.

Tolkien was indeed troubled by the ugly aspects of industrialism and a pattern of city growth in the England of his day that demonstrated too little regard for beauty or the contours and rhythms of the English countryside. But his answer wasn't population control or a return to the Stone Age. It was to inspire his readers to imagine realms that grow and build in harmony with the natural order—the elven civilizations of

Lothlórien and Rivendell; the hobbits with their round windows and doors leading from their homes built into the hillsides of the rolling and beautifully gardened Shire; and even the humans of Gondor with their capitol city built in striking harmony with the great stone shoulder (like the prow of a ship) stretching from the Hill of the Guard to the great mountain at its back. After all, the story of Tolkien's religion begins in a garden and ends in a great city, one with mighty walls, a river, and the Tree of Life.

It wasn't that Tolkien loved mankind too much to be a thoroughgoing environmentalist. His vision was not one of lukewarm compromise between the needs of nature and the needs of human civilization. Rather, it was a vision of integration and enrichment for both—an integration made possible because of his understanding of humans as creatures made in the image of *the* divine maker, the culmination of the Creation week and the world's chosen stewards.

Chapter 8

The Fellowship of the Localists

In the prologue to *The Lord of the Rings*, Tolkien's narrator tells us that hobbits "love peace and quiet and good tilled earth: a well-ordered and well-farmed countryside was their favorite haunt. They do not and did not understand or like machines more complicated than a forge-bellow, a water-mill, or a hand-loom, though they were skillful with tools." Peter Jackson's movies nicely portray the abiding charm of this Shire culture, with its rolling hills, snug hobbit holes, stone bridges, lush green lawns, water wheels, gardens, and wildflowers encircled by farms in the distance. We also learn from Tolkien's novels that the hobbits of the Shire consume mainly locally grown food and tobacco, and have a marvelous knack for living in harmony with their surroundings. That they go barefoot is very much apiece with their relationship with the land around them. They are "in touch" with the land, literally and figuratively, rooted and contented to garden their little corner of Middle-Earth.

Since Tolkien modeled the Shire on one of his favorite childhood homes and described himself as "a hobbit (in all but size)", preferring "gardens, trees and unmechanized farmlands", a pipe, and "good plain food (unrefrigerated)",[1] it's clear that the Shire gives us more than a whimsically round window onto a lovely landscape. It also gives us a window onto its author. The love for communities living in rooted harmony with their geographies—so evident in the Shire and elsewhere in Tolkien's writings—has inspired millions of readers to reflect on their own cities and towns, especially today, when there is growing interest in the virtues of a "local" lifestyle. Grocery stores advertise the fact that they offer local produce, local milk, and local meat. The Chipotle restaurant chain uses its locavore credentials in its advertising.[2] And Michelle Obama keeps a garden with arugula at the White House.

There is more to localism than this brief listing, of course. A classic source for localist principles is the collection of essays by economist E.F. Schumacher, *Small Is Beautiful*, first published in 1973.[3] Schumacher argued that modern capitalist economies were unsustainable, since they produce larger and larger industries, which use up more and more resources. Such economies also create a dehumanizing workplace for most people, and should be replaced with smaller, localized, "human-sized" work environments, like villages, that are more dignified and sustainable.

Many are now convinced that they have a moral and economic obligation[4] to buy locally, and to avoid stores owned by big companies outside their communities.[5] These ideas became even more popular in the wake of the 2008 financial crisis. This has fueled renewed talk of a "third way" between capitalism and socialism, as there was a century ago.

Much of this trend is surely wholesome. You're not a Luddite just because you prefer fresh local produce and fish to canned, or organic milk from a local dairy to powdered milk from who knows where.[6] To avoid being carried away by a spirit of the age, though, we need to view this trend dispassionately. Similarly, to understand what Tolkien has to tell us about these matters, we have to approach his writings with something more than a simple equation of Tolkien = Shire = Localism. A personal affinity is not a programmatic agenda, and even the author's personal affinities may be more complex than they seem at first blush.

Starbucks Localism

Sometimes it makes sense to buy locally—much more on that below—but often it has severe limits. I (Jonathan) live on an old farm in west Michigan where my family and I keep a decent-sized garden, laying hens, wild turkeys, and deer that visit our backyard occasionally; cherry and apple trees; volunteer blackberries; and sons who are learning how to spot edible wild plants, and who are using the rest of the family as guinea pigs to try them out. We enjoy providing some of our own sustenance, but it isn't a full-time job, and the yield of all this is miniscule compared to the needs of our family. If we had to subsist entirely on what we could harvest or hunt, there would soon be five fewer Witts in the world.

You might think this is only because there is heavy snow on the ground for a third of the year in Michigan, so consider another example from a more temperate climate. In summer 2013, I (Jay) lived with my family at Mileta Farm, overlooking Quartermaster Harbor, on Vashon Island. The island is in the middle of Puget Sound, just a few miles by ferry to Seattle, but it is still isolated. Think of the Shire, with soil so rich and moisture so plentiful that even the driveways get overrun with moss and weeds, if left to their own devices. Now, put the Shire on an island in the middle of a temperate zone, where temperature extremes are rare, with a view of the sea and snow-peaked mountains beyond it. It's hard to imagine any place on Earth more likely to cultivate nostalgia for the agrarian way of life.

Mileta Farm is no longer a working farm except for flowers and a garden. We have friends on the island, however—the Maderases and the Dalys—who really farm. They have sheep, goats, chickens, and even some crops. Cheese made from their goats' milk is as smooth and sweet as can be had anywhere on the planet. But even in one of the most temperate and fertile places on earth, and using modern technology—electricity, cars, tools, tractors, electric saws, and a thousand other conveniences we all take for granted—the Maderases and the Dalys could not live beyond mere subsistence if they had to rely solely on the income and produce of their individual farms. Both families still rely on a steady stream of food from the local Thriftway, along with countless goods and services from other sources, made possible by a global system of trade.

Colin Maderas has a landscaping business that helps keep his growing family afloat. Marcus Daly spends most of his days building handmade, wooden coffins, similar to the coffin in which John Paul II was buried.[7] (A few years back, he cut off his right ring finger with a table saw—the same finger Frodo lost on Mount Doom. By getting to Seattle in time, he was able to have it reattached. He now calls the saw "Gollum".)

These families, who live in a farmer's paradise and could serve as poster children for the localist lifestyle, nevertheless remain firmly tied to a global marketplace that richly benefits them. If this is the case with them, how much more so with people living in less hospitable locations for growing food? For people in these other places, the advice to always "buy local" lacks even a superficial credibility.

If buying local was intrinsically superior to distant trade, Americans would be better off if we had stayed separate colonies trading goods, services, and capital internally and coming together only in cases of a direct military threat from outside. For that matter, the towns in the colonies would be better if they just traded within their borders.[8] Swiss Family Robinson would be the ideal.

Few take the local-is-better philosophy to such an extreme, of course. The point of the *reductio ad absurdum* is to get clear on the cost and benefits of trading with people beyond our corner of the world, and the costs and benefits of refusing to do so. Seven billion people trading only with their families and neighbors would not create seven billion self-sufficient people. It would create several billion dead people, and leave the rest to eke out a meager existence as subsistence farmers, hunter-gatherers, or scavengers.

This sounds harsh because the reality of shifting to such an economy would be harsh, almost unimaginably so. Specialization and division of labor allows individuals, cultures, and countries to specialize in the things they do best—or at least better than many others—and trade for other things. This has created vast wealth by allowing us to share and coordinate our gifts.[9] That isn't to say there aren't grave injustices and dire poverty in the world. It's rather to state a point that's wholly noncontroversial in economics: supporting seven billion people without the global division of labor isn't feasible.

Okay, but isn't buying local better for the environment? Actually, it's not so simple. Shipping a freight of bananas from Costa Rica is much less energy- and labor-intensive than growing them in Duluth, Minnesota. A *single* twenty-foot container can hold about forty-eight thousand bananas. And a ship such as the EMMA MÆRSK can carry eleven thousand full twenty-foot containers. That equals a train seventy-one kilometers long. So, in theory, a vessel could transport about 528 million bananas in a single voyage. That's enough to give every person in Europe or North America a banana for breakfast.[10] That's part of why bananas are so economical. If it's energy-intensive to get something to your local store, it shows up in the price, provided the government isn't masking that cost through subsidies (more on this in a bit).

Although now-developed countries have benefited the most, even the poorest parts of the world have gained dramatically from industrialization and globalization. Economist Martin Wolf notes, "Africa's average real income per head is perhaps three times higher than it was a century or so ago. Asia's as a whole is up six-fold since 1820 and Latin

America's nine-fold. In 1900, life expectancy was a mere twenty-six in today's developing world. It was sixty-four in 1999. This is much the same as the sixty-six achieved by today's advanced countries as recently as 1950."[11] To those of us living comfortable middle-class lives in developed economies, it's easy to miss the billions of concrete personal dramas involved here—the untold number of parents who did not have to bury a child, the countless children who could begin to dream about something larger than their next good meal, the half-grown girls and boys who were not turned out on the streets, because their parents didn't die.

What's particularly telling is that it's those developing economies most connected to the global economy that have delivered the most economic progress to their citizens. Of course, this development exacts costs, sometimes severe ones,[12] but those costs must be weighed against the unprecedented benefits in health, life expectancy, mobility, and income to billions of people.[13]

For the "bottom billion", bare subsistence on local goods is a bitter reality, not an ideal. In Middle-Earth the equivalent would be the Wild Men of the Woods,[14] who do seem to have a wholly localist economy. The other free peoples of Middle-Earth—hobbits, dwarves, elves, and humans—clearly benefit from trade and division of labor. Take dwarves and hobbits. Hobbits love to farm, but we have no hints of smelters or metal smithing in the Shire. Dwarves mine stones and forge metal, but don't do much farming.[15] This makes far more sense than if the Shire-hobbits, with no access, interest, or skill in stonecraft, were to mine and carve precious gems, while dwarves, who prefer caves, were to raise tobacco and garden vegetables.

Similarly, Aragorn employs elves and dwarves to help rebuild Minas Tirith at the beginning of the Fourth Age. Elves make waybread and the finest swords and rope. And as we have already seen, after the tyrannical Smaug is overthrown in *The Hobbit*, trade expands in the valley, with dwarves joining the elves of Mirkwood and the men of Lake-town in trading goods up- and downriver—not just international trade but inter-species trade!

When Bigger Is Beautiful

All this beneficent free trade among free peoples should remind us that, while small can be beautiful, so too can bigness. Sometimes, bigger is better. Almost any affordable piece of modern technology you can think of—not just high-tech gadgets like computers, smart phones,[16] and medical devices, but fairly simple things like lattes and pencils—is possible not only because of division of labor, but because of economies of scale. If a company can find one million customers for a product, then it's worth investing in sophisticated "labor-saving" equipment for mass production. If a company produces just six typewriters, the cost per typewriter would be astronomical, as they were in the early days of the technology. But when the development of interchangeable parts led to mass-production techniques, the approach soon spread to typewriters, dramatically lowering their cost,[17] so that even a cash-strapped Englishman of the 1920s could get his hands on one.

It's one thing to have a healthy appreciation for skillfully handcrafted, custom-made goods. But for some, it's de rigueur to sniff at mass-produced goods. This is shortsighted. Even granting that the mass-produced version is often inferior, it's undeniable that the techniques of mass production have allowed middle- and lower-class people to enjoy goods they never could have afforded otherwise—everything from typewriters and sewing machines to bicycles and CD players. Nor are mass-produced goods necessarily cheap in the pejorative sense of the term, since the quality of the outcome, as with smartphones, sometimes vastly exceeds what could be accomplished locally or by hand.

The long and short of it is this: many successful companies grow because they create wealth and serve their customers well. Large chain stores like Costco, Target, or Walmart grow not by some evil conspiracy but because they enjoy greater economies of scale. They can buy, sell, and distribute in bulk, and they can negotiate lower prices with suppliers, not only because of the leverage they bring to the negotiating table, but because they vastly simplify marketing for the wholesalers selling to them. If you produce undershirts, and Walmart offers to buy ten million of them, you can afford to sell your shirts near your cost of production and still make a handsome profit. And now more undershirts are available to low-income customers.

When Small Is Beautiful

There's a tension here: we want lower-income people to be able to buy products that once would have been out of their reach. And most of us shop at discount stores at least on occasion. But let's face it: for most of us, a Walmart is not the favorite place to hang out. It isn't the least bit Shire-like. It's drab and fluorescent lit. Fortunately, no one is forced at gunpoint to shop or work at Walmart.

We don't even have to worry about big box stores swallowing up all the small stores. That's because just as there are economies of scale, so too are there *diseconomies* of scale. Larger companies are generally more bureaucratic, top-heavy, and slower to adapt. "What small companies give up in terms of financial clout, technological resources, and staying power," Thomas Sowell writes, quoting an Indian entrepreneur, "they gain in flexibility, lack of bureaucracy, and speed of decision-making."[18] That's why new companies spring up all the time (Google and Facebook), and big companies disappear (Circuit City, Borders, Lehman Brothers).

Bigger is plainly not better for some things. Small, local charities, for instance, tend to help the needy who face long-term problems more effectively than big, impersonal bureaucracies. Small, young companies are often better able to think outside the box and innovate. The proliferation of Shirriffs in the Shire at the end of *The Lord of the Rings* is not a welcome development. And small private and home schools can better tailor teaching strategies to individual students. (We both homeschool our children.)

Bigness Good and Bad

So there's room for both big and small. And certainly we find positive examples of each in Middle-Earth. The scale of the Shire is an obvious example of smallness done well. But there are some big things that are also given their due. The underground city of the dwarves in Moria no doubt required labor and coordination on a massive scale, as did the mountain fortress of Erebor, the walled city of Minas Tirith, the watchtower Orthanc built by the Dúnedain, and the enormous stone Argonath guarding the river on the northern border of Gondor. Even the modest water mill at the heart of Hobbiton was no weekend project of the miller and his sons. Smelting and smithing labor (stone and metal) were needed to make the grinding wheel and metal parts, skills we have no indication are local to the Shire.

Taken together, these various lines of evidence suggest that Tolkien clearly didn't see bigness as intrinsically bad. There is a uniformly bad kind of bigness, however. Sometimes companies grow, not so much by creating value for customers, but by making backroom deals with government. This is growth by collusion and coercion rather than fair competition. Such cronyism contradicts the free market, inhibits innovation, and undermines local and agrarian economic patterns by unfairly favoring big corporations.

We saw this during the financial crisis, and afterward, when politicians left and right came together to bail out certain large financial institutions with taxpayer money, while leaving small ones to struggle. In a similar fashion, in agriculture, corn and rice subsidies—a political rather than a market invention—often go disproportionately to corporate farms, which encourage agribusiness monocultures in large sections of the Midwest while hurting small farmers, especially in the developing world.

Farmers Gene Logsdon and Joel Salatin—both champions of environmentally sensitive agriculture and the benefits of robust regional food markets—show in their writings how pastoral life is undermined by big government in cahoots with corporations.

Salatin has been featured in Michael Pollan's *The Omnivore's Dilemma* and in the popular documentaries *Food, Inc.* and *Fresh.* In one of his own books, *Everything I Want to Do Is Illegal,* Salatin tells harrowing tales of how much freedom has been taken away from farmers and food producers who simply want to exercise their creative freedom and compete, but are battered and suppressed by food and agricultural bureaucracies that often seem designed to eradicate small operations.[19] The picture he paints is of a government that has gotten so large that many agricultural companies prefer to curry favor with federal regulators rather than compete fairly for customers.

Gene Logsdon is equally critical of the federal government's interference with regional farming markets. In *The Contrary Farmer,*[20] he explores how government manipulation of agricultural markets has led to costly, hare-brained, and environmentally damaging practices. For example, farmers are tempted by government subsidies to grow corn on land far better suited for other, unsubsidized crops. The end result: the agricultural and economic diversity of whole regions of the United States is diminished. This has the knock-on effect of undermining opportunities for people in these regions to obtain a variety of affordable, locally grown produce.

People talk about addressing such problems by further regulating lobbyists, but every new wave of regulations seems only to make matters worse. The best way to avoid cronyism and the government manipulation of markets in favor of corporate bigness is to have big government shrunk down to size and hemmed in by severe limits. Tolkien, as we've seen, beat the drum of small government when the rest of the world was running headlong into arms of Big Brother.

Nature, the Teacher

Recently, I (Jay) had the chance to spend an afternoon with one of the farmers mentioned above, Joel Salatin. After he served my colleagues and me a lunch of raw milk, apple cider, cheese omelets, and apples, we enjoyed a lengthy tour of his Polyface farms—a reference to the many different kinds of animals on the farm, including cows, pigs, turkeys, and chickens. The farm is nestled in a valley in rural Virginia amid green fields, rolling hills, large patches of trees, and some farmhouses that date to the Revolutionary War. If you picture the Shire, you won't be too far off.

Salatin has a robust Christian understanding of stewardship and animal husbandry. He's said, famously, that he "respects the pigness of pigs". He's committed to biomimicry, a trend in fields as diverse as medicine, robotics, transportation, and farming. The basic idea is to develop methods with special attention to the preexisting patterns of nature. Industrial farms tend to pack cattle together with only the occasional herding dog or quarter horse to lend variety. But if you watch almost any nature documentary about the African savannah, you know there always seem to be birds hanging out with the bovines. That's because they live in a win-win "symbiotic" relationship. So taking a cue from nature, Salatin, rather than isolating his chickens in a coop, has them in the pasture following the cattle from paddock to paddock in a rotational grazing system. The hens break up the cow manure as they look for worms, which helps to accelerate the process of the manure decaying into fertilizer. He also adds some "watch geese" to the mix to protect the chickens from predators.

Like any good rancher, he also works to cultivate certain natural symbiotic relationships between plant and animal. For example, cattle, when herded wisely, graze on the grass at an optimal height for the grass' health, which both nourishes the cattle and encourages the grass to grow. Unlike much modern industrialized farming, Salatin assumes that chickens are meant to eat in a field, and pigs to root in the mud. This doesn't lead him to abandon technology, but to seek technology that harnesses these natural designs, as with his use of portable electric fencing to efficiently move his chickens from paddock to paddock. We see something like this in the artistry of the eco-friendly elves, who are not low-tech but high-tech. Their swords, clothing, and architecture are vastly superior to the blunt machetes, animal skins, and crude cave holes of the orcs. The elves' technology is superior in part because elvish artifice builds on and harmonizes with natural patterns.

Interestingly, too, biomimicry may allow a favorite element of localist subculture to spread to the wider culture. At the moment, the products of local, free-range, organic farming are essentially luxury goods. The raw milk, eggs, beef, and pork from Joel Salatin's Polyface farms are three to four times more expensive than what you would find in a Walmart supercenter. That's no big deal when food is a tiny fraction of your income. But it *is* a big deal if 30 percent of your budget goes to food.

This could change, however. Salatin says the techniques that he and other biomimetic farmers are developing are scalable—up and down—which could lower their costs. The best way to find out is to let a thousand entrepreneurial flowers bloom. Unfortunately, the biggest challenge he and his fellow innovators face—and the reason he wrote *Everything I Want to Do Is Illegal*—is that the biggest business of all, the federal government, has made it hard for farmers to innovate and deliver finished goods to area customers, thanks to a byzantine regulatory regime that stacks the deck in favor of corporate agriculture. Here the obvious cure is something the Shire has in abundance—less government.

A Diverse Culture

Despite Tolkien's provocative complaints against the ugly elements of industrialism, he did not embrace a lifestyle of pastoral primitivism. Though he showed a deep appreciation for pastoral life in both his fiction and his personal correspondence, his thought taken as a whole is quite pluralistic. He dignified other ways of living, including the city life of Minas Tirith, the equestrian culture of Rohan, the cavern-dwelling and stone craft of Erebor, the merchant culture of Bree, the contemplative and intellectual culture of Rivendell, the suburban seaside community Tolkien and his wife retired to, and his own professorial life at Oxford

University. So of course Tolkien respected various ways of life besides the pastoral. Indeed, he would have been ungrateful not to. The division of labor and the hustle and bustle of commercial cities make places like Oxford University possible. That institution provided Tolkien with the financial stability, intellectual resources, and some of the time to create his Middle-Earth novels.

Moreover, in a very real sense trade created Tolkien's readers. Contrary to popular impression, at the cultural level, wealth precedes education, not the other way around.[21] Western civilization's trade of goods, services, and ideas beyond the local level helped to generate the broad middle class essential to a novel-creating and novel-reading culture, along with the technology necessary to mass-produce and distribute affordable books.

Tolkien understood what some localists seem to have forgotten. To use terms from Catholic social teaching, the principle of subsidiarity (which gives priority to the competent authority closest to a problem) needs to be balanced by the principle of solidarity. People in every part of the world are creatures made in the image of God and so are worthy of joining us not only in global networks of charity but also in our circles of productivity and exchange. While no one, at least no head of a household, would want to depend absolutely on another human being for his survival, we live in a deeply *inter*dependent world, and that has many benefits. John Paul II celebrated this fact in *Centesimus Annus*: "More than ever, work is *work with others* and *work for others*" (emphasis in original).[22]

Is the localist agrarian lifestyle choice superior, say, to one dedicated to enriching the culture in a densely populated city through service, innovation, art, or music? Is the life of the small farmer superior to that of a priest in Des Moines or a medical missionary in Mumbai? Tolkien probably would have regarded these as prudential questions best answered by particular individuals and families in conversation with wise friends and mentors. We should strive for a society in which those who wish to embrace an agrarian, locavore life should be free to do so, but avoid one in which it is compulsory or paraded about as morally superior.

Distributism

Closely related to localism is distributism, an economic view proposed by early twentieth-century English Catholic thinkers Hilaire Belloc and

G. K. Chesterton.[23] Some Tolkien scholars have identified Tolkien with this view as well.

Before we consider that, we should first lay out what exactly distributism is. Presented as a "third way" between capitalism and socialism, distributism is marked by a deep nostalgia for pastoral life.[24] It seeks to move society toward more local, agrarian, small-scale, and family-centered practices reminiscent of the English Middle Ages. This earlier period is said to be marked by the wide distribution of productive property (land, tools to cultivate the land, and tools to practice a trade), and guilds that maintained standards and wages for different trades. The original distributist idea is not that everyone should be a full-time farmer, but that every family should have "productive property" so it could have a sense of independence and security, knowing that, if need be, the family could grow its own food.[25]

In his *Essay on the Restoration of Property*, Hilaire Belloc described his ideal as one in which "property is so well distributed and so large a proportion of families in the State severally own and therefore control the means of production as to determine the general tone of society."[26] Belloc's concern was that wealth and power tend to become concentrated in the hands of a few owners or capitalists in the modern age, with the vast majority of people barely eking by as "wage slaves". In *The Servile State*, first published in 1912, before the communist revolution in Russia and two world wars, he argued that modern capitalism leads to concentrations of wealth and monopoly, and "is tending to reach a condition of stable equilibrium by the establishment of compulsory labor legally enforceable upon those who do not own the means of production for the advantage of those who do."[27]

Was Tolkien a Distributist?

In his excellent work *J. R. R. Tolkien's Sanctifying Myth*, Bradley Birzer explores the similarity between Tolkien and the early distributists, but leaves open the question of whether Tolkien actually was a distributist. Some of our other favorite Tolkien interpreters have gone further.[28] Peter Kreeft states simply, "Tolkien's political philosophy had a name: distributism."[29] Joseph Pearce, in *Tolkien: Man and Myth*, provides more detail, pointing to a key passage from *The Lord of the Rings*, which Pearce thinks shows the "distributist credo": "Deep down in him [Sam

Gamgee] lived still unconquered his plain hobbit-sense. The one small garden of a free gardener was all his need and due, not a garden swollen to a realm, his own hands to use, not the hands of others to command."[30] Pearce shows the affinities between Tolkien's and Chesterton's work, and demonstrates that Tolkien knew, and for the most part admired, Chesterton's writings. He offers no direct evidence, though, that Tolkien was a distributist.

The connection to the Shire is easy enough to recognize. The hobbits live an idyllic life uncluttered by the excesses of modern big city capitalism, a life with the qualities that distributists hope to cultivate in contemporary life. But concluding that Tolkien was a distributist is unwarranted.

Nostalgia and Idealized History

Despite its initial appeal, distributism has attracted relatively few supporters over the years, due to the many problems critics have raised since it was first proposed. Belloc and Chesterton wrote at a time when land laws made it very hard for the ordinary Englishman without land to get ahead. It was also a time when some historians were painting a rosy picture of the lives of farmers and laborers in the Middle Ages. This led Belloc and Chesterton to romanticize the English Middle Ages. The medieval period was certainly more fruitful and civilized than the "Dark Ages" stereotype invented by modernists; and life was better for the average English family than it was for slaves during the Roman Empire. Nevertheless, historians now recognize that the typical life of the medieval European, and Englishman, was, to quote Thomas Hobbes, "poor, nasty, brutish, and short".[31] Nathan Rosenberg and L. E. Birdzell put it bluntly in their 1986 book: "The romantic view that workers in pre-Industrial Europe lived well may safely be dismissed as pure fantasy.... The early factories were able to attract workers with low wages because the wages were still ... better than anything available elsewhere to an impoverished agricultural population."[32]

The notion that small farmers and craftsmen generally live a secure life is the sort of thing that only nonfarming writers living in verdant England could believe. Even today, small farming is vulnerable to all sorts of contingencies—droughts, hail, locusts, aphids. An old joke in west Texas defined a successful farmer as one whose wife has a job in town. Farming can be far more stressful and far less secure than an ordinary nine-to-five job. Owning a business of any kind is risky, and many people prefer a regular wage to the vicissitudes of entrepreneurship.

As for the agrarian Shire, there are lessons in it, but we need to be cautious. Tolkien emphasized that the preindustrial life of the Shire hobbits was not meant to function as "a Utopian vision" or to encourage us to return to preindustrialism and freeze in time a particular historical moment.[33] This, he explained, was the "weakness" of the elves, who "regret the past", and "become unwilling to face change: as if a man were to hate a very long book still going on, and wished to settle down in a favourite chapter. Hence they fell in a measure to Sauron's deceits: they desired ... to make their particular will to preservation effective: to arrest change, and keep things always fresh and fair."[34]

Tolkien even referred to elves as "embalmers":

> They wanted to have their cake and eat it: to live in the mortal historical Middle-earth because they had become fond of it (and perhaps because they there had the advantages of a superior caste), and so tried to stop its change and history, stop its growth ... and they were overburdened with sadness and nostalgic regret. In their way the Men of Gondor were similar: a withering people whose only "hallows" were their tombs.

To make crystal clear the daylight between him and the elves on this score, he insisted, "I am not a reformer nor an 'embalmer'! I am not a 'reformer' (by exercise of power) since it seems doomed to Sarumanism. But 'embalming' has its own punishments."[35]

The Elusive Middle Way

Distributism's problems run deeper than a tendency toward "embalming". At least in Belloc's formulation, it is also beset by serious economic problems. And even the claim that distributism is a third way between capitalism and socialism depends upon a definition of *capitalism* that no defender would embrace. The common contrast between capitalism and socialism is itself of socialist pedigree. It was Marx who popularized the word *capitalism*. Though its champions now use the word as a synonym for property rights, limited government, and economic freedom, Marx defined capitalism as a system that must lead to the exploitation of the poor at the hands of the rich.

In *The Communist Manifesto*, written in 1848, Marx and his coauthor, Friedrich Engels, argued that under capitalism the vast majority of the wealth in the economy would be transferred to a few capitalists who owned the means of production, and away from the growing throng of the proletariat, "wage slaves" who would get poorer and poorer.

Marx and Engels' argument in *The Communist Manifesto* is strikingly similar to Belloc's argument in *The Servile State*. Both failed to understand that free exchange benefits both parties.[36] Both held to what is called the labor theory of value, roughly the idea that something is worth economically just how much it cost to produce it.[37] As a result, both viewed profit as the result, not of customer satisfaction and prudent production, but of what Marx called "surplus value", by which the capitalist exploits both the worker and the customer. This follows by definition. If a car is worth just as much as it costs to produce it, then any profit is essentially theft. In other words, both books depict the relationship between "capitalist" and "proletariat" as a zero-sum game.

Marx and Engels predicted that capitalism would destroy itself, because over time the capitalists would extract more and more wealth from the laborers, driving wages down and down until a few semimonopolist islands would be engulfed by a vast and revolutionary proletarian sea. In reality, while Marx was writing the *Manifesto*, the wages of workers near his apartment in London were going up, not down. Marx didn't know this, because he never bothered to study local factories. If he had, he might have concluded that, perhaps, even when employers own most of the "means of production", as those means improve due to innovation, they increase the output and value of labor. This leads to higher wages.

The similarity between Marx's and Belloc's arguments does not mean that Belloc was a Marxist, but rather that he unwittingly shared some economic assumptions with the founder of modern Communism. In fact, though he officially accepted the need for a division of labor, Belloc seemed to understand its value less well than Marx did. Tolkien nowhere expressed similar opinions.

The Distributist Paradox

Belloc was right to criticize certain elements of nineteenth-century England, with its privileged aristocracy and giant landed estates maintained by stiff laws of entail and enclosure. However, he went well beyond advocating a legal system purged of class favoritism. An aspiration or good intention is one thing, a policy is quite another. In the form proposed by Belloc,[38] distributism calls for the machinery of the state to actively redistribute "productive property" and then keep it well-distributed through a variety of taxes and regulations. "We must seek political and economic reforms," he wrote in his *Essay on the Restoration of Property*, "which shall tend to distribute property more and more widely until the owners of sufficient Means of Production (land or capital or both) are numerous enough to determine the character of society."[39] The implication is plain: if land and capital are "unequally" owned, the state needs to equalize the situation by using its coercive powers to confiscate private property and redistribute it along presumably more egalitarian lines.

Lest anyone miss the point, Belloc goes on to insist that "the effort at restoring property will certainly fail if it is hampered by a superstition against the use of force as the handmaid of Justice." All this dividing and sharing, you see, requires "gatherers and sharers" with the power to gather and share.

Note the irony: Belloc wanted to distribute the power and wealth of a few actors—large landowners and capitalists—in order to avoid concentrations of power in the hands of the few. But Belloc seemed to realize the only feasible way to accomplish and maintain this end is to permanently grant power over private property to the national government. This means giving more power to the entity that already possesses the most power in society, the same entity that enjoys a near monopoly on coercion: the government. Call this the distributist paradox: to disperse concentrations of power in the private sector (the realm of voluntary exchange), we must concentrate power in the political sector (the realm of coercion).

To be sure, Belloc proposed a gradual though persistent use of state power for these purposes, not the radical collectivization attempted by Lenin and Stalin. And later distributists have sought to resolve this contradiction.[40] Nevertheless, Belloc seems to have unwittingly embraced what Austrian economist F. A. Hayek observed and lamented: "A claim for equality of material position can be met only by a government with totalitarian powers."[41] Perhaps this goes some way toward explaining why Belloc, Chesterton, and other distributists, such as A. J. Henty, were sympathetic to the French Revolution and to the Fascism of Mussolini's

Italy (though Chesterton changed his mind on that more quickly than Belloc did).[42] Tolkien's views, in contrast, were poles apart from both Fascism and the French Revolution.[43]

Now, Tolkien surely knew more than a little about the views of Belloc and Chesterton. Both men were prolific writers in England during Tolkien's lifetime, and the spheres of their influence overlapped with Tolkien's world. Belloc went to Newman's Oratory School in Birmingham, where Tolkien later spent nine years of his childhood as a parishioner, and then attended Balliol College, Oxford, where he was part of the small Catholic minority that later included Tolkien. Chesterton—like Tolkien—was instrumental in C. S. Lewis' conversion to Christianity (by way of his book *The Everlasting Man*), and parts of Chesterton's *Orthodoxy* read like prolegomena for the aesthetic program of Tolkien and Lewis. In short, Tolkien surely knew of the writings of distributists of his day and frequently commented on matters political and economic. This is why it is so significant that *no* endorsement of the distributist program has ever been discovered in Tolkien's writings. It's akin to the Sherlock Holmes story involving a stolen racehorse and a dead trainer. A crucial key to unraveling the case is a dog *not* barking when he might have been expected to bark.[44] Sometimes the absence of evidence is evidence.

And in the case of Tolkien and the distributists, it isn't just the telling absence of explicit approval. Tolkien expressed views that run counter to the distributist program. For instance, guilds, much beloved by Belloc and other distributists, are effectively powerful cartels that control prices and restrict entry into various trades, thus preventing less skilled workers from competing, and becoming more skilled, by accepting lower wages. Guilds, like any cartel, need coercion to be sustained. In modern societies, this means the state would need to enforce the guild rules—essentially corporatism, or what we have already called cronyism—unfit men bossing other men around, to borrow Tolkien's description.[45] Indeed, Tolkien articulated—clearly and on several occasions—a deep and wide-ranging hostility to plans that would further empower government bureaucrats to reform society, however nobly intentioned.

Try to picture Tolkien as a hobbit, pipe in hand, standing on the stump of the party tree at Bilbo's Eleventy-First Birthday Party, or on a platform in Minas Tirith or Rivendell or Edoras, pointing out certain well-heeled figures in the crowd—the Tooks, Faramir, Elrond,

Éomer—and declaring, as Belloc did, that "the effort at restoring property will certainly fail if it is hampered by a superstition against the use of force as the handmaid of Justice!"[46]

Tolkien advocated the use of force for self-defense from violent aggression, but he never recommended that the state make its regular and ongoing business to redistribute legally owned property in the pursuit of equality. Just the opposite: he was opposed to governments punishing economic success, exclaiming to his son Michael after *The Lord of the Rings* had begun to earn him a comfortable and rising income, "Don't speak to me about 'Income Tax' or I shall boil over. They had all my literary earnings until I retired."[47] Elsewhere he referred to "the claws" of England's "Taxgatherers".[48] More than this, he found the whole mindset of pursuing aggressive reform through the coercive arm of the state fraught with danger. He warned of " 'reformers' who want to hurry up with 'reconstruction' and 'reorganization' ", and of their pursuing their goals innocently enough, but only "before pride and the lust to exert their will eat them up".[49]

At the end of *The Hobbit*, recall, Tolkien lampoons the impulse to divvy up the wealth of the well-to-do. Bilbo arrives home to find his property being auctioned off, and, of course, he wants his stuff back. And while there's a good bit of grumbling and complaining, and a few dishonest folks who sneak off with what isn't theirs, the common opinion is that Mr. Baggins' stuff is Mr. Baggins' stuff, even if he did return from his adventures with more treasure than he knows what to do with. It never crosses the hobbits' collective mind that some government official should have the power to appropriate a sizable portion of Bilbo's property and distribute it more equitably throughout the community.

The scene by itself doesn't show that Tolkien wasn't a distributist, of course, but certainly it's an odd plot element for a follower of Belloc's political program to squeeze into his novel at the eleventh hour; and taken together with the other lines of evidence, it points us in a very different direction from the early distributist program of reform.

The Family

All that said, distributists have called attention to some truths often overlooked by economists. Contemporary distributists, such as Dale Ahlquist and Allan Carlson, argue for a more family-centered view of economics.

They rightly regard the family as the most important human institution for bearing and raising children, and as a bulwark against a state seeking to expand its reach over society. The family-oriented economy of the Shire is a fitting example.

Unfortunately, distributists often yoke this insight to flawed policy prescriptions. For example, many distributists call for a family living wage, in which the government, or a cartel-like guild with government support, would stipulate the minimum salary employers could pay an employee who has a wife and children.[50] The goal is to increase family ties by building an economy in which a man can make enough to support his family without having to take a second job, and in which his wife would not, at least by necessity, have to work outside the home.

The goal is surely worthy. The problem is that the policy would yield a very different result. Just think about it from the perspective of the employer. John owns a pizza restaurant and needs to hire a chef. For John, paying a chef is a cost. Three equally qualified men apply for the position. The first is single with no marital prospects, the second is married with no kids, and the third is married with six kids. If John hires the man with the large family, the law will require John to pay his employee a much higher wage than if he hires either of the other two men. As a result, hiring the single man would be John's most economical choice, since the single man's salary and insurance premiums would be the least expensive. So an enhanced minimum wage designed to help men with large families earn more would in fact do the opposite. This is what happens when you ignore unintended consequences and focus only on the good ends you want to achieve. Economic realities—in this case, scarcity and the price function—can't be wished away.[51]

Widespread Ownership of Property

Another good distributist intuition is that ownership of property should be widespread. And we certainly see something like that in the Shire. But there's a difference between a right to lawfully acquire and own property—one of the foundations of a free and flourishing society—and a right to have someone else's property. You don't have the right to your neighbor's Aston Martin any more than the other hobbits had a right to Bilbo's fortune. And if you have properly purchased a Mini Cooper, your neighbor doesn't have a right to that, either.

Belloc and Chesterton seemed to identify "productive property" with land and equipment. This is understandable. When they were writing, a large segment of the British and global population still lived on farms. As recently as 1900, half of all Americans lived in rural settings. At the time of the American founding, over 90 percent of the labor force was farming. Today, that percentage has dropped to about 2 percent both here and in England.[52] Recently, as a result of the growing demand for local food, the net number of farms in the United States has increased slightly for the first time since the Great Depression.[53] But even if the number of Americans living on farms doubles or triples, that would still be only 4 to 6 percent of the labor force. Most upper middle class people, if they wanted to, could take a cue from Sam Gamgee and buy a small farm. Apparently they don't want to. So it's very unlikely, short of a population-destroying global catastrophe, that people in advanced societies will freely return to a largely agrarian lifestyle.[54] Most people don't want to be farmers or live on farms. Like Tolkien, they find their calling by doing something else.

Chesterton and Belloc failed to see that the earlier agrarian and later industrial stage of the economy in England near the turn of the century were just that—stages. Advanced societies have moved from agrarian to industrial to service and now to information economies. Can you think of a living billionaire entrepreneur who reached that rarified elevation through agriculture? Probably not. Pope John Paul II made just this point in *Centesimus Annus*: "Whereas at one time the decisive factor of production was *the land*, and later capital—understood as the total complex of the instruments of production—today the decisive factor is increasingly *man himself*, that is, his knowledge, especially his scientific knowledge, his capacity for interrelated and compact organization, as well as his ability to perceive the needs of others and to satisfy them" (emphasis in original).[55]

Chesterton and Belloc also seemed to treat as permanent a corporate structure with a clean divide between wage-earning laborers and capitalist owners. But there's nothing immutable about such a structure. Like everything else in an economy, corporate governance evolves over time as long as it is allowed to do so. Even the traditional joint stock company doesn't fit the tidy taxonomy of capitalists-and-proletariat. Factory workers in a GE plant that makes light bulbs can buy GE stock, and many do. Profit sharing is now increasingly common. And most modern tech start-ups compensate employees through a combination of wages, salary, and stock options. Who are the proletariat at Microsoft and Google?[56]

Catholic Social Teaching and Distributism

Distributists hold what they believe is a final trump card in favor of distributism generally, and in favor of the more specific claim that the orthodox Catholic Tolkien was himself a distributist. They argue that distributism is *the* economic view consistent with Catholic social teaching. Allan Carlson, following G. K. Chesterton, claims its origins lie in the 1891 encyclical *Rerum Novarum*, issued by Leo XIII.[57] Many also include the later encyclical *Quadragesimo Anno*, issued by Pope Pius XI in 1931. It's plausible to see sympathy for a third way in *Rerum Novarum* and *Quadragesimo Anno*, but to conclude that Catholic social teaching endorses or requires the distributist model is an unwarranted leap.[58] Pope John Paul II betrayed no awareness of building on such a vision when he penned *Centesimus Annus* in 1991. There he wrote that "the Church has no models to present" and that "the Christian faith does not presume to imprison changing sociopolitical realities in a rigid schema."[59] And in his 1987 encyclical *Sollicitudo Rei Socialis*, he wrote, "The Church's social doctrine is not a 'third way' between liberal capitalism and Marxist collectivism, not even a possible alternative to other solutions less radically opposed to one another: rather it constitutes a category of its own."[60]

He went on to ask in *Centesimus Annus* if there was a model that could be commended to "the countries of the Third World which are searching for the path to true economic and civil progress." His response is worth quoting at length:

> The answer is obviously complex. If by "capitalism" is meant an economic system which recognizes the fundamental and positive role of business, the market, private property and the resulting responsibility for the means of production, as well as free human creativity in the economic sector, then the answer is certainly in the affirmative, even though it would perhaps be more appropriate to speak of a "business economy," "market economy" or simply "free economy." But if by "capitalism" is meant a system in which freedom in the economic sector is not circumscribed within a strong juridical framework which places it at the service of human freedom in its totality, and which sees it as a particular aspect of that freedom, the core of which is ethical and religious, then the reply is certainly negative.[61]

What's particularly telling is that Pope John Paul II's social encyclicals frequently refer to the earlier encyclicals' emphasis on property rights, economic freedom, subsidiarity, and limited government. The message is clear: the encyclicals have identified a core role for government and, at the same time, have consistently promoted local initiative and political and economic freedom over and against grandiose political planning.

Distributists pursue many worthy social goals, goals in keeping with our nature as creatures made in the image of God. The difficult but vital task for all Christians is to integrate the truths of theology with the discoveries (rather than the ideologies) of economics.[62] Joseph Ratzinger (Pope Benedict XVI) emphasized the point explicitly:

> A morality that believes itself able to dispense with the technical knowledge of economic laws is not morality but moralism. As such it is the antithesis of morality. A scientific approach that believes itself capable of managing without an ethos misunderstands the reality of man. Therefore it is not scientific. Today we need a maximum of specialized economic understanding, but also a maximum of ethos so that specialized economic understanding may enter the service of the right goals. Only in this way will its knowledge be both politically practicable and socially tolerable.[63]

It may seem astounding that thinkers such as G.K. Chesterton and Hilaire Belloc, who were such insightful guides on so many topics, could still make major economic blunders. But history is filled with good and generally insightful people with blind spots in this or that area of their thinking, and economic reality is often counterintuitive.[64]

In all this, we would do well to remember the sage advice of Pope John XXIII, spoken to Catholics but applicable to all people of good will: "Differences of opinion in the application of principles can sometimes arise even among sincere Catholics. When this happens, they should be careful not to lose their respect and esteem for each other."[65] Tolkien would surely agree.

Chapter 9

Love and Death in Middle-Earth

Behold! we are not bound for ever to the circles of the world, and beyond them is more than memory.

—Aragorn speaking to Arwen on his deathbed, *The Lord of the Rings*

Tolkien once insisted that the central theme of *The Lord of the Rings* is "Death and the desire for deathlessness", or as he put it elsewhere, "the hideous peril of confusing true 'immortality' with limitless serial longevity."[1] At virtually every point in the novel we find ourselves bumping into characters and events related to the subject: the many battle-related deaths and scrapes with death; the companions' brush with a kind of living death at the hands of the Barrow-wights; the immortality of Tom Bombadil and the elves; Gandalf's death and resurrection; the longevity of the Ents who are nevertheless doomed to extinction because of their estrangement from the Entwives; Aragorn's ride through the Paths of the Dead; the White Tree of Gondor standing dead in the palace courtyard of Minas Tirith; the nihilistic suicide of Denethor, the Steward of Gondor; Sam and Frodo's walk through "the Mere of Dead Faces"; Frodo's envenomed and deathlike sleep in Mordor; the elven maiden Arwen choosing a mortal life as Aragorn's wife; the quality of the One Ring and the nine rings of the Nazgûl to grant extreme longevity—on and on we could go. This final chapter focuses on the theme both because Tolkien's exploration of it is worth tending in its own right, and because his insights into the matter bear directly on the question of the free society.

Death and Dominion

If one were to read the whole of *The Lord of the Rings* and miss the centrality of death, the final pages might serve as a wake-up call. Sharkey (Saruman) has been defeated by the hobbits, the Shire has been scoured and restored, and now Sam hopes that Frodo can "*live happily ever after to the end of his days*"[2] there at Bag End. But Frodo's wounds from the Morgul-blade and from bearing the ring to Mount Doom have taken a toll, and eventually he seeks the sea, which to hobbits, we are told, stands as "a token of death".[3] With Bilbo, Gandalf, and the high elves, Frodo sails into the West. Although not the same as death in Tolkien's Middle-Earth geography, this final journey does serve as a powerful figuration of what awaits the blessed after death. It suggests the passage of death so strongly that Peter Jackson's cinematic retelling takes the novel's description of Frodo's destination—"white shores and beyond them a far green country under a swift sunrise"[4]—and places it in the mouth of Gandalf as he offers a battle-frightened Pippin a comforting glimpse of life after death.

In Tolkien's biography, we find a correspondence with Frodo's woundedness along with ample explanation for the novel's preoccupation with death. Tolkien lost his father when he was five, his mother when he was twelve, faced the imminent threat of death in the trenches of World War I, and in that same war lost most of his closest friends. As we saw in chapter 1, Tom Shippey has noted that Tolkien, for all his originality, employed a literary mode characteristic of the twentieth century, "writing about worlds and creatures which we know do not exist", and that the leading practitioners of this mode had all lived through extraordinarily traumatic events.[5] Maybe those experiences were too painful to approach directly. Maybe the authors sensed that to describe the experiences directly would lead to morbidity rather than illumination. Perhaps they were trying to say things that are almost unsayable and using the tools of the fantastic to better communicate the almost ineffable.

Whatever the reasons, a letter of Tolkien's concerning his relationship with his late wife, Edith, seems to confirm Shippey's argument. Tolkien is describing how much Edith meant to him, and telling Christopher that he should like to have a long talk with his son before too long:

> For if as seems probable I shall never write any ordered biography—it is against my nature, which expresses itself about things deepest felt in

tales and myths—someone close in heart to me should know something about things that records do not record: the dreadful sufferings of our childhoods, from which we rescued one another, but could not wholly heal the wounds that later often proved disabling; the sufferings that we endured after our love began—all of which (over and above our personal weaknesses) might help to make pardonable, or understandable, the lapses and darknesses which at times marred our lives—and to explain how these never touched our depths nor dimmed our memories of our youthful love.[6]

When Tolkien says he won't unpack his painful experiences in an autobiography because "it is against my nature, which expresses itself about things deepest felt in tales and myths", he's as good as begging us to look for resonances between his life and his fiction. And it's easy to find them. The letter, for instance, calls to mind the final chapter of *The Lord of the Rings*, where we learn that Frodo has been "too deeply hurt" by wounds "that will never really heal",[7] wounds that led to "dreadful sufferings" and "lapses and darknesses".

When we turn from the novel's central hero to its central plot device, the rings of power, we find the death and deathlessness themes equally in evidence and now connected to the accompanying theme of domination. The rings of power are part of Sauron's scheme to dominate the free peoples of the West, and they link the themes of domination, death, and deathlessness by curiously halting the aging of any mortal who possesses one of them. As Tolkien explains, "The chief power (of all the rings alike) was the prevention or slowing of *decay*. . . . But also they enhanced the natural powers of a possessor—thus approaching 'magic,' a motive easily corruptible into evil, a lust for domination."[8]

The connection is further explored in a backstory covered briefly in *The Lord of the Rings* and more fully in *The Silmarillion*.[9] Long ago Sauron came to the elves disguised as "the Lord of gifts" and, offering them his ring lore, enabled them to forge

Three Rings for the Elven-kings under the sky,
Seven for the Dwarf-lords in their halls of stone,
Nine for Mortal Men doomed to die.

Sauron then returned to his stronghold and forged the "*One ring to rule them all*", a ring designed to control the other rings and so dominate the free peoples of Middle-Earth. The scheme was only partially successful.

The elves had made their three rings without Sauron's direct involvement, and, sensing his evil plan as soon as he put the One Ring on his finger, the Elven-Kings quickly removed their rings. The dwarves, for their part, were incited to "wrath and an overmastering greed of gold" by their rings, but being a race that "ill endure the domination of others", they too eluded Sauron's control.

Humans fared less well. The nine who possessed the "*Nine for Mortal Men*" were lured by the promise of power and immortality and successfully brought under Sauron's dominion, "for Men proved in this matter as in others the readiest to his will." The power of the rings helped the nine gain "glory and great wealth, yet it turned to their undoing", we learn. "They had, as it seemed, unending life, yet life became unendurable to them." One after another they "fell under the thraldom of the ring". Becoming invisible except to Sauron, "they entered into the realm of shadows".

From the first stages of the hobbits' quest in *The Lord of the Rings*, they are pursued by these black riders, the Ringwraiths, the Nazgûl "who cried with the voices of death".

The Fall of Númenór

Three of the Nazgûl were once "great lords of Númenórean race",[10] significant in this context because the story in *The Silmarillion* of Sauron leading Númenór astray and its ensuing fall links the themes of human mortality, political power, and the desire for ageless life unending.

Númenór was a great island, closer than the mainland of Middle-Earth to the Blessed Realm over the sea where dwelled the highest servants of the Creator, the angel-like and immortal Valar. The Creator, Eru Ilúvatar, had declared this distant realm off limits to the seafaring Númenóreans, but the Númenóreans grow obsessed with youth and vainglorious projects, and begin to toy with the idea of voyaging to this forbidden land of immortal life. To avert disaster, messengers are sent to remind them of the Creator's will and to ease their temptation by explaining that even if the Númenóreans could reach the land, they would not enjoy life everlasting. It is the created nature of those who dwelled there—rather than anything in the air or soil—that grants immortality.

The warning of the messengers to the King of Númenór is unambiguous but also leavened with hope:

> Beware! The will of Eru may not be gainsaid; and the Valar bid you earnestly not to withhold the trust to which you are called, lest soon it become again a bond by which you are constrained. Hope rather that in the end even the least of your desires shall have fruit. The love of Arda [the world] was set in your hearts by Ilúvatar, and he does not plant to no purpose. Nonetheless, many ages of Men unborn may pass ere that purpose is made known; and to you it will be revealed and not to the Valar.[11]

Notice here the role they give to faith in resisting the desire to try to elude death and create a perfect and ageless existence in this world. Tragically, King Atanamir "was ill pleased with the counsel of the Messengers and gave little heed to it, and the greater part of his people followed him; for they wished still to escape death in their own day, not waiting upon hope." Atanamir doesn't hazard a voyage to the Undying Lands, but he does remain obsessed with extending life as long as possible, "clinging to his life beyond the end of all joy; and he was the first of the Númenóreans to do this, refusing to depart until he was witless and unmanned, and denying to his son the kingship at the height of his days."[12]

In the generations that follow, the Númenóreans construct "great houses for their dead" and grow ever more fearful of death. They seek to extend their lives by any and all means such that "their wise men laboured unceasingly to discover if they might the secret of recalling life, or at the least of the prolonging of Men's days." They neglect worship of the Creator and, instead, are drawn into a worship of dark things and into a hedonistic fixation with power, riches, and glory for their own sake. Beginning with Atanamir, their rule is also marked by the tyrannical abuse of political authority—they are "proud men, eager for wealth" who "laid the men of Middle-earth under tribute, taking now rather than giving." Desiring "wealth and dominion in Middle-Earth ... they appeared now rather as lords and masters and gatherers of tribute than as helpers and teachers." In time, "they hunted the men of Middle-Earth and took their goods and enslaved them."

Eventually, goaded by Sauron, they set sail for the undying realm to conquer and occupy it. Appalled by their wickedness and folly, the Creator opens up a great rift in the sea, and the ships of Númenór are drowned along with their great island civilization, with only a small number of Númenóreans—who had remained faithful to Ilúvatar—saved.[13]

In this tragic tale are combined several themes: cultural decadence; faithlessness; spiritual rebellion; the swelling of abusive, centralized political authority; fertility decline; and a fixation on cheating death. It's no coincidence that this web of cultural pathologies maps so closely onto many of the pathologies that Tolkien saw sprouting all around him. It's also not a coincidence that the story resembles the Greek myth of Atlantis, a myth that some have seen as a warning against the excesses of imperial power.

Númenór, Atlantis, Babel

Tolkien was explicit about the Atlantis story as a source for Númenór, though in *The Silmarillion* he ingeniously has his narrator position the Númenórean version as the true but long-lost tale that came down to us in corrupted form as the story of the destruction of Atlantis.[14]

Plato provides our earliest account of any detail of the Atlantis myth—briefly in the *Timaeus* dialogue and at greater length in the subsequent *Critias*, written about 360 B.C.[15] The final portion of that unfinished dialogue makes it easy to see the Atlantis story as a warning against the decline from virtue to moral decadence. For several generations the people of Atlantis prized nothing so highly as virtue, and "neither were they intoxicated by luxury; nor did wealth deprive them of their self-control; but they were sober, and saw clearly that all these goods are increased by virtue and friendship with one another." In time, however, "when the divine portion began to fade away, and became diluted too often and too much with the mortal admixture, and the human nature got the upper hand, they then, being unable to bear their fortune, behaved unseemly, and to him who had an eye to see grew visibly debased, for they were losing the fairest of their precious gifts." They had grown full of "unrighteous power" and greed; divine intervention followed swiftly:

> Zeus, the god of gods, who rules according to law, and is able to see into such things, perceiving that an honourable race was in a woeful plight, and wanting to inflict punishment on them, that they might be chastened and improve, collected all the gods into their most holy habitation, which, being placed in the centre of the world, beholds all created things.

Since the dialogue is unfinished, we lack Plato's account of how things degenerated from a divine attempt to chasten Atlantis to the decision to destroy it. Even so, the similarities in the stories of these two great island civilizations, Atlantis and Númenór, are obvious. In both, their great ones are of mixed mortal and immortal blood. In both, the admixture of immortal blood wanes with the passing of generations. In both, the civilizations, in the course of moral decline, grow imperialistic and abusive toward the nations under their rule. And in both, divine action wipes the mighty island civilizations off the map because of a fall from virtue.

There are also parallels between these sister stories and the Genesis story of the Tower of Babel. In the Babel story, the descendants of Noah have multiplied and migrated to the plain of Shinar. The genealogical account stretching from Noah to the time of Abraham traces a decline in the lifespan of men—from Noah's 950 years to Seth's 600 years, down and down until a lifespan over 200 years becomes unusual. It is in this context that the human family gets the bright idea to build a great tower reaching to Heaven in order to make a name for themselves—immortality through renown. Seeing the evil this act of hubris is bound to lead to, God turns their single common language into several distinct languages. In the babble of confusion that follows, they abandon their great project and scatter throughout the earth, their proud civilization brought to an end.

Add to this picture the Flood narrative that precedes it in Genesis and you have several points of connection with Atlantis and Númenór. One can only conjecture about the curious similarities between the Atlantis myth and the Noah and Babel stories (Genesis probably wasn't translated into Greek until some two centuries after Plato); but the Genesis stories were part of Tolkien's mental furniture from childhood, so it's hardly strange that his story of Númenór parallels both the story of Babel with its cautionary tale of a civilization destroyed for its hubris, and the story of Noah, in which a remnant is saved by ship from a great flood sent to destroy a society grown violent and impious.

The Shadow of Númenór

The lessons for modernity aren't difficult to trace. Already by Tolkien's youth—and increasingly as he grew older and continued work on his Middle-Earth world—Western society was turning away from religion and growing increasingly worldly and obsessed with youth and agelessness. Tolkien tinkered long on an ultimately unfinished work involving time travel from modern England back to various points in the past. The story culminates in a trip back to Númenór, as if Tolkien wanted to further press the connection between that mythical tragic civilization and ours.[16] Happily, the Númenórean practice of sacrificing children in the flames (Sauron's helpful religious innovation) hasn't caught on (yet), but already in Tolkien's day the West was turning away from the high value it had placed on fertility and children and beginning to embrace minimal fertility, infertility, and even abortion as the easy path to idleness and a higher standard of living.

Tolkien reflected those existing trends in his mythology, but his tale of Númenór was also prescient. In Tolkien's twilight years and increasingly since then, techno-utopians such as Ray Kurzweil have pursued human immortality through high technology, limning the dream of sloughing off "this mortal coil" and escaping "the thousand natural shocks that flesh is heir to" (*Hamlet*, 3.1.67, 63–64), not through death, as Prince Hamlet envisages, but through human ingenuity.

Kurzweil and his fellow transhumanists go so far as to champion an imminent future in which we can upload our minds into ultra-powerful computers to live indefinitely as sentient software. Their aspirations have received increasing traction in the popular imagination even as the fertility rate in the developed world has slipped below the replacement threshold (Israel being the lone exception at the time of this writing). In essence, as developed countries have grown more and more youth- and leisure-obsessed, we have grown less and less interested in the work and cost of raising the next generation, much less in sacrificing our lives for the greater good. The upshot is a low-fertility culture increasingly fixated on technologies to delay and even cheat death, resulting in the looming and grimly ironic prospect of demographic winter—an aging and declining population with too few young people to take care of the old.

Here, again, Tolkien's work offers insights into what ails us. In *The Philosophy of Tolkien*, Peter Kreeft explores the significance of the One Ring and suggests that the perennial fixation on cheating death is a sinful attempt to elude a key consequence of the Fall, an attempt that leads only to the death of conscience. "Tolkien does not condemn the desire for true immortality, an immortality consonant with our nature and our destiny as designed by a wise divine providence", Kreeft adds, but condemns rather "the depraved desire for a false and unnatural immortality under our own foolish control."[17]

This was, of course, how Satan tempted Eve in the Garden. When she explained that God had told them they would die if they ate from the Tree of the Knowledge of Good and Evil, Satan replied, "You will not die. For God knows that when you eat of it your eyes will be opened, and you will be like God, knowing good and evil."[18] Satan, in the form of a serpent, promised Eve deathlessness, secret knowledge, and enhanced power if she would disobey God and eat of the forbidden fruit. In Middle-Earth, the Dark Lord Sauron promises much the same as he tempts the kings of Númenór to turn from the worship of Eru Ilúvatar, set sail for the Undying Lands forbidden to them, and claim the immortality he suggests is theirs by right of their greatness.[19] It's all a lie, of course, and leads to their destruction. The Creator, in his wisdom, decreed that humans would be mortal, and the Númenóreans' attempt to circumvent the decree is depicted as the utmost folly.

The warning is clear enough, but Tolkien's mythology involves an additional layer of complexity in the immortal elves. They view human mortality as a gift, for without it the passing of all things mortal around them becomes a source of grief and weariness. In his collected letters, Tolkien explains that the elven perspective on death isn't meant to represent the whole truth about human mortality, or to contradict the Judeo-Christian doctrine that human death is a curse put on us for the sin of Adam and Eve in the Garden. Through the various peoples of his imagined world, Tolkien can explore differing perspectives, some of them flatly contradictory, others only seemingly so. Through the elves he explores a tension in the sentence of death that follows the original sin of Adam and Eve: death was a negative consequence of man's fall into sin, but because he was now sinful, death was also a gift. God uses it as a means of chastening sinful humanity, allowing those of us who learn "to number our days" to "get a heart of wisdom",[20] as Moses says in the Psalm.

"A divine 'punishment' is also a divine 'gift,' if accepted," Tolkien wrote, "since its object is ultimate blessing, and the supreme inventiveness of the Creator will make 'punishments' (that is changes of design) produce a good not otherwise to be attained."[21] Paradoxically then, death is a blessing as well as a curse, and Tolkien's dialogic imagination, far from introducing heterodoxy, takes us deeper into biblical orthodoxy, into the mystery of death. Death is the final and implacable rebuke to all who would seek to deny the Fall, including those who imagine that man can build a "new man" and with him a Heaven on earth.

The book of Proverbs reminds us that a wise rebuke is a gift to the righteous but an insult to the wicked.[22] The techno-utopian, ignoring the rebuke of inevitable death, along with the clear evidence of the Fall, believes falsely that human ingenuity can cure sin and its effects, quite apart from the Creator's grace and authority. The story of Númenór suggests otherwise, and as if to drive home the point, Tolkien refers to its tragic end as "the Second Fall of Man".[23]

The lesson conveyed negatively in the story of Númenór is conveyed positively through the actions of several heroic characters in *The Lord of the Rings*. Aragorn, in the royal line of Númenórean kings, might have seized the One Ring from Frodo in a bid for glory and immortality. Instead he takes the Paths of the Dead—the path, if you will, of suffering and self-denial. Gandalf rejects the path of Saruman, who invites Gandalf to combine their wizardly powers to lay hold of the Ring of Power, sweep aside their incompetent allies, and set the world right. Instead, Gandalf chooses death in battle with the Balrog to save the quest. Frodo and Sam are perhaps the preeminent examples, humble servants of the good marching to what looks like certain death to destroy the one thing that seems able to hold aging and death at bay.

Tolkien summed up the pattern in a lecture on the epic of *Beowulf*: "the wages of heroism is death."[24]

Then, too, there is the story of Aragorn and Arwen, hinted at in the body of the novel and completed in the appendix. Arwen is the Evenstar of her people, in whom the great beauty of their ancestor Lúthien shines again. As an elf, Arwen is immortal, but out of love for Aragorn she lays down her immortality to wed him, a choice she possesses as a daughter of Elrond and descendant of an earlier marriage of a man and elf, Beren and Lúthien.[25] Arwen's choice serves as a mirror opposite of the Númenórean kings who are bewitched by Sauron's rings of power and the promise of immortality, only to become hateful wraiths. They pursued dominating power animated by hatred; Arwen chooses a mortal life out of love.[26]

Sub-Creation in Eternity

We could end the chapter here, but there is another element Tolkien connected to the theme of mortality: his identity as a sub-creator. He was absorbed for long years in the artistic labors of creating his secondary world, and he explored the matter explicitly in connection with the theme of death in one of his rare forays into allegory, "Leaf by Niggle".[27]

The short story tells of a modest fellow named Niggle who lives in the country and loves to paint, but there's a long journey he knows he'll eventually have to make. The problem is he's constantly being interrupted by his various obligations, and he desperately wants to finish a favorite painting before the journey. It is a picture of a great tree with a forest in the distance, a work that absorbs more and more of his attention until it becomes his one creative endeavor. His other paintings are either abandoned or fitted into this single grand work. This, of course, parallels Tolkien the writer, for whom Middle-Earth became his central artistic preoccupation.

There are other parallels. Niggle and Tolkien each has difficulty ever completing his great work, partly because it keeps branching out and out, partly because the artist was at times dilatory in his work, and partly because of all the blasted duties and disturbances. For Niggle, a repeated interruption comes in the form of the crippled Mr. Parish, his nearest neighbor. Mr. Parish isn't a bad man, but he considers Niggle's painting an idle hobby, so he's never shy about interrupting Niggle to ask for help with something urgent that his handicap won't allow him to do himself.

One time, in particular, Mr. Parish bothers Niggle about a leak in his roof, imploring Niggle to ride over and fix it before it threatens the health of Mr. Parish's wife. Grudgingly Niggle puts down his paint brush, bicycles over in a cold rain, and makes the repair, all the while cursing the delay and worrying that the long journey he'll have to go on before too long will prevent him from ever finishing his painting. To make matters worse, he catches a nasty chill from the bicycle trip, leading to more frustrating delays on the painting.

Eventually, feeling a bit better, he starts back to work, but then the Inspector of Houses shows up and informs him that Mr. Parish's house is again in a poor state due to the recent flood, and that Niggle will be required to help his neighbor weather the situation.

Niggle tries to fob the responsibility for Mr. Parish off on the local government, but the Inspector will have none of it. He insists that Niggle has an obligation to come to Mr. Parish's assistance even if it means giving up some of his beloved paint and canvas to help with the repairs. It's tempting to take this new visitor for a bossy government bureaucrat, but there is something uncanny, perhaps even supernatural, about this Inspector. More on that in a moment, but first notice how overtly the scene promotes the principle of subsidiarity, with the Inspector of Houses pressing Niggle to stop it with all his talk of licensed builders and government agencies, and insisting that "you should have helped your neighbor."[28]

The principle of subsidiarity, recall, emphasizes that social problems are generally best handled by those closest to the problem and that government, however well-intentioned, should not arrogate to itself the role of remedying these problems when individuals and institutions closer to the situation are available to help.

Caring people readily grasp the complementary principle of solidarity—that as the old saying has it, "we are all God's children"—but many times entirely overlook subsidiarity. For Christians this is an odd oversight, since the Bible repeatedly stresses it.[29] It's a doubly odd oversight for Catholics conversant with papal social encyclicals, because it's emphasized repeatedly there. In *Quadragesimo Anno*, published in 1931, Pope Pius states, "It is an injustice, a grave evil and a disturbance of right order for a larger and higher organization to arrogate to itself functions which can be performed efficiently by smaller and lower bodies. This is a fundamental principle of social philosophy, unshaken and unchangeable, and it retains its full truth today."[30]

Or to take a more recent example, Pope John Paul II's 1991 *Centesimus Annus* warns that the welfare state ignores the principle of subsidiarity by intervening aggressively in local communities. This leads to "a loss of human energies and an inordinate increase of public agencies, which are dominated more by bureaucratic ways of thinking than by concern for serving their clients, and which are accompanied by an enormous increase in spending."[31]

As for Niggle, his debate with the Inspector over the principle of subsidiarity is cut short, along with his work on the Tree painting:

> Niggle said no more, for at that moment another man came in. Very much like the Inspector he was, almost his double: tall, dressed all in black.
>
> "Come along!" he said. "I am the Driver."
>
> Niggle stumbled down from the ladder. His fever seemed to have come on again, and his head was swimming; he felt cold all over.

Soon it becomes clear that the Inspector of Houses is no ordinary Inspector; his near double, the Driver, no ordinary Driver; and the long expected journey, no ordinary journey. Niggle boards the train and is dropped off at a mysterious place called the Workhouse Infirmary. Soon it becomes obvious that the journey Niggle is on is the final journey that is death. The Infirmary is the first stage of Niggle's purgatory, where an unpleasant but beneficent daily regimen gradually sanctifies him until he is ready to continue on to the next stage. When Niggle disembarks the train at this second stage, he finds himself out in the countryside where he climbs on his old bicycle and rides along in the spring sunshine "over a marvelous turf".[32]

Before long the countryside begins to seem familiar, and then "a great green shadow came between him and the sun." Niggle looks up and tumbles off his bicycle in shock:

> Before him stood the Tree, his Tree, finished. If you could say that of a Tree that was alive, its leaves opening, its branches growing and bending in the wind that Niggle had so often felt or guessed, and had so often failed to catch. He gazed at the Tree, and slowly he lifted his arms and opened them wide.
>
> "It's a gift!" he said. He was referring to his art, and also to the result; but he was using the word quite literally.[33]

Every branch and leaf was there as he had imagined them, as well as "others that had only budded in his mind, and many others that might have budded, if only he had had time". Even more astonishingly, "Some of the most beautiful—and the most characteristic, the most perfect examples of the Niggle style—were seen to have been produced in collaboration with Mr. Parish: there was no other way of putting it."[34]

Eventually a much-sanctified Mr. Parish joins Niggle, and they set to work rounding out the forest that serves as the background for the Tree. There isn't anything wrong with the forest, "but it needed continuing up to a definite point", so two companions happily dive into the task of sub-creation. This, of course, was the very thing Niggle had been about with his old portrait, the difference being that now they can pursue a riper and more vivid fulfillment of it, and do so cooperatively.

As they work, Niggle notices, off in the distance, beyond even the forest, a range of mountains, and he realizes these are part of a different portrait. And yet, as he also learns, his portrait is connected to those distant mountains, and soon he's called to journey on to them. And what of Niggle's original canvas painting? As the story explains, only a corner of his great canvas is preserved. "Most of it crumbled; but one beautiful leaf remained intact." It is framed and placed in the town museum. Later the museum catches fire and burns to the ground, "and the leaf, and Niggle, were entirely forgotten in his old country."

That is not the end of the story, however. The landscape of green country around Niggle's Tree that he and Mr. Parish complete proves "very useful indeed" for travelers on their way to the mountains. It works wonders for many of them, such that more and more are being sent there as a stage on their journey, with few of them ever having to return to an earlier stage for remedial work. The "First Voice" figures it's time to give the place a name and asks the Second Voice for a suggestion. " 'The Porter settled that some time ago,' said the Second Voice. '*Train for Niggle's Parish in the bay.*' "

"Leaf by Niggle" takes on a double resonance when we learn that Tolkien wrote it during a particularly tough stretch of his work on *The Lord of the Rings*. The book had kept growing beyond what he had expected; he was years past his deadline, and suddenly he was stuck cold. Add to this his many obligations as a professor, husband, and parent, and he may have faced the prospect of his great work never being completed. Happily, the act of writing "Leaf by Niggle" seems to have helped break Tolkien's creative log jam,[35] and sent his sub-creation of hobbits, dwarves, wizards, men, and elves bobbing along the running river of his extraordinary imagination till their quest and the novel were completed.

Tolkien, however, never completed his mythology of the many branching stories set in the first and second ages of Middle-Earth, a great canvas near and dear to his heart. What we have in *The Silmarillion* is his son Christopher's valiant attempt to pull together the many boxes of poems and stories of Middle-Earth, involving numerous drafts and partial drafts of various tales, the drafts often in no easily discernible order of composition. Tolkien very much wanted to finish it, but in his last years he felt his energies fading and the work still to be done overwhelming.

At such a time Tolkien surely felt the age-old desire to extend one's strength and mortal life far into the future. But he met the prospect of approaching death with the reassurance at the heart of "Leaf by Niggle", the same reassurance carried by the messengers to the King of Númenór. Rather than trying to conquer that great limit that is death, they exhorted him, "Hope rather that in the end even the least of your desires shall have fruit." As they go on to say, humanity's love for the earth and the breath of life was set in our hearts by the Creator, "and he does not plant to no purpose".

It's true that "many ages of Men unborn may pass ere that purpose is made known", they tell the people, but "to you it will be revealed".[36]

Although widely ignored in Tolkien's century and ours, the substance of that message is indispensable to every sub-creator seeking to work well and humbly (if also boldly and daringly) within the fitting limits of our fallen and properly mortal natures. The message is this: there is a place beyond death where our good endeavors and good creations—often left incomplete and imperfect in this life—will be brought to full flowering through the grace of God and the ongoing labors of the redeemed, where "he will wipe away every tear", where "death shall be no more",[37] and where, perhaps even more mysteriously, we "shall reign with him".[38]

We began this final chapter looking at the final chapter in Frodo's story, which tells of something often emphasized in Tolkien, the woundedness of the human soul. There are hints throughout his mythology that the world of Middle-Earth will one day be renewed, will be mended and perfected. *The Lord of the Rings* and the Middle-Earth tales set before *The Hobbit* make a place for human artifice and healing, but they warn against attempting to achieve by human effort a perfection reserved only for the next life. As Tolkien understood, and history vividly attests, the grand schemes of the political planners to build a Heaven on earth, to immanentize the eschaton,[39] have led to the greatest horrors. The faithful life of Tolkien the husband, father, scholar, novelist, and servant of God, in contrast, illustrates a contrasting and paradoxical truth that his friend C. S. Lewis memorably articulated:

> If you read history you will find that the Christians who did most for the present world were just those who thought most of the next. The Apostles themselves, who set on foot the conversion of the Roman Empire, the great men who built up the Middle Ages, the English Evangelicals who abolished the Slave Trade, all left their mark on Earth, precisely because their minds were occupied with heaven. It is since Christians have largely ceased to think of the other world that they have become so ineffective in this. Aim at Heaven and you will get earth "thrown in": aim at earth and you will get neither.[40]

The End of Man

Tolkien understood that human death is a consequence of our Fall into sin, a final rebuke to every utopian planner seeking to fashion *the new man* through either politics or science. At the same time, he saw the sentence of death as a limit meant for our ultimate good, a gift. We're reminded of a pair of verses from the Hebrew Scriptures. One is a prayer: "So teach us to number our days that we may get a heart of wisdom."[41] The other is a meditation on God, mortality, and eternity: "He has made everything beautiful in its time; also he has put eternity into man's mind."[42] The foolish person is the one who forgets both his physical mortality and his spiritual immortality, while the "heart of wisdom" holds a pair of truths in tension before it: "All flesh is grass",[43] and yet the spirit of man is immortal.

For Tolkien, of course, the hope runs deeper than "serial longevity", as he put it. In trying to explain what that deeper thing is, he spoke of the "good catastrophe" and said that fairy-stories were especially suited to evoke it:

> The consolation of fairy-stories, the joy of the happy ending: or more correctly of the good catastrophe, the sudden joyous "turn" ... is not essentially "escapist," nor "fugitive." In its fairy-tale—or otherworld—setting, it is a sudden and miraculous grace: never to be counted on to recur. It does not deny the existence of *dyscatastrophe*, of sorrow and failure: the possibility of these is necessary to the joy of deliverance; it denies (in the face of much evidence, if you will) universal final defeat and in so far is *evangelium*, giving a fleeting glimpse of Joy, Joy beyond the wall of the world, poignant as grief.[44]

Tolkien goes on to elaborate his point about the *evangelium*. The perfect tale of the "good catastrophe", the one that "entered History and the primary world", is the story of the Incarnation, Crucifixion, and, when all hope was lost among the apostles, the Resurrection of the Son of God.[45] In Tolkien's secondary world of Middle-Earth, it's the eleventh hour and a happy reversal when the old thrush lights on Bard's shoulder when all seems lost and the arrow from the great Yew bow speeds through the air and finds the hollow on the belly of the dragon. It's the shout of hope, "The Eagles are coming! The Eagles are coming!"[46] just when all hope seems lost. And it's Frodo, defeated by the ring in the final pinch, placing it on his finger only to have the wicked

Gollum tackle him, bite the ring off his finger, and, cackling in victory, stumble and fall into the flames of Mount Doom, destroying Sauron's ring and saving the West—not by mere chance but rather, as Gandalf explained to Frodo, because another and higher purpose, quite apart from the workings of darkness, is also at work in the world.

A perfect healing and an immortality, beyond the tiresome longevity offered by the rings of power, is the faith and hope of Frodo, Bilbo, Gandalf, and the elves who together set sail from the Grey Havens at the end of *The Lord of the Rings*. On this voyage, when the elven ship has "passed on into the West, . . . on a night of rain" and with a sweet fragrance in the air, suddenly, "The grey rain-curtain turned all to silver glass and was rolled back", and the wounded Frodo beholds "white shores and beyond them a far green country under a swift sunrise." Here is a glimpse of something indispensable; but not just here in Tolkien. His life and work, taken as a whole, clearly reflected his belief in "a far green country", in a "better country"[47] beyond death—a belief, moreover, that a steadfast hope in both it and its maker could lend one the courage to pursue good in the face of evil, to work patiently and humbly in whatever plot of ground one is tending by choice, calling, and circumstance; and that, in looking forward to that better country, where our good works will find their full flowering, we will have the patience and wisdom to avoid the folly of pursuing a Heaven here on Middle-Earth, even as we labor creatively for the greater good.

EPILOGUE: FRODO IS WITH US

In a speech at the University of Munich in 1918, German sociologist Max Weber spoke of the "disenchantment" of the West. He described that growing conviction in Western man that virtually every mystery has or would surrender to scientific calculation and analysis—would be subsumed within a wholly blind and mechanistic understanding of reality. Tolkien also lamented this cultural descent, convinced that it could only end in a false and emaciated view of the world as a purposeless collection of material parts.

Tolkien called for escape from this cultural procrustean bed and rejected the pejorative tone of critics in their use of the term *escapism*. In his view, we shouldn't conflate the "Escape of the Prisoner with the Flight of the Deserter"[1] or "real-life" with smokestacks and industrial machinery:

> Not long ago—incredible though it may seem—I heard a clerk of Oxenford declare that he "welcomed" the proximity of mass-production robot factories, and the roar of self-obstructive mechanical traffic, because it brought his university into "contact with real life." ... The notion that motor-cars are ... more "real" than, say, horses is pathetically absurd.[2]

The remedy for the clerk's disenchanted way of seeing the world is what Tolkien refers to as "recovery". "We should look at green again, and be startled anew (but not blinded) by blue and yellow and red", he said. "We should meet the centaur and the dragon, and then perhaps suddenly behold, like the ancient shepherds, sheep, and dogs, and horses—and wolves. This recovery fairy-stories help us to make."[3]

Tolkien also employed the language of enchantment and disenchantment, describing the former as a deep rapport with the created order, characterized by a sense of wonder too often missing from modern life.

In Middle-Earth, the elves exemplify this condition of enchantment, and the elven realm of Lothlórien perhaps most of all, so much so that its very soil has the power of reenchantment. We see this near the end of *The Lord of the Rings* when Frodo's gardener and faithful companion, Samwise Gamgee, takes a box of soil brought from Lothlórien and sprinkles it all about the despoiled Shire, setting in motion its swift reenchantment.

Of course, there is far more of this enchanted soil in Lothlórien, but significantly, the hobbits were not meant to remain in that most enchanted of realms. They're meant to use what they gained there to recover and enrich the extraordinary that persists in the ordinary world of their homeland. Part of what the hobbits carry back from Lothlórien is the truth that the fleeting world of the Seen is enveloped by the much vaster world of the Unseen and derives its meaning from the realm beyond. This notion differs from the Gnostic's disdain for the material world. In Tolkien's figuration, the truth is manifested in seed and soil. Having sprinkled little pinches of the Lothlórien loam all about the Shire and set in motion its swift reenchantment, Sam then takes the single seed given to him by Galadriel and plants it in the place of the party tree, cut down by hooligans. Soon a much larger and grander tree, a Mallorn, grows up to take its place, a glimpse and share of the grace of Lothlórien transplanted into the heart of the Shire.

For the Christian, we might see this as a metaphor for the resurrection of the blessed. The analogy isn't quite perfect since we're dealing with two seeds from two different trees (the old party tree and the new Mallorn); but the whole work of Sam and soil and sunshine—of sowing and waiting, of sprouting and blossoming and reenchantment, all in the context of the wounded Frodo choosing to sail into the West—calls to mind the apostle Paul's description of our bodies as akin to seeds that die and then sprout and flourish in a far more glorious form. "It is sown in dishonor, it is raised in glory", he tells the Corinthian Christians. "It is sown in weakness, it is raised in power. It is sown a physical body, it is raised a spiritual body."[4] The story of the cultural and physical destruction of the Shire and its recovery through seed and soil opens onto this hope, as well as onto Tolkien's hopes and fears for the West of our age. Tolkien spoke of the many Sarumans at work among us.[5] He could be pessimistic at times, but he wasn't one to surrender. As he made clear in word and deed, he believed that to seek our culture's reenchantment was a fitting labor for our time.

Each of us is called to enter into that labor according to our calling, gifts, and situation; but Tolkien's writings suggest that the larger contours of that labor involve, among other things, an escape from the materialist flatland that consigns the transcendent to the realm of irrational faith. And if Tolkien's animus against the political "gatherers and sharers" is any indication, it also involves an escape from what economist Friedrich Hayek called *The Road to Serfdom*, a path Robert Nisbet also warned against in *The Quest for Community*. It goes by many names but always ends in greater centralized political authority at the expense of individuals, families, and the Church. The work of reenchantment begins, in other words, by rejecting not just an ideology but a subtle process, long at work among Western democracies, that leads by slow degrees from a free Shire to a place where creative energy and opportunity give way before the twin opiates of false equality and an all-embracing administrative bureaucracy.

Hayek and Nisbet wrote their seminal books when Tolkien was writing *The Lord of the Rings*, in the midst of, and motivated by, the great clash of ideas that shaped so much of the twentieth century. That clash created some strange bedfellows. It divided military ally from military ally as often as it did enemy from enemy. On one side was an allegiance to freedom and limited government; on the other was a commitment to state-sponsored collectivism in the name of the common good. The West can pat itself on the back for throwing off the German National Socialism of Hitler and, later, the socialism that was the Soviet death machine. But while those great Saurons of our age have been overthrown, there remain the many soft voices that draw us toward the soft tyranny of the "gatherers and sharers".

This is the soft despotism that an earlier writer, Alexis de Tocqueville, warned could "take hold in the very shadow of the sovereignty of this people". He foresaw in the "nations of Christendom ... an innumerable crowd of men, all alike and equal" and above them "stands an immense and protective power which alone is responsible for looking after their enjoyments and watching over their destiny. It is absolute, meticulous, ordered, provident, and kindly disposed", a ruling power that "spreads its arms over the whole of society, covering the surface of social life with a network of petty, complicated, detailed, and uniform rules" until it "reduces each nation to nothing more than a flock of timid and hard-working animals with the government as shepherd."[6]

Tolkien opposed this soft despotism because he opposed with his whole being the modern cult of the planners in whatever guise they appeared. "I am not a 'socialist' in any sense," he wrote in 1956, "being averse to 'planning' (as must be plain) most of all because the 'planners,' when they acquire power, become so bad."[7] The Soviet Politburo seemed to have understood this about him and his work, because they banned the publication of *The Lord of the Rings* in the Soviet Union. The ban compelled Soviet dissidents to pass around an illegal, and inferior, mimeographed translation. Yet even in this diminished form, the stories and the characters of the book resonated with Soviet dissidents longing to be free of Communist tyranny.

For these "Tolkienisti",[8] as they were called, the character of Frodo came to serve as a symbol for the deepest values of the novel. And so it was that in August 1991, when the Soviet experiment was taking its last, gasping breaths, anti-Communist groups in Moscow raised up a banner over barricades they erected as Communist tanks were closing in on them. "Frodo is with us!" the banner read.[9]

It was not long before the megalith of Soviet Communism collapsed, like Barad-dûr, in a moment, but with far less bloodshed than anyone predicted. The whole world seemed to breathe a sigh of relief.

The image is inspiring to those who remember it; and yet its meaning seems not to have worked its way into the bones of Westerners, or Russians, who often seem all too eager to give up liberty for a chimerical security. Despite the swelling hope that followed the historic events in Moscow, the collapse of Communism did not usher in the end of history in which representative democracy, human rights, and economic freedom would become the new and permanent world order (as Francis Fukuyama predicted a year later in his book *The End of History and the Last Man*).

Tolkien understood what Fukuyama missed: freedom is always at risk, and democracy is no cure-all. It's been said that "a democracy cannot exist as a permanent form of government" because eventually "voters discover that they can vote themselves largesse from the public treasury ... with the result that a democracy always collapses over loose fiscal policy, always followed by a dictatorship."[10] Tolkien was a first-hand witness of English democracy being put to just such ends, so his pessimism isn't surprising. As he explained in a letter drafted in 1956, "I am *not* a democrat only because 'humility' and equality are spiritual principles corrupted by the attempt to mechanize and formalize them, with the result that we get not universal smallness and humility, but universal greatness and pride, till some Orc gets hold of a ring of power—and we get and are getting slavery."[11]

This isn't to say that Tolkien opposed representative government. As we have seen, he offered good and bad examples of representative governance in *The Hobbit* and *The Lord of the Rings*. What he consistently opposed was democracy put in the service of socialism and the tyranny of the majority, and he tended to fear the worst in such matters.

Had he lived to see the Soviet Union collapse, he would have doubted the sanguine belief that freedom would then triumph permanently. He would not have been surprised to hear Hal Colebatch later comment, "The fall of Communism, like the death of Smaug, appears to have unleashed armies of petty goblins.... It proved ... sinister and depressing, for many men showed that they were unqualified for the opportunity that had been given them to rebuild the world."[12]

Tolkien knew fallen human nature. After the success of *The Lord of the Rings*, he started a sequel situated in the Fourth Age of Middle-Earth, a century after the destruction of Sauron. In it, the city of Minas Tirith is still free and powerful, but it has begun to drift into decadence and "Satanistic religion", with bored young people getting their kicks by imitating orcs.[13] He never finished it, but his thought was prophetic. The victory over Communism, like the victories over Smaug and Sauron, is not permanent. It is not the ultimate victory over evil, but one battle in a long war that stretches from the dark past unto the end of the world.

The quest for freedom, like the quest to destroy the ring, traverses the edge of a knife, even as shouts of "freedom" proliferate on all sides. In 1944, at the height of World War II, Tolkien wrote to his son Christopher, then serving in the Transvaal in South Africa. He described a conversation he had had with C.S. Lewis, Lewis' brother, and Charles Williams, which turned "on the difficulties of discovering what common factors if any existed in the notions associated with *freedom*, as used at present." Tolkien concluded that "I don't believe there are any, for the word has been so abused by propaganda that it has ceased to have any value for reason and become a mere emotional dose for generating heat."[14] Tolkien and his great story of the free peoples of the West should summon us to recover the meaning and purpose of freedom.

And what of that ragged banner waved at the fall of Soviet Communism, declaring, "Frodo is with us!"? It inspires hope; but in an age when more and more of us have made our peace with the growing "network of petty, complicated, detailed, and uniform rules" of the "gatherers and sharers", perhaps we should turn around the banner's message and ask: Are we still with Frodo?

ENDNOTES

Chapter 1: In a Hole in the Ground There Lived an Enemy of Big Government

[1] There are various chapters and articles on the topic. A particularly fine one that anticipates some of the themes in the present book is John West's "*The Lord of the Rings* as a Defense of Western Civilization" in the short anthology *Celebrating Middle-Earth:* The Lord of the Rings *as a Defense of Western Civilization*, ed. John G. West Jr. (Seattle, Wash.: Inklings Books, 2002), pp. 15–30. West argues that the novel ably articulates "four overarching themes that serve as cornerstones for the entire Western tradition": natural law, freedom, the transcendent, and the doctrine of the Fall.

[2] Joseph Pearce, *Literary Giants, Literary Catholics* (San Francisco: Ignatius Press, 2005), pp. 259–60.

[3] Tolkien to Deborah Webster, October 25, 1988, in *The Letters of J. R. R. Tolkien*, ed. Humphrey Carpenter (New York: Houghton Mifflin, 2000), p. 288.

[4] Tolkien to Christopher Tolkien, November 29, 1943, in *Letters*, p. 63.

[5] Ibid.

[6] Robert Stark, "Tolkien versus the Frankfurt School: The Good, the Bad, and the Ugly of the Left", *All Right Magazine*, August 16, 2011, http://www.allrightmagazine.com/politics/tolkien-versus-the-frankfurt-school-the-good-the-bad-the-ugly-of-the-left-10346/.

[7] Jack Zipes, *Breaking the Magic Spell: Radical Theories of Folk and Fairy Tales*, rev. and exp. ed. (Lexington, Ky.: University Press of Kentucky, 2002), pp. 165, 171. For more on Marxist engagement of Tolkien, see David D. Oberhelman, "Marxist Readings of Tolkien", in *J. R. R. Tolkien Encyclopedia: Scholarship and Critical Assessment*, ed. Michael D. C. Drout (New York: Routledge, 2007), pp. 410–11.

[8] Leo XIII, Encyclical Letter *Rerum Novarum*, May 15, 1891, no. 15, http://www.vatican.va/holy_father/leo_xiii/encyclicals/documents/hf_l-xiii_enc_15051891_rerum-novarum_en.html.

[9] Pius XI, Encyclical Letter *Quadragesimo Anno*, May 15, 1931, nos. 117, 120, http://www.vatican.va/holy_father/pius_xi/encyclicals/documents/hf_p-xi_enc_19310515_quadragesimo-anno_en.html.

[10] J. R. R. Tolkien, *The History of Middle-Earth: Vol. 9: Sauron Defeated*, ed. Christopher Tolkien (New York: Houghton Mifflin, 1992), p. 225.

[11] In his foreword to the second edition of *The Lord of the Rings*, Tolkien commented, "I much prefer history [to allegory], true or feigned, with its varied applicability to the thought and experience of readers. I think that many confuse 'applicability' with 'allegory'; but the one resides in the freedom of the reader, and the other in the purposed domination of the author" (J. R. R. Tolkien, foreword to *The Lord of the Rings*, 2nd ed. [New York: Houghton Mifflin, 1994], p. xvii. *Lord of the Rings* hereafter).

[12]Tolkien to Hugh Brogan, September 18, 1954, in *Letters*, p. 186.

[13]Tolkien believed that the mode of the fairy-story, properly understood (close to Shippey's notion of the fantastic), was well-suited to estrange. This is in line with the critical tradition of formalism, and most obviously with the Russian formalists Victor Shklovsky and Boris Eichenbaum. As Shklovsky argued, the technique of art "is to make objects 'unfamiliar'". See Victor Shklovsky, "Art as Technique", in *Critical Theory Since Plato*, ed. Hazard Adams, trans. Lee T. Lemon and Marion J. Reis, rev. ed. (New York: Harcourt Brace Jovanovich College Publishers, 1992), pp. 750–59. Also see Boris Eichenbaum, "The Theory of the 'Formal Method'", in ibid., pp. 801–16. Closer to home for Tolkien if further away in time is English Romantic Samuel Taylor Coleridge, who said of the poet as poet, "What is old and worn-out, not in itself, but from the dimness of the intellectual eye, produced by worldly passions and pursuits, he makes new" (see "A Report by J. P. Collier of a Lecture Given by Coleridge, 1811–1812", *Coleridge's Writings on Shakespeare*, ed. Terence Hawkes [New York: G. P. Putnam's Sons, 1959], pp. 43–44).

[14]Tom Shippey, *J. R. R. Tolkien: Author of the Century* (New York: Houghton Mifflin, 2001), p. vii.

[15]Ibid., pp. vii–viii.

[16]See Fred Sanders' online essay "T. S. Eliot: Things That Can Just Barely Be Said", *Scriptorium*, April 12, 2007, http://www.scriptoriumdaily.com/2007/04/12/t-s-eliot-things-that-can-just-barely-be-said/. The essay offers a good discussion of the poetic task of "naming the just barely nameable". As the title suggests, Sanders is enthusiastic about T. S. Eliot's talent for doing just this: "Civilians work with the easily labeled things, but when something just barely describable confronts us, we call in the language marines: poets. But then, out beyond that, there's Eliot and the type of poetry he represents. It's another step beyond. It agrees that special tactics need to be applied to the nearly-unspeakable." What we're suggesting is that while Eliot was using devices to achieve this at the level of the line and phrase, Tolkien and other skilled artisans of the fantastic were using poetic devices at the level of plot or world building.

[17]All quotations from *Hamlet* are from the edition published by Ignatius Press: *Hamlet*, ed. Joseph Pearce, Ignatius Critical Editions (San Francisco: Ignatius Press, 2008).

[18]The discipline of political economy wasn't an invention of the secular Enlightenment but has its roots in Medieval and Renaissance thought. Prior to the modern age, it reached its high point in the School of Salamanca. These Spanish Scholastics explored the political-economic order of their day from within a framework richly informed by Christian theology and moral philosophy, and anticipated many of the central insights of modern economics. See Stephen J. Grabill, ed., *Sourcebook in Late-Scholastic Monetary Theory* (Lanham, Md.: Lexington Books, 2007). Then, too, the man often considered the father of modern economics, Adam Smith, was a professor of moral philosophy, and heavily influenced by the School of Salamanca, absorbing their insights from the seventeenth-century natural law philosophers Hugo Grotius and Samuel von Pufendorf. Smith's *The Theory of Moral Sentiments* (1759) preceded his more famous *The Wealth of Nations* (1776) and provides useful foundation material for the later book specifically and the field of political economy generally. Knowing all of this helps us to see what Tolkien had in common with these founders of the discipline of political economy. All of them took physical reality seriously, all of them were interested in human nature and human action as they play themselves out in history, and all proceeded from a worldview richly informed by centuries of Christian philosophical and theological reflection.

[19]*Lord of the Rings*, prologue.

[20]Tolkien to Milton Waldman (undated, late 1951) in *Letters*, p. 153.

[21]Shippey, *Author of the Century*, pp. 18, 23.

[22]Ibid., p. 5.

[23] Alexis de Tocqueville, *Democracy in America*, trans. Gerald E. Bevan (1835, 1840; New York: Penguin, 2003), pp. 805–6.

[24] From a public hearing, July 13, 2010, in Traci D. Joseph, "Neiman Marcus Chicken Coops: Exploring Class and Identity through Backyard Chicken Keeping and the Contemporary Food Movement" (master's thesis, Western Michigan University, 2013), p. 96, http://scholarworks.wmich.edu/cgi/viewcontent.cgi?article=1182&context=masters_theses.

[25] Ibid., pp. 74, 106–7.

[26] Ibid., pp. 137, 140.

[27] "When a single factory is grinding 20 million hamburger patties in a week or washing 25 million servings of salad, a single terrorist armed with a canister of toxins can, at a stroke, poison millions. Such a system is equally susceptible to accidental contamination: the bigger and more global the trade in food, the more vulnerable the system is to catastrophe. The best way to protect our food system against such threats is obvious: decentralize it" (Michael Pollan, "Farmer in Chief", *New York Times Magazine*, October 9, 2008, Reregionalizing the Food System section, par. 2, http://www.nytimes.com/2008/10/12/magazine/12policy-t.html?pagewanted=all&_r=0).

[28] For a concise overview of economic freedom in Middle-Earth, see Hal G. P. Colebatch, "Capitalism", in Drout, *Tolkien Encyclopedia*, pp. 83–85.

[29] "$500 Fine for Lemonade Stand", UPI, June 18, 2011, http://www.upi.com/Odd_News/2011/06/18/500-fine-for-lemonade-stand/UPI-76201308380400/.

Chapter 2: Adventure, Inc.

[1] J. R. R. Tolkien, *The Hobbit*, rev. ed. (1937; repr., New York: Ballantine, 1981), chap. 2. *Hobbit* hereafter.

[2] See an illuminating discussion of this history in chapters 1–5 of Rodney Stark, *The Victory of Reason: How Christianity Led to Freedom, Capitalism, and Western Success* (New York: Random House, 2006).

[3] All quotations in this and the next subsection are from chap. 1 of *The Hobbit*.

[4] *Lord of the Rings*, bk. 1, chap. 7.

[5] See J. R. R. Tolkien and Christopher Tolkien, *The Return of the Shadow: The History of* The Lord of the Rings, *Part One* (Boston: Houghton Mifflin, 1988), pp. 115–16.

[6] Tolkien to Naomi Mitchison, April 25, 1954, in *The Letters of J. R. R. Tolkien*, ed. Humphrey Carpenter (New York: Houghton Mifflin, 2000), p. 174.

[7] Tolkien, notes on W. H. Auden's review of *The Return of the King*, in *Letters*, p. 244. The editor comments that the notes were "a rewriting at some later date of an earlier version, now lost, that was in all probability written 1956".

[8] *Hobbit*, chap. 1.

[9] Adam Szirmai lists punctuality as one of many "modernization ideals" that contribute to an advanced and prosperous economy in *The Dynamics of Socio-Economic Development* (Cambridge: Cambridge University Press, 2005), p. 8.

[10] Walt Whitman, "Song of Myself", line 19, in *Leaves of Grass* (Philadelphia, Penn.: David McKay, 1891–1892).

[11] Bradley J. Birzer, *J. R. R. Tolkien's Sanctifying Myth: Understanding Middle-Earth* (Wilmington, Del.: ISI Books, 2002), p. 127.

[12] William E. Ratliff and Charles G. Flinn, "The Hobbit and the Hippie", *Modern Age*, Spring 1968, p. 144.

[13] Ibid., p. 145.

[14]Ken Myers, "Waiting for Epimenides", *Touchstone*, July/August 2009, pp. 9–11.

[15]John McWhorter, *Doing Our Own Thing: The Degradation of Language and Music, and Why We Should, Like, Care* (New York: Gotham Books, 2003), pp. xxi–xxii.

[16]George Steiner, *Real Presences* (Chicago: University of Chicago Press, 1989), pp. 147–48.

[17]Steiner's work in *Real Presences* is aimed at reviving the old custom of magnanimous hospitality that Abraham and Hamlet assumed, with Steiner applying it to the way we invite the great authors into our lives. As Steiner puts it, "The numinous intimations which relate hospitality to religious feeling in countless cultures and societies, the intuition that the true reception of a guest, of a known stranger in our place of being touches on transcendent obligations and opportunities, helps us to understand the experiencing of created form" (Steiner, p. 155). In other words, we shouldn't approach a great work of art cynically or violently, as many postmodern critics do when they dive into a work of literature in order to "deconstruct" it and hold up the remaining parts as evidence of sexism, classism, the patriarchal superstructure, et cetera, ad nauseam. Instead, we should recall that we have a moral obligation, informed and enriched by our religious traditions, to engage the artist attentively and respectfully—not in a way that checks our own moral intuitions and convictions at the door, but also not in a way that expects only to find dated ideas with the scent of mothballs about them.

[18]Aurelie A. Hagstrom, "Christian Hospitality in the Intellectual Community", in Douglas V. Henry and Michael D. Beaty, eds., *Christianity and the Soul of the University* (Grand Rapids, Mich.: Baker Academic, 2006), pp. 119–20.

[19]G.K. Chesterton, *Orthodoxy* (1908; repr., San Francisco: Ignatius Press, reprint edition 1995), p. 53.

[20]Ibid., p. 6.

[21]Ibid., p. 7.

[22]An important caveat in all this is that hospitality has existed outside the Judeo-Christian tradition. Natural law and common grace, along with various religious traditions, have encouraged hospitality across cultures and ages, as even a cursory study of human history shows. But we can recognize this while also acknowledging that Christianity leavened human society in unique and powerful ways. It isn't simple coincidence that Christianity gave the world its first truly global religion—of Jew and Greek, barbarian, Scythian, slave, and free (see Col 3:11)—or that, for instance, both hospitals and universities are the invention of Christendom. See, for instance, Rodney Stark, *The Victory of Reason* (New York: Random House, 2006), pp. 226–29. Christianity was not the inventor of hospitality in the West, but it did become its lodestar.

[23]Tolkien to Milton Waldman, est. date late 1951, in *Letters*, p. 144.

[24]Tolkien to Robert Murray, S.J., December 2, 1953, in *Letters*, p. 172.

[25]If we turn to Tolkien's published letters, we find an emphasis on propriety that echoes and extends the theme as it manifests itself in his Middle-Earth novels. A perusal of the collected letters turns up at least forty-five nonironic occurrences of the terms *proper/improper/properly/improperly*. Some of these refer to social mores or professional standards of work. Many are connected with the philological vision that gives Tolkien's Middle-Earth world its sense of substance and rootedness, a vision that included an abiding attention to selecting the appropriate words from the appropriate etymological lineage for a given cultural context. These passages from his letters, along with his academic-philological work, testify of a writer who went to extraordinary lengths to select the names of the people and places in Middle-Earth, along with the common objects of those places, so that they fit their etymological origin, their cultural and ethnic roots. He did this partly out of commitment to sub-creation done well, and partly so that the words would feel fitting and proper to readers, even if purely at a subconscious level. Ernest Hemingway compared good imaginative writing to an

iceberg. The seven-eighths or more of the iceberg below the surface gives the visible part its air of imperturbable solidity. A successful work of literature is akin to this, Hemingway argued, with the words on the page connected to a rich, unseen substratum of knowledge about the characters and context. In essence, Tolkien took a similar aesthetic and applied it philologically to the process of world building, a commitment driven by his high regard for the customs, traditions, and semantic propriety inherent in language and its slow development from older languages. (For Hemingway's discussion, see his work *Death in the Afternoon* [1932; New York: Scribner, 1999], p. 116.)

[26] Theodore Dalrymple gives a surgical, and harrowing, description of such characters in *Life at the Bottom: The Worldview That Makes the Underclass* (Chicago: Ivan Dee, 2003). See also Charles Murray, *Coming Apart* (New York: Crown Forum, 2013).

[27] The singing elves who poke fun at Bilbo and the dwarves as they enter Rivendell could hardly be considered the height of courtesy, but their humor is gentle and gives way to the high courtesy of Elrond's house, where hospitality reaches perhaps its greatest breadth and richness in Middle-Earth.

[28] *Hobbit*, chap. 4.

[29] Ibid.

[30] Ibid., chap. 5.

[31] Ibid., chap. 7.

[32] Ibid.

[33] Ibid., chap. 7.

[34] Ibid., chap. 18.

[35] Ibid.

[36] See Jay W. Richards, *Infiltrated* (New York: McGraw-Hill, 2013).

Chapter 3: The Lonely Mountain versus the Market

[1] Significantly, trade not only becomes their means of escape from the Elvenking's palace (barrels on the river); it also strengthens the bonds between Lake-town and the elven realm, leading them to feast together in the scene where Thorin announces his return, and motivating the Master of Lake-town to maintain good relations with his major trading partner, the Elvenking.

[2] *Hobbit*, see chap. 9.

[3] Ibid., chap. 10.

[4] Ibid.

[5] Ibid.

[6] The terminology is taken from Lajos Egri, *The Art of Dramatic Writing* (New York: Simon and Schuster, 1946).

[7] See Pope Benedict's incisive exploration of what he called the "crisis of reason" in his Regensburg address on September 12, 2006, http://www.vatican.va/holy_father/benedict_xvi/speeches/2006/september/documents/hf_ben-xvi_spe_20060912_university-regensburg_en.html.

[8] 2 Peter 3:4 (Revised Standard Version, Second Catholic Edition; all subsequent references are from this version).

[9] We see the Master's keen interest in keeping "the rafts running on time" when, for instance, the narrator comments that he was eager for the dwarves to leave because "their arrival had turned things into a long holiday in which business was at a standstill" (*Hobbit*, chap. 10).

[10] Tom Shippey, *J. R. R. Tolkien: Author of the Century* (New York: Houghton Mifflin, 2001), p. 37.

[11] Hal G. P. Colebatch, *The Return of the Heroes:* The Lord of the Rings, Star Wars, Harry Potter, *and Social Conflict*, 2nd ed. (Christchurch, New Zealand: Cybereditions Corporation, 2003), p. 82.

[12] Michael Novak in the Effective Stewardship DVD Series, Session 1: Talents (Grand Rapids, Mich.: Zondervan, 2009). See also Novak's lengthier discussion of this in his book *The Spirit of Democratic Capitalism* (New York: Simon and Schuster, 1982), chap. 7.2, "The Assault on the Bourgeoisie", pp. 150–55.

[13] Jack Zipes, *Breaking the Magic Spell: Radical Theories of Folk and Fairy Tales*, rev. and exp. ed. (Lexington, Ky.: University Press of Kentucky, 2002), p. 171. At times Zipes ably clarifies some of the differences between Tolkien and his own socialist vision. At other times his desire to appropriate Tolkien leads him into strange and demonstrably false interpretations, as when he asserts that "Bilbo is described as a lower middle-class shop-keeper" (p. 170) and his "hesitation to join the dwarfs, i.e., the working class, is understandable since the lower middle class has always preferred to move upward and side with the ruling forces in society, namely the dragons" (p. 171). This interpretation is confused. The aristocratic dragon is a plundering miser, not an investing and enterprising capitalist. Thorin son of Thrain is dispossessed royalty, rather than "working class". And Bilbo is one of the wealthiest hobbits in the Shire and, until Gandalf awakens his Tookish side, an idle country gentleman. Since these pesky facts do not map neatly onto Marxism's historical caricature of uncreative capitalist exploitation, Zipes—in good Marxist fashion—revises them into oblivion.

[14] *Hobbit*, chap. 12.

[15] The language here echoes the counsel found in Ecclesiastes 11:1: "Cast your bread upon the waters, for you will find it after many days."

[16] For this detail, Shippey, in his *Author of the Century*, cites Humphrey Carpenter, *Tolkien: The Authorized Biography* (Boston: Houghton Mifflin, 1977), p. 106.

[17] Shippey, *Author of the Century*, p. 10.

[18] Ibid.

[19] *Hobbit*, chap. 12. The *Hobbit* quotations that follow in this subsection are all from chapter 12.

[20] Quoted in Shippey, *Author of the Century*, p. 10.

[21] Ibid.

[22] Novak, *Spirit*, p. 153.

[23] Shippey, *Author of the Century*, p. 11.

[24] *Hobbit*, chap. 15.

[25] Ibid., chap. 17.

[26] Anthony Bloom, *Beginning to Pray* (New York: Paulist Press, 1982), p. 35.

[27] *Lord of the Rings*, bk. 1, chap. 2.

[28] *Hobbit*, chap. 18.

[29] Aurelie A. Hagstrom, "Christian Hospitality in the Intellectual Community", in Douglas V. Henry and Michael D. Beaty, eds. *Christianity and the Soul of the University* (Grand Rapids, Mich.: Baker Academic, 2006), p. 121. She adds that Christian hospitality is further differentiated from mere tolerance in that it "grows out of the morally rigorous demands of Jesus Christ's unsurpassable example".

[30] Novak, *Spirit*, p. 152.

[31] *Hobbit*, chap. 18.

[32] Ibid., chap. 19.

[33] Ibid.

[34]Ibid.

[35]Ibid.

Chapter 4: The Ring of Power Corrupts Absolutely

[1]John Emerich Edward Dalberg, Lord Acton, to Bishop Mandell Creighton, April 5, 1887, in Online Library of Liberty, http://oll.libertyfund.org/titles/acton-acton-creighton-correspondence#lf1524_label_010.

[2]*Lord of the Rings*, bk. 1, chap. 2.

[3]Ibid.

[4]Tolkien to Eileen Elgar, drafts, September 1963, in J. R. R. Tolkien, *The Letters of J. R. R. Tolkien*, ed. Humphrey Carpenter (New York: Houghton Mifflin, 2000), p. 332.

[5]*Lord of the Rings*, bk. 2, chap. 2.

[6]Ibid., chap. 7.

[7]Ibid., chap. 2.

[8]Ibid., chap. 10.

[9]Ibid., chap. 2.

[10]J. R. R. Tolkien, *The Silmarillion* (1977; repr., New York: Ballantine, 1979), "Of the Rings of Power and the Third Age". *Silmarillion* hereafter.

[11]Tolkien to Robert Murray, S.J., draft, November 4, 1954, in *Letters*, p. 202.

[12]Mason Harris, "The Psychology of Power in Tolkien's *The Lord of the Rings*, Orwell's *1984*, and Le Guin's *A Wizard of Earthsea*", *Mythlore* 55 (Autumn 1988): 50.

[13]Tolkien to Naomi Mitchison, draft, September 25, 1954 (final version), in *Letters*, p. 200.

[14]The 2000 Hollywood movie *The Hollow Man* was billed as inspired by *The Invisible Man*. In the film, the title character uses his newly acquired invisibility first for sexual voyeurism and sexual molestation before going onto the requisite murder rampage.

[15]*Lord of the Rings*, bk. 1, chap. 2.

[16]Ibid., bk. 4, chap. 9.

[17]Plato, *Republic*, trans. Benjamin Jowett, *The Dialogues of Plato,* 3rd ed. (Oxford University Press, 1892), bk. 2, http://oll.libertyfund.org/?option=com_staticxt&staticfile=show.php%3Ftitle=767&chapter=93808&layout=html&Itemid=27.

[18]Ps 111:10.

[19]Eccles 12:14.

[20]If that hymn isn't creepy enough by itself, imagine how it goes down for a boy who has just read *The Lord of the Rings*! As it turns out, the effect on rowdy boys at church gatherings was specifically intended, since, according to the New Georgia Encyclopedia entry on the hymn's author, J. M. Henson, "The song was inspired by one revival service in particular that Henson attended. The revival leader told a group of young boys whose unruly conduct had been the source of trouble at previous services, 'We're expecting order here and you had better be careful, because there's an all-seeing eye watching you tonight.' That eye belonged to the county sheriff, who was at the meeting by invitation. Henson, reflecting on the parallel between the sheriff and the Lord, wrote a song in which the 'all-seeing eye' is God's." Of course, the idea of divine omniscience is an ancient one, both within and outside the Judeo-Christian tradition. "The Eye of God" entry in *The Oxford Dictionary of Christian Art* notes that the specific symbol of an eye with rays emanating from it, inside a triangle, has been used for centuries as "a symbol of the Holy Trinity, for example in the lantern of the dome of San Carlo alle Quattro Fontane in Rome" and "in Pontormo's altarpiece of the Supper at Emmaus, painted in 1525". The entry further notes that use of a single eye to symbolize

God was generally avoided in the Medieval period, since it was equated with "the Evil Eye," though it "has been connected with Masonic ritual, since the medieval masons' guilds were often dedicated to the Holy Trinity". *Oxford Dictionary of Christian Art* (New York: Oxford University Press, 2004), p. 190.

[21] *Lord of the Rings*, bk. 2, chap. 2; bk. 2, chap. 7; bk. 6, chap. 3.

[22] Ibid., bk. 2, chap. 7.

[23] Ibid., chap. 10.

[24] Ibid., bk. 4, chap. 2. Mason Harris considers Sauron's evil gaze in "Psychology of Power", p. 49.

[25] *Lord of the Rings*, bk. 5, chap. 6.

[26] Ibid., bk. 6, chap. 3.

[27] Ibid., bk. 3, chap. 11.

[28] Ibid., bk. 4, chap. 9.

[29] Ibid., bk. 6, chap. 1.

[30] Gollum, as it turns out, gets the climactic moment of gloating. Grappling with Frodo above the chasm, he bites off the hobbit's ring finger, seizes the "Precious", and then, "even as his eyes were lifted up to gloat on his prize, he stepped too far, toppled, wavered for a moment on the brink, and then with a shriek he fell" (*Lord of the Rings*, bk. 6, chap. 3).

[31] Allison Harl, "The Monstrosity of the Gaze: Critical Problems with a Film Adaptation of *The Lord of the Rings*", *Mythlore* 25, nos. 3–4 (Spring/Summer 2007): 64.

[32] *Lord of the Rings*, bk. 2, chap. 7.

[33] Harl, "Monstrosity of the Gaze", p. 64.

[34] J.R.R. Tolkien, "On Fairy-Stories", *The Tolkien Reader* (New York: Ballantine, 1966), p. 80.

[35] *Lord of the Rings*, prologue.

[36] Harris, "Psychology of Power", p. 47.

[37] W.H. Auden, "The Quest Hero", ed. Neil d. Isaacs and Rose A. Zimbardo, *Tolkien and the Critics* (Notre Dame, Ind.: University of Notre Dame Press, 1968), p. 57.

[38] Humphrey Carpenter, *J.R.R. Tolkien: A Biography* (1977; repr., New York: Houghton Mifflin, 2000). Carpenter writes that Tolkien "delighted his friends with recitations from Beowulf, the Pearl, and Sir Gawain and the Green Knight, and recounted horrific episodes from the Norse Völsungasaga, with a passing jibe at Wagner whose interpretation of the myths he held in contempt" (p. 54).

[39] Tolkien to Allen and Unwin, February 23, 1961, in *Letters*, p. 306. In his biography of Tolkien, Carpenter comments, "The comparison of his Ring with the *Nibelungenlied* and Wagner always annoyed Tolkien" (*A Biography*, p. 206).

[40] Edward R. Haymes, "The Two Rings: The Lord of the Rings; The Ring of the Nibelung", speech given to the Wagner Society of New York, New York, January 4, 2004, http://de-vagaesemhybrazil.blogspot.com/2008/12/two-rings-tolkien-and-wagner-dc-before.html.

[41] For an argument that the ring offered to Gawain possessed powerful protective properties, see Jessica Cooke, "The Lady's 'Blushing' Ring in *Sir Gawain and the Green Knight*", *Review of English Studies* 49, no.193 (1998): pp. 1–8.

[42] At one point Sam fails to follow his right inclination to stick by Frodo even when Frodo is seemingly dead. However, Sam's inclination is one developed through long and loyal service—a virtuous habit, in other words, rather than a natural instinct.

[43] Tom Shippey argues that it's unlikely that something like hobbits, celebrated for their humility, could "possibly ever find a place in Wagner's conception". Shippey also touches on the controversial matter of Wagner's alleged anti-Semitism and the uses made of Wagner by

the Nazis: "It might or might not be possible to excuse Wagner for the uses made of his work by the Nazis after he was dead, but from Tolkien's perspective, perhaps even more than from ours, the seeds of horror were there in Siegfried's causal and uncondemned brutality [particularly toward a vulnerable dwarf character], in the picture of a divine/heroic world constantly threatened by cunning, sneaking dwarf-shapes, so easily converted ideologically into *Untermenschen*, sub-humans. The least one can say of this is that Wagner and Tolkien were on opposite sides of a great divide created by two world wars and all that went with them.... If Tolkien did take anything from Wagner, it was perhaps no more than the idea that something could be done with the idea of the Ring of Power, something more, and more laden with significance, than anything in an ancient source, but at the same time and very definitely *not* what Wagner had done with it" (Tom Shippey, "The Problem of the Rings: Tolkien and Wagner", *Roots and Branches: Selected Papers on Tolkien by Tom Shippey* [Zollikofen, Switzerland: Walking Tree Publishers, 2007], p. 113).

[44] Alex Ross, "The Ring and the Rings: Wagner vs. Tolkien", *The New Yorker*, December 22, 2003, http://www.newyorker.com/archive/2003/12/22/031222crat_atlarge ?currentPage=all.

[45] Ibid.

[46] Ibid.

[47] Come to think of it, the ents *are* star-crossed. There's also Eowyn's attraction to Aragorn, Wormtongue's lustful designs on Eowyn, and the romantic relationships between Aragorn and Arwen, Eowyn and Faramir, and Sam Gamgee and Rosie Cotton. None of these end in illicit love affairs, however. For that, one must turn to *The Silmarillion*, where one may be further surprised to encounter evidence that an author who married his beloved after a forced separation of several years, and had four children with her, actually knew a little something about eros.

[48] Ross, "The Ring and the Rings".

Chapter 5: The Free Peoples and the Master of Middle-Earth

[1] *Lord of the Rings*, bk. 2, chap. 10.

[2] Thomas Shippey, *The Road to Middle-Earth: How J. R. R. Tolkien Created a New Mythology* (Boston: Houghton Mifflin, 2003), pp. 140–41.

[3] Ibid., p. 140.

[4] *Lord of the Rings*, bk. 5, chap 4.

[5] As quoted in Shippey, *Road to Middle-Earth*, p. 141.

[6] *Lord of the Rings*, bk. 3, chap. 4.

[7] Ibid., bk. 2, chap 2.

[8] Shippey, *Road to Middle-Earth*, p. 142.

[9] Ibid.

[10] Thomas Shippey, *J. R. R. Tolkien: Author of the Century* (Boston: Houghton Mifflin, 2002), p. 141.

[11] Matthew Dickerson, *Following Gandalf: Epic Battles and Moral Victory in* The Lord of the Rings (Grand Rapids, Mich.: Brazos Press, 2003), p. 81.

[12] Bertrand Russell, "Has Religion Made Useful Contributions to Civilization?" in *Why I Am Not a Christian* (New York: Simon and Schuster, 1967), pp. 37–38, quoted in Dickerson, *Following Gandalf*. The giveaway that Russell is talking rubbish is the final phrase, "by any stretch of the imagination." The human imagination, of even the feeblest intellect, naturally and easily imagines that others are responsible for evil actions, no stretching required. It's only

by the most assiduous effort that one imagines one's way out of such a natural conviction. An example was the psychology teacher the two of us had our senior year in high school. If his course content was any indication, he was dedicated to the proposition that all men are created automata, the products of genetics and environment. And yet he could never fully suppress his sense of moral outrage when his students wandered in late to class or kept chattering after the opening bell. We both want to go back and ask him: If we are all just automata, why the righteous indignation?

[13] B. F. Skinner, *Beyond Freedom and Dignity* (Indianapolis, Ind.: Hackett Publishing, 1971), pp. 200–201, quoted in Dickerson, *Following Gandalf*, pp. 15–16.

[14] *Lord of the Rings*, bk. 3, chap. 2.

[15] Jn 15:13.

[16] Michael Ruse and E. O. Wilson, "The Evolution of Ethics", *Religion and the Natural Sciences: The Range of Engagement*, ed. J. E. Huchingson (Orlando, Fla.: Harcourt and Brace, 1991), p. 51.

[17] *Hobbit*, chap. 12.

[18] Nassim Nicholas Taleb, *Antifragile: Things That Gain from Disorder* (New York: Random House, 2012).

[19] *Lord of the Rings*, bk. 2, chap. 5.

[20] This is based on a private conversation that Tolkien had with Clyde Kilby in the summer of 1966. Kilby wrote about it in Clyde Kilby, *Tolkien and the Silmarillion* (Wheaton, Ill.: Harold Shaw, 1976), p. 59.

[21] Gen 1:26.

[22] Shippey, who occupied Tolkien's chair of philology at Oxford at one time, ably explores this connection in *Author of the Century*, pp. 90–98.

[23] Of course, there were soldiers in Christendom who behaved this way, but in pagan European cultures this was viewed as the normal, religiously justified behavior of conquering soldiers, not as an evil that soldiers indulged in because they felt like ignoring the teachings of their religion.

[24] Dickerson called our attention to this point in *Following Gandalf*, pp. 104–5.

[25] The question doesn't arise for God, since he exists eternally. The question needing an answer is the origin of finite creatures that begin to exist. How could true freedom emerge as an effect from a lesser cause that lacked freedom? For a rigorous defense of the argument that reason, freedom, and agency are very unlikely to emerge from a blind material process, see Alvin Plantinga, *Where the Conflict Really Lies: Science, Religion and Naturalism* (New York: Oxford University Press, 2010), pp. 307–50.

[26] Ayn Rand, "The Objectivist Newsletter", August 1962, p. 35.

[27] Saint Thomas Aquinas, *Summa Theologica* I, q. 22, a.3.

[28] *Lord of the Rings*, bk. 1, chap. 2.

[29] For more on this, see Benjamin Wiker and Jonathan Witt, *A Meaningful World: How the Arts and Sciences Reveal the Genius of Nature* (Downers Grove, Ill.: InterVarsity Press, 2006).

[30] This is often attributed to historian Arnold Toynbee, but Toynbee attributes the quote to H. A. L. Fisher in Arnold J. Toynbee, *A Study of History, Volume 2* (Oxford, UK: Oxford University Press, 1957), p. 257.

[31] *Lord of the Rings*, bk. 2, chap. 2.

[32] Ibid., bk. 4, chap. 8.

[33] In his *Summa Theologica*, Thomas Aquinas argues that Creation refers "properly" only to God, who creates from nothing, and he tends to avoid the word when referring to human production. In modern English, however, the word has much broader connotations and isn't explicitly theological.

[34]For details, see Economic Freedom in the World, at http://www.freetheworld.com, and the complementary Index of Economic Freedom, at http://www.heritage.org/index/. See also the new resource, HumanProgress, at http://humanprogress.org.

[35]*Lord of the Rings*, prologue.

[36]For example, John Adams said, "Our Constitution was made only for a moral and religious people. It is wholly inadequate to the government of any other."

[37]This is from *The Federalist*, no. 51. Madison exaggerated a bit. Even if we weren't sinners, we would still need some rules for traffic and whatnot; but without sin, we wouldn't need a government to bear the sword and coerce us.

[38]Lord Acton, "The History of Freedom in Antiquity" (address delivered to the members of the Bridgnorth Institute, February 26, 1877), http://www.acton.org/research/history-freedom-antiquity.

Chapter 6: The Just War of the Ring

[1]James Person mentions Edmund Wilson, John Le Carre, and Germaine Greer, who "smelled the transcendent element in Tolkien's works the way a dog smells death—and with the same response. Only they called it not *the transcendent*, but craven *escape* and *fascism*—apparently believing that the taking down of weapons from the wall to defend one's home and land is the first step on the road to becoming a goose-stepping worshipper of the total state", in "The Transcendent in Tolkien", *The Imaginative Conservative*, http://www.theimaginativeconservative.org/2012/12/the-transcendent-in-tolkien.html.

[2]Matthew Dickerson, *Following Gandalf: Epic Battles and Moral Victory in* The Lord of the Rings (Grand Rapids, Mich.: Brazos Press, 2003), p. 25. There is a revised edition of this book, written in 2012, *A Hobbit Journey: Discovering the Enchantment of J. R. R. Tolkien's Middle Earth* (Grand Rapids, Mich.: Brazos Press).

[3]Ibid.

[4]Ibid., p. 26.

[5]Ibid., p. 30.

[6]Tolkien to Robert Murray, S.J., draft, November 4, 1954, in *The Letters of J. R. R. Tolkien*, ed. Humphrey Carpenter (New York: Houghton Mifflin, 2000), p. 202. Quoted in ibid., p. 49.

[7]Dickerson, *Following Gandalf*, p. 50. In the revised and expanded 2012 edition of this book, *A Hobbit Journey*, Dickerson removed this sentence. This revised edition, however, still flatly states, "Gandalf is sent to Middle-earth to provide wisdom, not to provide 'power on the physical plane', or what one might call 'military might'" (p. 68). Continuing to put the matter this baldly risks clouding Tolkien's more nuanced depiction of a wizard who is sent "primarily" to "train, advise, instruct, arouse", but who is also intended to judiciously employ his considerable physical might.

[8]Ibid., p. 41.

[9]Ibid., p. 42.

[10]Perhaps the most prominent secular Just War proponent at the moment is the American political philosopher Michael Walzer. See, for instance, Michael Walzer, *Just and Unjust Wars: A Moral Argument with Historical Illustrations* (New York: Basic Books, 2006).

[11]Brian Orend, "War", *Stanford Encyclopedia of Philosophy*, Fall 2005, http://plato.stanford.edu/entries/war/.

[12]Matthew Dickerson shows that for Tolkien, the One Ring doesn't represent "mere power, but the power to enslave: to rule over other wills"; it is the "lust for domination" (*Following Gandalf*, pp. 96–101).

[13]That is, in a way that doesn't require one to engage in intrinsically evil acts.

[14]Tom Shippey, *The Road to Middle-Earth: How J. R. R. Tolkien Created a New Mythology* (Boston: Houghton Mifflin, 2003), p. 345.

[15]*Lord of the Rings*, bk. 3, chap. 7.

[16]Alfred Duggan, review of *The Fellowship of the Ring* by J. R.R. Tolkien, August 27, 1954, *The Times Literary Supplement*, http://www.the-tls.co.uk/tls/public/article1124990.ece.

[17]Quoted in Shippey, *Road to Middle-Earth*, p. 174.

[18]Gandalf explains later that Aragorn had said, "There is no doubt that he was tormented, and the fear of Sauron lies black on his heart." Sauron extracts two words: "Baggins" and "Shire". He then sends the Black Riders (later identified as the Nazgûl) to the Shire to capture the ring. Gollum is apparently then allowed to escape in the hope that he will lead Sauron's spies directly to the ring (*Lord of the Rings*, bk. 2, chap. 2).

[19]Gandalf tells Frodo that he had to "put the fear of fire on him" (*Lord of the Rings*, bk. 1, chap. 2).

[20]*Lord of the Rings*, bk. 3, chap. 8.

[21]Ibid., bk. 5, chap. 5.

[22]Ibid., bk. 4, chap. 4.

[23]Ibid., chap. 5.

[24]Ibid., bk. 1, chap. 2.

[25]Brian Rosebury, *Tolkien: A Critical Assessment* (New York: St. Martin's Press, 1992), p. 36.

[26]*Lord of the Rings*, bk. 5, chap. 1.

[27]Ibid.

[28]Tom Shippey, *J. R. R. Tolkien: Author of the Century* (Boston: Houghton Mifflin, 2002), p. 166.

[29]The reason is another principle of the Just War tradition—namely, the requirement that a people have some probability of success. For a nation to ride to the rescue anywhere and everywhere is a sure recipe for overextension, decline, and ultimate collapse. To put it in nakedly economic terms, capital that can be used for justice is a scarce resource (at least this side of the Second Coming). Even a powerful nation has only so much of it. This means that the more wisely the nation uses that capital, the further that justice-defending capital will stretch.

So, for instance, imagine there are two international conflicts, both involving a grave injustice against an innocent group. In one case, the probability of a successful intervention is low and success would serve the altruistic but not the political and economic interests of the intervening country. In the second case, the probability of a successful intervention is high and victory would protect crucial economic interests, as well as serve humanity. To forego the first conflict and intervene in the second might strike some as craven and self-serving; but the country that routinely dives into the first sort of conflict would quickly find itself politically, economically, and militarily shipwrecked, and thus unable to defend justice even inside its own borders.

[30]*Lord of the Rings*, bk. 5, chap. 4.

[31]In Tolkien's celebrated lecture on *Beowulf*, quoted in Shippey, *Author of the Century*, p. 149.

[32]Ibid., p. 150.

[33]*Lord of the Rings*, bk. 6, chap. 3.

[34]Ibid., bk. 5, chap. 4.

[35]Shippey, *Author of the Century*, p. 40.

[36]*Lord of the Rings*, bk. 2, chap. 2.

[37]Ibid., bk. 5, chap. 3.

[38]Ibid., chap. 4.

[39]Colin Duriez, *Tolkien and C. S. Lewis: The Gift of Friendship* (Mahwah, N.J.: Hidden Spring, 2003), p. 15.

[40]Probably the definitive treatment of this part of Tolkien's life, from which we draw here, is John Garth, *Tolkien and the Great War: The Threshold of Middle-Earth* (New York: Houghton Mifflin Harcourt, 2003).

[41]Quoted in Charles C.W. Cooke, "Liberty in the Tentacular State", *National Review Online*, June 10, 2013, http://www.nationalreview.com/article/350609/liberty-tentacular-state-charles-c-w-cooke.

[42]See Samuel Gregg, *Becoming Europe* (New York: Encounter, 2013), introduction.

[43]Quoted in ibid.

[44]*Lord of the Rings*, bk. 6, chap. 8.

Chapter 7: The Scouring of the Shire

[1]*Lord of the Rings*, bk. 3, chap. 4.

[2]Ibid., foreword to the second edition.

[3]"It was a kind of lost paradise", Tolkien said in an interview with the *Guardian* newspaper. "There was an old mill that really did grind corn with two millers, a great big pond with swans on it, a sandpit, a wonderful dell with flowers, a few old-fashioned village houses and, further away, a stream with another mill" (quoted by John Ezard, "Tolkien's Shire", *Guardian*, December 28, 1991, http://www.theguardian.com/books/1991/dec/28/jrrtolkien.classics).

[4]Humphrey Carpenter, *J. R. R. Tolkien: A Biography* (1977; repr., New York: Houghton Mifflin, 2000), pp. 129–30.

[5]Ibid., p. 40.

[6]Quoted by Karen Wynn Fonstad, *The Atlas of Middle-Earth* (Boston: Houghton Mifflin, 1991), p. ix. From Henry Resnick, "An Interview with Tolkien", *Niekas*, 1967, pp. 37–47.

[7]Of course, Rousseau could trust this sudden feeling that man is naturally good because man *is* naturally good, and so, naturally, he could trust his sudden inspiration that man is naturally good! Not the most rigorous of philosophers, Rousseau made up for it in cultural influence.

[8]Theodore Dalrymple film interview with Coldwater Media, Birmingham, England, Summer 2004. Portions of this material appear in *The Truth Project*, Part 3 (Coldwater Media, 2007).

[9]Chris Baratta, "'No Name, No Business, No Precious, Nothing. Only Empty. Only Hungry': Gollum as Industrial Casualty", in *Environmentalism in the Realm of Science Fiction and Fantasy Literature*, ed. Chris Baratta (Newcastle upon Tyne, England: Cambridge Scholars, 2012), p. 33.

[10]*Lord of the Rings*, bk. 1, chap. 2.

[11]Mathew Dickerson and Jonathan Evans, *Ents, Elves and Eriador: The Environmental Vision of J. R. R. Tolkien* (Lexington, Ky.: University of Kentucky Press, 2011).

[12]Lynn White Jr., "The Historical Roots of Our Ecologic Crisis", *Science* 21 (June 1969): 42–47.

[13]*Ents, Elves and Eriador*, p. 63.

[14]Ps 24:1.

[15]See for example chapter 2 of *Ents, Elves and Eriador*, "Gandalf, Stewardship, and Tomorrow's Weather", pp. 37–67.

[16]See Rev 13:1.

[17]See Mk 5:1–20 and Lk 8:26–39.

[18]Dickerson and Evans, *Ents, Elves and Eriador*, p. 265.

[19] Ibid., p. 266.

[20] So for instance, after summarizing cases of attacks by rabid wolves and by wolves defending themselves, the staid and academic Norwegian Institute for Nature Research (NINA) describes its findings on documented cases of healthy wolves preying on humans: "Predatory attacks appear to usually involve single wolves, or single packs, that learn to exploit humans as prey. In these cases the victims are usually directly attacked around the neck and face in a sustained manner. The bodies are often dragged away and consumed unless the wolves are disturbed." See John D. C. Linnell et al., "The Fear of Wolves: A Review of Wolf Attacks on Humans", *The Norwegian Institute for Nature Studies*, January 2002, p. 16, http://digitalcommons .unl.edu/cgi/viewcontent.cgi?article=1026&context=wolfrecovery. On page 3 of the report, the researchers note that it "was financed by the Ministry of the Environment with the purpose of providing a foundation for the process of reducing people's fear of wolves", so any temptation the researchers may have faced would have been in the direction of minimizing the threat of wolf attacks on humans. To their credit, the authors frankly concede that even healthy wolves do occasionally attack humans, leading to the second purpose of the report: to "make some management recommendations to reduce the risks of attacks".

[21] *Lord of the Rings*, bk. 2, chap. 3.

[22] Alfred Lord Tennyson, *In Memoriam A. H. H.*, canto 56.

[23] Edgar Allen Poe, "The Raven", st. 1, line 6.

[24] Jesus describes Satan thus in John 12:31, 14:30, and 16:11 (see Douay-Rheims, KJV, NIV, Jerusalem).

[25] *Lord of the Rings*, bk. 6, chap. 3.

[26] Quoted in Ishay Landa, "Slaves of the Ring: Tolkien's Political Unconscious", *Historical Materialism* 10, no. 4 (2003): 122.

[27] See the details graphically depicted in "Wealth and Health of Nations", *Gapminder*, www .gapminder.org/world/.

[28] For the gory details of environmental devastation under Communism, see Nicholas Eberstadt, *The Poverty of Communism* (Piscataway, N.J.: Transaction Publishers, 1988).

[29] Chris Brawley, "The Fading of the World: Tolkien's Ecology and Loss in *The Lord of the Rings*", *Journal of the Fantastic in the Arts* 18, no. 3 (2007).

[30] Carpenter, *Tolkien: A Biography*, pp. 150–52.

[31] Tolkien to Naomi Mitchison, September 25, 1954, in J. R. R. Tolkien, *The Letters of J. R. R. Tolkien*, ed. Humphrey Carpenter (New York: Houghton Mifflin, 2000), p. 178.

[32] Brawley, "Fading of the World".

[33] Michael Polanyi, *Personal Knowledge: Towards a Post-Critical Philosophy*, corr. ed. (Chicago: University of Chicago Press, 1974). He wrote this in many places. He discussed the idea in detail on pp. 61–99.

[34] Patrick Curry promotes a similar attitude toward language in an essay exploring the idea of enchantment in Tolkien, quoting Jan Zwycky, who writes, "Lyric springs from the desire to recapture the intuited wholeness of the non-linguistic world, to heal the slash in the mind that is the capacity for language" (p. 230 of Zwicky). Curry and Zwicky avoid falling into a position allergic to stewardship by distinguishing between exploitation and the idea of the domestic, which is willing to live apart from absolutes—to leave Lothlórien when duty calls, as Curry suggests—and, in Zwicky's words, to "accept the essential tension between lyric desire and the capacity for technology" (p. 258). What's missing from this analysis, we would suggest, is the theological and specifically Christological category of the *Logos*. This was part of Tolkien's understanding of reality generally and of language specifically. On this understanding our present linguistic capacity is not "a slash" across the human mind. Rather, we are a finite and fallen language animal groping toward the Word and ground of all being, in whom

and through whom language is an intrinsic and permanent characteristic of reality. The biblical story of the sinless Adam naming the animals and then the sinful Adam being driven from paradise may have played a significant role in Tolkien's thinking. This is suggested by a passage from his lecture "On Fairy-Stories". There he writes that the perennial human interest in beast fables and in talking with animals reflects a desire to recover a lost time when man communed more closely with animals. "A vivid sense of that separation is very ancient," he writes, "but also a sense that it was a severance: a strange fate and a guilt lies on us" (*The Tolkien Reader* [New York: Ballantine, 1966], p. 66). See Patrick Curry, "Enchantment in Tolkien and Middle-Earth", *Tolkien's* The Lord of the Rings*: Sources of Inspiration*, ed. Stratford Caldecott and Thomas Honegger (Zurich, Switzerland: Walking Tree Books, 2008); and Jan Zwicky, *Lyric Philosophy* (Toronto: University of Toronto Press, 1992).

[35] Brawley, "Fading of the World".

[36] Rev 2:17.

[37] Ps 46:10.

[38] Brawley, "Fading of the World".

[39] Ibid.

[40] *Lord of the Rings*, prologue.

[41] Ibid., bk. 6, chap. 8.

[42] *Hobbit*, chap. 19.

[43] Robert Plank, "'The Scouring of the Shire': Tolkien's View of Fascism", in Jared Lobdell, ed., *A Tolkien Compass*, 2nd ed. (Chicago: Open Court, 2003), p. 107.

[44] See Carpenter, *Tolkien: A Biography*, pp. 129–30. Notice that Tolkien's comment doesn't rule out the possibility that later events inspired at least some of the details of the chapter. Understand, too, that Tolkien often resisted efforts to draw parallels between events in *The Lord of the Rings* and the political figures and events of his day, while privately drawing just such parallels in his letters, for example, between Hitler and Sauron (see Tolkien to Christopher Tolkien, May 6, 1944 [FS 22], in *Letters*, p. 78).

[45] Hal Colebatch, "Communism", in *J. R. R. Tolkien Encyclopedia: Scholarship and Critical Assessment*, ed. Michael D. C. Drout (New York: Routledge, 2007), p. 109.

[46] In *Liberal Fascism: The Secret History of the American Left from Mussolini to the Politics of Change* (New York: Three Rivers Press, 2009), Jonah Goldberg demonstrates that Fascism was and is a product of the progressive left. We miss this point because we fail to distinguish the Fascism in Nazi Germany and Fascist Italy from what is called "liberal Fascism", the softer version that went to seed in much of Western Europe and North America.

[47] Tom Shippey, *J. R. R. Tolkien: Author of the Century* (New York: Houghton Mifflin, 2001), p. 171, quoted in Brawley, "Fading of the World".

[48] Brawley, "Fading of the World".

[49] For links to reports corroborating this description of the event, see "*Statement from Forrest Mims, Letters from UT's Dr. Kenneth Summy:* Support for Mims on Dr. 'Doom' Speech", *The Pearcey Report*, April 12, 2006, http://www.pearceyreport.com/archives/2006/04/press_release_u.php. Also see Eric Pianka's response to the controversy, "What Nobody Wants to Hear, but Everyone Needs to Know", http://uts.cc.utexas.edu/~varanus/Everybody.html. There Pianka clarifies his position, stating that humans "are behaving like bacteria growing on an agar plate", and "I do not bear any ill will toward people. However, I am convinced that the world, including *all humanity*, WOULD clearly be much better off without so many of us" (emphasis in original).

[50] *Lord of the Rings*, bk. 5, chap. 1.

[51] Ibid., appendix A, iv.

[52] Ibid., bk. 4, chap. 5.

[53] Ibid., bk. 5, chap. 9.

[54] Ibid., bk. 6, chap. 7.

[55] See Julian Simon, *The Ultimate Resource II* (Princeton, N.J.: Princeton University Press, 1998).

[56] This is referred to as the Environmental Kuznets Curve. In early stages of industrialization, countries are hard on the environment, but as they grow more prosperous, environmental protection becomes a higher priority. Subsistence farmers, for example, don't have the time or resources to remove infinitesimal impurities from gasoline and monitor the precise composition of their drinking water. But countries with economic freedom move from poverty to prosperity, and in the process have shown a remarkable capacity and interest in making the natural environment around them healthier and more pleasant. See Bruce Yandle, Maya Vijayaraghavan, and Madhusudan Bhattarai, "The Environmental Kuznets Curve: A Primer", *PERC Research Study* 2, no. 1 (May 2002), http://perc.org/sites/default/files/Yandle_Kuznets02.pdf. For years, Steve Hayward published an annual "Index of Leading Environmental Indicators", which showed the overall improvement of tangible environmental problems in developed nations. The most recent Index is from 2008 (Pacific Research Institute, April 21, 2008), at http://special.pacificresearch.org/pub/sab/enviro/2008/study.html.

[57] David Goldman, *How Civilizations Die: And Why Islam Is Dying Too* (Washington, D.C.: Regnery, 2011).

[58] See Ps 127:3–5.

[59] For the book review discussing this, see Jonathan Witt, "Oh Brave New Abundance!" *Religion and Liberty* 22, no. 2, http://www.acton.org/pub/religion-liberty/volume-22-number-2/o-brave-new-abundance.

[60] *Lord of the Rings*, bk. 2, chap. 2.

[61] *Silmarillion*, "Of the Rings of Power and the Third Age".

[62] Bradley Birzer, *J. R. R. Tolkien's Sanctifying Myth* (Wilmington, Del.: ISI Books, 2002), pp. 127–29.

[63] J. R. R. Tolkien, "The Istari", *Unfinished Tales of Númenór and Middle Earth*, ed. Christopher Tolkien (Boston: Houghton Mifflin, 1980), p. 390.

[64] Gen 1:1, 27.

[65] Dorothy Sayers, *The Mind of the Maker* (1941; repr., San Francisco: Harper and Row, 1979), pp. 21–22.

[66] In his private correspondence, Tolkien often spoke of humans and many of his characters as "sub-creators". See, for instance, his letters to Milton Waldman, 1951, pp. 145–46, and to Peter Hastings, draft, September 1954, pp. 187–89, in *Letters*.

Chapter 8: The Fellowship of the Localists

[1] Tolkien to Rhona Beare, draft, October 25, 1958, in *The Letters of J. R. R. Tolkien*, ed. Humphrey Carpenter (New York: Houghton Mifflin, 2000), pp. 288–89.

[2] See, for instance, http://www.relevantmagazine.com/current/chipotle-fast-food-and-theology-what-we-eat.

[3] E. F. Schumacher, *Small Is Beautiful* (London: Hartley and Marks, 2000).

[4] For instance, in *Deep Economy* Bill McGibben argues that the "Wal-Mart Nation" is unsustainable and needs to be replaced by a human-scaled, sustainable "Farmers' Market Nation" (Bill McGibben, *Deep Economy: The Wealth of Communities and the Durable Future* [New York: Times Books/Henry Holt, 2007]).

[5]There's even a Web site, Delocator (http://www.delocator.net/index.php), where you can type in your zip code and find "independent", locally owned coffee shops, bookstores, and movie theaters. The Web site explains, "Corporate industries invading American neighborhoods, from coffee chains to bookstore chains, music chains and movie theatre chains, pose a threat to the authenticity of our unique neighborhoods" (http://www.delocator.net).

[6]In the mid-twentieth century, it was progressive to feed babies formula rather than nursing them. We now know better.

[7]You can read about his Vashon Island Coffin Company and even order one of his beautiful coffins over the Internet, that ubiquitous icon of the global marketplace. See the Web site at http://islandcoffins.com/Home.html.

[8]Martin Wolf offers a similar illustration in his *Why Globalization Works* (New Haven, Conn.: Yale Nota Bene, 2005), p. 3.

[9]Adam Smith put it best when he said: "What is prudence in the conduct of every family can scarce be folly in that of a great kingdom. If a foreign country can supply us with a commodity cheaper than we ourselves can make it, better buy it of them with some part of the produce of our own industry, employed in a way in which we have some advantage." This is true in everything from agriculture to the newest information technology. See "Food Politics", *The Economist*, December 7, 2006, http://www.economist.com/node/8380592.

[10]Thanks to Vikram Pimplekar of MÆRSK for this information.

[11]Wolf, *Why Globalization Works*, pp. 44–45.

[12]Much, but not all, of the costs to the poor are due to a lack of property rights and rule of law. Where these exist, many of the costs of economic development are mitigated even as the rate of economic development for the poor accelerates (see Paul Collier, *The Bottom Billion* [Oxford: Oxford University Press, 2007]). For more on this, see the PovertyCure DVD Series (particularly Part 4) and other material available at Povertycure.org. Also see Hernando De Soto, *The Mystery of Capital* (New York: Basic Books, 2000).

[13]In *The Bottom Billion*, Oxford development economist Paul Collier explores what has worked and hasn't worked to lift the world's poor out of poverty. In an interview about the book, he discussed the idealism of those who would protect the world's poor by keeping them isolated in their rural, localist economies:

> One careless romantic vision of the poor is that they're being so exploited that they should just be left to retreat into self-sufficiency, you know, the organic holistic peasant uncontaminated by the dirty business of a market economy. And of course that is just romantic nonsense. People who retreat into subsistence disconnected from the market are poor. The only ones who are not start off as investment bankers and then go and live out this romantic fantasy, and that's fine for them; it's no good for today's poor. Today's poor need all the connections they can get. ("Paul Collier—Improving Aid with Smarter Compassion", interview, http://www.povertycure.org/voices/paul-collier/)

[14]These are the Woses who help the army of Rohirrim on their march to Minas Tirith (bk. 5, chap. 5), the short men who resemble the Pukel-men statues that Merry saw earlier on the journey.

[15]In a 1954 letter, Tolkien connected the dots: "The Shire-hobbits have no very great need of metals, but the Dwarfs are agents; and in the east of the Mountains of Lune are some of their mines (as shown in the earlier legends): no doubt, the reason, or one of them, for their often crossing the Shire" (Tolkien to Naomi Mitchison, September 25, 1954, in *Letters*, p. 196). Tolkien is underscoring what one can infer from the novels: the free peoples of Middle-Earth enjoy division of labor and trade with each other.

[16]To get a sense of what is involved in bringing a smartphone to market, see "I, Smartphone" at http://www.tifwe.org/smartphone.

[17]The Smithsonian Education Web site describes how one of the early patent holders for the typewriter, Christopher Sholes, sold his patent in 1873 because he couldn't make his typewriter affordably, and was bought out by a company that applied the method of interchangeable parts and mass production to dramatically lower prices; see http://www.smithsonianeducation.org/idealabs/ap/essays/looking6.htm. For a more in-depth treatment of how the development of interchangeable parts spread through various technologies and lowered prices, see David Hounshell, *From the American System to Mass Production, 1800–1932: The Development of Manufacturing Technology in the United States* (Baltimore: John Hopkins University Press, 1984). Also see Thomas Sowell, *Basic Economics* (New York: Basic Books, 2004), p. 85.

[18]Sowell, *Basic Economics*, p. 86.

[19]Joel Salatin, *Everything I Want to Do Is Illegal* (Swoope, Va.: Polyface, 2007).

[20]Gene Logsdon, *The Contrary Farmer* (White River Junction, Vt.: Chelsea Green Publishing, 1995), pp. 95–96, 149, 155–56.

[21]Nassim Nicholas Taleb provides the surprising evidence for this in *Antifragile: Things That Gain from Disorder* (New York: Random House, 2012), pp. 202–6.

[22]John Paul II, Encyclical Letter *Centesimus Annus*, May 1, 1991, no. 31, http://www.vatican.va/holy_father/john_paul_ii/encyclicals/documents/hf_jp-ii_enc_01051991_centesimus-annus_en.html.

[23]The affinities between Belloc's and Chesterton's thought on these matters led Fabian socialist George Bernard Shaw to coin the term "Chesterbelloc".

[24]For more background of the views of contemporary distributists, see the *Distributist Review* at http://distributistreview.com/mag/. Chesterton wrote on distributism in several places. Three major publications, *What's Wrong with the World?*, *The Outline of Sanity*, and *Utopia of Usurers*, have been reprinted in a single volume, *Three Works on Distributism* (Create Space Independent Publishing Platform, 2009).

[25]Chesterton and Belloc sometimes included tools for a trade in this category, even when such tools weren't strictly farm related.

[26]Hilaire Belloc, *Essay on the Restoration of Property* (Norfolk, Va.: IHS Press, 2009), p. 6.

[27]Hilaire Belloc, *The Servile State* (Indianapolis, Ind.: Liberty Fund, 1977), p. 39.

[28]See his nuanced discussion in *J. R. R. Tolkien's Sanctifying Myth: Understanding Middle Earth* (Wilmington, Del.: ISI Books, 2003, 2009), pp. 120–26.

[29]Kreeft doesn't elaborate. In fact, immediately after identifying Tolkien as a distributist, he quotes, not Tolkien, but C. S. Lewis. See Peter Kreeft, *The Philosophy of Tolkien: The Worldview behind* The Lord of the Rings (San Francisco: Ignatius Press, 2005), p. 164.

[30]See the discussion in Joseph Pearce, *Tolkien: Man and Myth* (San Francisco: Ignatius Press, 1998), pp. 159–64. Pearce is building on the opinion of Charles A. Columbe. Stratford Caldecott also identifies Tolkien with distributism, but argues that forcible redistribution of land is not part of the distributist program. Of course, that depends on the definition of distributism. But in any case both the logic and explicit details of Belloc's argument involve a vast exercise of state power. See Stratford Caldecott, *The Power of the Ring: The Spiritual Vision behind the Lord of the Rings* (New York: Crossroad Publishing, 2005), appendix, "Tolkien's Social Philosophy".

[31]See details and references in Thomas E. Woods Jr., *Beyond Distributism*, Christian Social Thought, Series 13 (Grand Rapids, Mich.: Acton Institute, 2008), pp. 22–26.

[32]Nathan Rosenberg and L. E. Birdzell, *How the West Grew Rich: The Economic Transformation of the Industrial World* (New York: Basic Books, 1986), p. 173. Quoted in Maciej Zięba, *Papal Economics: The Catholic Church on Democratic Capitalism from* Rerum Novarum *to* Caritas in Veritate (Wilmington, Del.: ISI Books, 2013), p. 102.

[33]Tolkien to Naomi Mitchison, September 25, 1954, in *Letters*, p. 197.

[34]Tolkien to Michael Straight, draft, probably January or February 1956, in *Letters*, p. 232.

[35]Tolkien to Naomi Mitchison, September 25, 1954, in *Letters*, p. 197.

[36]For example, if the owner of a Papa John's pizza franchise hires Sarah to deliver pizza, he'll only do it if he thinks he, or his franchise, will be better off as a result. In other words, he'll only do it if he prefers having her deliver pizzas for him rather than keeping the, say, twelve dollars an hour he'll pay her. And Sarah will only accept the job if she thinks she'll be better off. By coordinating their actions, Sarah and the pizza guy are able to engage in a free and mutually beneficial exchange. The point is simple enough to explain in one short paragraph, and yet some of history's greatest intellectuals have failed to get it.

[37]This was a widely held assumption up until the twentieth century. The theory leads to all sorts of predictions that conflict with observation, and generates insuperable paradoxes. For instance, imagine two identical cars, one made by a factory filled with an illogical and time-consuming assembly process, and the other by an orderly and efficient factory down the street. As a result, the first car took twice as much labor to produce. The labor theory should lead us to conclude that the first car is worth more than the latter. That's intuitively wrong, but why? What does it even mean to say that the first car is worth twice as much as the second?

Assume instead that the economic value of a car or other consumer good is determined by how much others will part with to acquire it. To determine the economic value of a car, we need a lawful and competitive environment where potential buyers can freely bid to purchase the car. In most cases, this will lead to a specific price, rather than a literal auction. Anyone producing a good or service, then, will want to produce something for less than potential customers will freely pay. If he succeeds, he will not only cover his costs, but also make a profit. But notice that the profit isn't something he "took" from the customer. He's simply applied his ingenuity and ability to anticipate the needs of others to the benefit of both himself and his customers.

This picture of economic value is, in a nutshell, the so-called subjective theory of economic value, which had precursors among the Spanish Scholastics, and others, but came into its own in the twentieth century through thinkers such as Carl Menger, Ludwig von Mises, and F. A. Hayek.

We can make the same point by comparing two goods produced by the same amount of labor. One man digs a hole in the desert that no one wants, and the other man digs an identical hole, which is to be used to build a pool. Clearly the economic value of the pool hole in a fancy estate in Beverly Hills will be much higher than the desert hole. Why? Because one contributes something that someone is willing to pay quite a lot for, and the other does not. Again, it is the subjective valuation of potential customers that determines economic value.

[38]Our purpose here is to consider distributism as Tolkien would have known it. We are focusing on Belloc because he commended certain policies quite clearly. Chesterton, in contrast, wrote more aphoristically and impressionistically on the subject. In this section, we are not passing judgment on the views of all contemporary thinkers who identify as distributist. There have been developments over the decades. The dilemma with modified distributism, however, is that it can quickly become indistinguishable from certain free market views. If distributism is merely a perspective that values limited government, widespread property ownership, strong families, and government policies that do not actively interfere with robust local food markets, etc., then we, Joel Salatin, F. A. Hayek, and Tolkien are all distributists.

[39]Belloc, *Essay on the Restoration of Property*, p. 6.

[40]See, for instance, John Creech, "An Evil Means to a Good End? Another Reflection on Hilaire Belloc's 'An Essay on the Restoration of Property'", *The Imaginative Conservative*,

September 9, 2010, http://www.theimaginativeconservative.org/2010/09/evil-means-to-good-end-another.html. The online magazine *The Imaginative Conservative* has many valuable discussions of distributism, written by champions and critics. Simply search for *distributism* at http://www.theimaginativeconservative.org.

[41] F.A. Hayek, *Law, Legislation and Liberty, Volume 2: The Mirage of Social Justice* (Chicago: University of Chicago Press, 1978), p. 83.

[42] See the discussion in David Deavel, "What's Wrong with Distributism", *Intercollegiate Studies Review* August 5, 2013, http://www.intercollegiatereview.com/index.php/2013/08/05/whats-wrong-with-distributism/.

[43] Hal G.P. Colebatch is incisive here: "The English political philosopher with whom Tolkien was most in harmony was probably Edmund Burke, a whig (i.e., 'Liberal' in the old sense which included minimal government, not the modern American sense of left-wing and State-interventionist). Burke saw society as an organic whole, whose liberties and rights were to be cherished and whose faults were to be remedied with the utmost care, not a machine that could be torn down and re-jigged by radical social engineering (Burke compared this latter to attempting to cure the wounds of one's father by chopping the old man to pieces and throwing the pieces into a magician's cauldron). Burke was horrified by the totalitarian nature of the French Revolution, which he predicted would end in terror and dictatorship, but regarded rebellion against tyranny as an ancient 'right.' (The orcs in *The Lord of the Rings* refer to the free people as 'cursed rebels,' which is presumably what Sauron had told them.) Like Tolkien, Burke rejected the doctrine of 'collective guilt,' stating he knew no way of drawing up an indictment against a whole people" (Hal G.P. Colebatch, "Politics", *J.R.R. Tolkien Encyclopedia: Scholarship and Critical Assessment*, ed. Michael D.C. Drout [New York: Routledge, 2007], p. 538).

[44] Arthur Conan Doyle, *The Memoirs of Sherlock Holmes*, "Silver Blaze", in *Adventures of Sherlock Holmes* (Norwalk, Conn.: Easton Press, 1981).

[45] Tolkien to Christopher Tolkien, November 29, 1943, in *Letters*, p. 64.

[46] Belloc, *Essay on the Restoration of Property*, p. 15.

[47] Tolkien to Michael Tolkien, November 1, 1963, in *Letters*, p. 340.

[48] Ibid., January 24, 1972, in *Letters*, p. 416.

[49] Tolkien to Peter Hastings, draft, September 1954, in *Letters*, p. 190.

[50] See Allan C. Carlson, *Third Ways: How Bulgarian Greens, Swedish Housewives, and Beer-Swilling Englishman Created Family-Centered Economies—and Why They Disappeared* (Wilmington, Del.: ISI Books, 2007), p. 178.

[51] Happily, there are some economists and sociologists who are now studying the crucial role healthy families play in sustaining a flourishing society, and who are suggesting ways to strengthen the family with attention to economic realities and the potential for unintended consequences. See, for instance, the work of economist Jennifer Roback Morse, and sociologist Bradley Wilcox, director of the National Marriage Project at the University of Virginia.

[52] See the progression at http://www.agclassroom.org/gan/timeline/farmers_land.htm.

[53] Natalie Kitroeff, "After Graduating from College, It's Time to Plow, Plant and Harvest", *New York Times*, September 24, 2012, http://www.nytimes.com/2012/09/25/nyregion/the-farm-life-draws-some-students-for-post-graduate-work.html?_r=0. See Stuart Staniford's correction of the statistics in this *New York Times* story at the Early Warning blog, September 26, 2012, http://earlywarn.blogspot.co.uk/2012/09/number-of-farms-in-united-states.html.

[54] When the German currency collapsed after World War I, peasants with land fared much better than the average city dweller. See Adam Fergusson, *When Money Dies*, repr. (New York: PublicAffairs, 2010).

[55] *Centesimus Annus*, no. 32, http://www.vatican.va/holy_father/john_paul_ii/encyclicals/documents/hf_jp-ii_enc_01051991_centesimus-annus_en.html.

[56] The financial crisis underscored the problem with some corporate management. Unlike entrepreneurial and privately owned companies, the short-term benefit for management and executives is not always aligned with the long-term health of the corporations they navigate. For instance, an executive may get bonuses and stock options that he can enjoy in the present and near future, even while his governance could destroy the company five years out. Unfortunately, these are precisely the companies likely to be bailed out by the federal government. Without such bailouts, the failure of companies with a bad corporate structure would encourage positive reform. Bailouts delay this painful but necessary process.

[57] See Carlson, *Third Ways*, p. 5.

[58] Maciej Zięba argues in *Papal Economics* that when looking at the century of encyclicals written from 1891 to 1991—*Rerum Novarum* to *Centesimus Annus*—"it is possible to discern an evolution in the Church's views on political-economic systems and in its postulated social solutions" (Wilmington, Del.: ISI Books, 2013). So to speak of a single view of a question in the papal encyclicals, one would need to take account of all of them and find the commonalities.

[59] *Centesimus Annus*, no. 46, http://www.vatican.va/holy_father/john_paul_ii/encyclicals/documents/hf_jp-ii_enc_01051991_centesimus-annus_en.html.

[60] John Paul II, Encyclical Letter *Sollicitudo Rei Socialis*, December 30, 1987, no. 41, http://www.vatican.va/holy_father/john_paul_ii/encyclicals/documents/hf_jp-ii_enc_30121987_sollicitudo-rei-socialis_en.html.

[61] *Centesimus Annus*, no. 42, http://www.vatican.va/holy_father/john_paul_ii/encyclicals/documents/hf_jp-ii_enc_01051991_centesimus-annus_en.html.

[62] For Catholics, at least, the goal should be to integrate the known truths and theoretical insights of economics with the normative truths and principles of ethics, Catholic social teaching, and ultimately, theology. That doesn't mean that thoughtful Christians must all study economics. Most of what we need to learn to do is not technical economics, but rather what Henry Hazlitt called the "art of economics", which "consists in looking not merely at the immediate but at the longer effects of any act or policy; it consists in tracing the consequences of that policy not merely for one group but for all groups" (*Economics in One Lesson*, repr. [New York: Three Rivers Press, 1988], p. 17).

To do this, we do need to understand well-established economic and historical truths, such as incentives matter, the relationship between supply and demand, price function (and the effect of price controls), the effects of specialization, the law of comparative advantage, analysis of economic value (such as discussed above), the win-win features of a free exchange, the cultural consequences of economic freedom, the insight that we can create new wealth rather than merely transfer it from one person or company to another, and so forth. These and most of the other insights into economics are summarized in many places, such as the (misnamed) *Common Sense Economics*, by James D. Gwartney, Richard L. Stroup, Dwight R. Lee, and Tawni H. Ferrarini (New York: St. Martin's Press, 2010). See also Jay W. Richards, *Money, Greed, and God* (San Francisco: HarperOne, 2009).

[63] Joseph Ratzinger, "Church and Economy: Responsibility for the Future of the World Economy", *Communio* 13, no. 3, pp. 199–204.

[64] Think of the trade-off between risk and return. An investor may be willing to risk his investment capital on a risky venture, if the potential return is great enough to offset the risk. Normally, a very low-risk bond will offer a more modest rate of return than a high-risk bond. Otherwise no rational investor would buy the high-risk bond. Every bond investor understands this point, yet as late as the second decade of the twentieth century, the leading British

economist John Maynard Keynes did not understand it. Sylvia Nasar describes this episode in *Grand Pursuit: The Story of Economic Genius* (New York: Simon & Schuster, 2012), chap. 34.

[65]John XXIII, Encyclical Letter *Mater et Magistra*, May 15, 1961, no. 238, http://www.vatican.va/holy_father/john_xxiii/encyclicals/documents/hf_j-xxiii_enc_15051961_mater_en.html.

Chapter 9: Love and Death in Middle-Earth

[1]Tolkien to C. Ouboter, Voorhoeve en Dietrich, April 10, 1958, in J. R. R. Tolkien, *The Letters of J. R. R. Tolkien*, ed. Humphrey Carpenter (New York: Houghton Mifflin, 2000), p. 267.

[2]*Lord of the Rings*, bk. 1, chap. 1. The phrasing is Bilbo's proposed ending to the book he putters away on but never finishes.

[3]We learn this in Tolkien's introductory material, before the beginning of the novel proper: "And as the days of the Shire lengthened they spoke less and less with the Elves, and grew afraid of them, and distrustful of those that had dealings with them; and the Sea became a word of fear among them, and a token of death, and they turned their faces away from the hills in the west."

[4]*Lord of the Rings*, bk. 6, chap. 9.

[5]See Tom Shippey, *J. R. R. Tolkien: Author of the Century* (Boston: Houghton Mifflin, 2002), pp. vii–viii.

[6]Tolkien to Christopher Tolkien, July 11, 1972, in *Letters*, pp. 420–21.

[7]*Lord of the Rings*, bk. 6, chap. 9.

[8]Tolkien to Milton Waldman, (undated, late 1951), in *Letters*, p. 152.

[9]*Silmarillion*, "Of the Rings of Power and the Third Age".

[10]Ibid., "Akallabêth".

[11]Ibid.

[12]The royal Númenórean line, unlike ordinary men, have been made stewards by the Creator of their end, a kind of complementary capacity balancing their gift of unusually long life. It is not meant to function as an advertisement for the virtues of suicide, both because the Númenórean kings do not choose death by any violent means but, as it seems, by simply and mysteriously allowing the course of death to move toward its natural end, and because Tolkien is careful to give us the negative example of Denethor, who is strongly rebuked by Gandalf for seeking suicide.

[13]*Silmarillion*, "Akallabêth".

[14]"And even the name of that land perished," the narrative informs us, "and Men spoke thereafter not of Elenna, nor of Andor the Gift that was taken away, nor of Númenórë on the confines of the world; but the exiles on the shores of the sea, if they turned towards the West in the desire of their hearts, spoke of Mar-nu-Falmar that was whelmed in the waves, Akallabêth the Downfallen, *Atalantë* in the Eldarin tongue" (emphasis added).

[15]Plato, *Critias*, trans. Benjamin Jowett, the Internet Classics Archives, http://classics.mit.edu/Plato/critias.html.

[16]See *Unfinished Tales of Númenór and Middle-Earth* (Boston, Mass.: Houghton Mifflin, 1980) and *The History of Middle-Earth* (New York: HarperCollins, collector's edition, 2011), vol. 5 and 9 for additional materials, unpublished in Tolkien's lifetime, on Númenór and Tolkien's attempt to create a bridge from modern England to Númenór ["The Lost Road" of vol. 5 and "The Notion Club Papers, (Part Two)" of vol. 9].

[17]Peter J. Kreeft, *The Philosophy of Tolkien: The Worldview behind* The Lord of the Rings (San Francisco: Ignatius Press, 2005), p. 97.

[18]Gen 3:4–5.

[19]Sauron seems to have made a career of misleading the kings of men. In *The Master of Middle-Earth* (Boston: Houghton Mifflin, 1972), author Paul Kocher points to a revealing scene in *The Fellowship of the Ring*, when Frodo, Merry, Pippin, and Sam are caught by the Barrow-wights: "The incantation chanted by the wight who is about to kill the hobbits specifically condemns them to death 'till the dark lord lifts his hand / over dead sea and withered land,' after the sun fails and the moon dies. Here a servant of Sauron (and maybe Sauron himself) is looking forward to a Black Resurrection at the end of the world, when the dead arise to face judgment not by Christ but by a triumphant Dark Lord who has taken his place. It is all nonsense, of course. Tom exorcises the wight to a prison 'darker than the darkness, / Where gates stand for ever shut, till the world is mended.' This mending of the world seems to refer to a Resurrection quite different from that anticipated by Sauron and his servants" (p. 74).

[20]Ps 90:12.

[21]Tolkien to Rhona Beare, unsent draft of a continuation of a letter sent October 14, 1958, in *Letters*, p. 284.

[22]For instance, "Do not reprove a scoffer, or he will hate you; reprove a wise man, and he will love you" (Prov 9:8).

[23]Tolkien to Milton Waldman, (undated, late 1951), in *Letters*, p. 154.

[24]J. R. R. Tolkien, *The Monsters and the Critics*, chap. 2, http://www.scribd.com/doc/11790039/JRR-Tolkien-Beowulf-The-Monsters-and-the-Critics. See also Bradley Birzer's helpful discussion of the death theme in Tolkien in *J. R. R. Tolkien's Sanctifying Myth* (Wilmington, Del.: ISI Books, 2002), chap. 2, "Myth and Sub-creation".

[25]Lúthien is actually half elf, half Maia. In Tolkien's legendarium, the Maiar are angelic-divine beings (created by Eru Ilúvatar), and through the marriage of Lúthien and the man Beren comes the royal line of Númenór. In this is an echo of another Genesis story, mentioned only in passing in Genesis 6:4: "The Nephilim were on the earth in those days, and also afterward, when the sons of God came in to the daughters of men, and they bore children to them. These were the mighty men that were of old, the men of renown." The Genesis reference is ambiguous as to the nature of these "sons of God". Some have suggested a reference to the line of Seth (with the daughters of men being from the wicked line of Cain), but others have supported the more mysterious possibility that these "sons of God" were angelic figures, cuing particularly off the use of the term "sons of God" in Job chapters 1, 2, and 38 where it seems to refer to beings able to appear before the throne of God in Heaven and who already existed when the "foundation of the earth" was laid (Job 38:4, 7), before the creation of mankind. Another ambiguity concerns the moral character of these mighty men, leaving open the possibility that some were morally upright. The Genesis verse that follows, however, gives the sense of moral decline and depravity: "The LORD saw that the wickedness of man was great in the earth, and that every imagination of the thoughts of his heart was only evil continually" (Gen 6:5).

In a similar vein, the kings of Númenór found in the Tolkien legendarium are mighty men of renown with divine blood in their lineage and who also fall into evil, both "in those days, and also afterward". However, the picture Tolkien offers is a bit less dark than what we find in the Genesis account. There were some mighty Númenórean kings who wielded their authority with modesty and restraint, exemplified in the character of Aragorn.

Tolkien was a fantasy novelist whose imagination was fired by his philological and literary studies of ancient texts, so it would have been in keeping with his creative modus operandi for him to leave an echo not only of the Atlantis myth, not only of the Babel story, not only of the account of Noah and the Flood, but also of this mysterious glimpse into the distant and mysterious past, hinting as it does to some true if only barely glimpsed and poorly understood source for all the tales about ancient humans with divine ancestry.

Tolkien was fastidious in his reimagining of older source material, so notice the important differences as well. First, in Tolkien's story of an angelic and human pairing, the male is elven rather than human. In Tolkien's legendarium, the elves, while not sinless, exist in closer proximity to the Creator. Also, the union involves a marriage in the Tolkien story while the Genesis story only mentions sexual union leading to childbearing. Finally, the Genesis account gives the impression of a powerful divine or angelic male figure taking advantage of a vulnerable human female. In the Tolkien tale, Lúthien is the offspring of a royal elven male warrior, Thingol, and a powerful female Maia, Melian, who fall in love, adore each other for many years, and are eventually joined in matrimony. These differences combine to create the effect of affection and wonder—in contrast to the biblical story's picture of lust-driven power—making for a more promising pedigree for the Númenóreans than for the Nephilim, although one where the Fall continues to play a role. Thus, the marriage of Thingol and Melian leads to various noble and good leaders but, in part because of their greater power and longevity, also to human kings corrupted by power.

[26]Tolkien moved this love story to the appendix not because he found the story unimportant but because *The Lord of the Rings* is hobbit centered and he felt that inserting it into the body of the novel would damage the work aesthetically. "I regard the tale of Arwen and Aragorn as the most important of the Appendices", he wrote; "it is part of the essential story, and is only placed so, because it could not be worked into the main narrative without destroying its structure: which is planned to be 'hobbito-centric,' that is, primarily a study of the ennoblement (or sanctification) of the humble" (his letter to Michael Straight, drafts, probably January or February 1956, in *Letters*, p. 237). In the writing business they call this "shooting your darlings", and we can get some sense of how dear this story was to Tolkien when we connect it to two backstories—his own life and his Middle-Earth legendarium. The story is an echo of the story of Beren and Lúthien, and Tolkien had these names inscribed on his and his wife's headstone. In a letter to his son Christopher, he explained that Lúthien wasn't a pet name he ever used for Edith but that she was the inspiration for the character. "In those days her hair was raven," he tells his son, "her skin clear, her eyes brighter than you have seen them, and she could sing—and *dance*." In the story of Beren and Lúthien, each saves the other, though interestingly Lúthien does more of the saving. Late in the story Beren dies in battle and Lúthien of grief. Her spirit departs to the Halls of Mandos, "the Doomsman of the Valar" and "keeper of the Houses of the Dead" (*Silmarillion*, "Valaquenta"), and through her tears and song of lament she is granted a choice. She can be "released from Mandos, and go to Valimar, there to dwell until the world's end among the Valar", though without Beren. Or "she might return to Middle-earth, and take with her Beren, there to dwell again, but without certitude of life or joy." This she chooses, and the two are restored to life as mortals together in Middle-Earth (*Silmarillion*, "Of Beren and Lúthien"). Tolkien was less fortunate with his Lúthien. As he told his son Michael after Edith's death, "In 1934 she was still with me, and her beautiful children. But now she has gone before Beren, leaving him indeed one-handed." Or as he put it in the letter quoted at the beginning of this chapter—where he spoke of "the dreadful sufferings of our childhoods, from which we rescued one another"—the story of Tolkien-Beren and Edith-Lúthien "has gone crooked, & I am left, and *I* cannot plead before the inexorable Mandos."

[27]There's a running debate as to whether Tolkien's short story, "Smith of Wooten Major" is also an allegory. Tom Shippey makes the case that it is in *The Road to Middle-Earth*, pp. 271–80.

[28]J. R. R. Tolkien, "Leaf by Niggle", *The Tolkien Reader* (New York: Ballantine Books, 1966), p. 95.

[29]The PovertyCure Web site provides a short introduction to the principle of subsidiarity in the Bible, in Protestant and Catholic social teaching, and as it relates to economics and the

poor: http://www.povertycure.org/issues/subsidiarity/. Also, *The Social Agenda: A Collection of Roman Catholic Magisterial Texts* explores further references to the theme of subsidiarity in Catholic social teaching, and to the complementary theme of solidarity: http://www.thesocialagenda.org/en/article-four-social-order.

[30]Pius XI, Encyclical Letter *Quadragesimo Anno*, May 15, 1931, no. 79, http://www.vatican.va/holy_father/pius_xi/encyclicals/documents/hf_p-xi_enc_19310515_quadragesimo-anno_en.html.

[31]John Paul II, Encyclical Letter *Centesimus Annus,* May 1, 1991, no. 48, http://www.vatican.va/holy_father/john_paul_ii/encyclicals/documents/hf_jp-ii_enc_01051991_centesimus-annus_en.html.

[32]Tolkien, "Leaf by Niggle", p. 103.

[33]Ibid., pp. 103–4.

[34]Ibid., p. 104.

[35]Humphrey Carpenter's biography of Tolkien (Boston: Houghton Mifflin, 1977) has an engaging discussion of Tolkien's fears of never finishing his mythology and the role "Leaf by Niggle" played in getting him back on track. In an interesting sidebar, Carpenter notes that at one point Tolkien's neighbor, Lady Agnew, bothered him about dealing with a poplar tree that she feared would wreck her house in a bad storm. Tolkien thought her fears misplaced, but grudgingly obliged, taking time out from his other obligations to prune back the tree. One morning not long after "he woke up with a short story in his head, and scribbled it down. It was the tale of a painter named Niggle" (p. 199).

[36]*Silmarillion*, "Akallabêth".

[37]Rev 21:4.

[38]Rev 20:6. See also 2 Tim 2:12.

[39]The phrase derives from the work of political philosopher Eric Voegelin who stated, "The problem of an eidos in history, hence, arises only when a Christian transcendental fulfillment becomes immanentized. Such an immanentist hypostasis of the eschaton, however, is a theoretical fallacy" (*The New Science of Politics* [Chicago: Chicago University Press, 1987], p. 120).

[40]C. S. Lewis, *Mere Christianity* (San Francisco: Harper San Francisco, 2001), p. 134, originally published in 1952 and based on a series of BBC recordings delivered during World War II.

[41]Ps 90:12.

[42]Eccles 3:11.

[43]Is 40:6.

[44]Tolkien, "On Fairy-Stories", *Tolkien Reader*, p. 68.

[45]Ibid., 71–72.

[46]*Lord of the Rings*, bk. 6, chap. 4.

[47]From the letter to the Hebrews: "These all died in faith, not having received what was promised, but having seen it and greeted it from afar, and having acknowledged that they were strangers and exiles on the earth. For people who speak thus make it clear that they are seeking a homeland. If they had been thinking of that land from which they had gone out, they would have had opportunity to return. But as it is, they desire *a better country*, that is, a heavenly one" (Heb 11:13–16; emphasis added).

Epilogue: Frodo Is with Us

[1]Tolkien, "On Fairy-Stories", *The Tolkien Reader* (New York: Ballantine Books, 1989), p. 60.

[2]Ibid., p. 62.

[3]Ibid., p. 57. The passage is reminiscent of a passage in G.K. Chesterton's *Orthodoxy* (San Francisco: Ignatius Press, reprint edition 1995), pp. 65–66:

> Because children have abounding vitality, because they are in spirit fierce and free, therefore they want things repeated and unchanged. They always say, "Do it again"; and the grown-up person does it again until he is nearly dead. For grown-up people are not strong enough to exult in monotony. But perhaps God is strong enough to exult in monotony. It is possible that God says every morning, "Do it again" to the sun; and every evening, "Do it again" to the moon. It may not be automatic necessity that makes all daisies alike; it may be that God makes every daisy separately, but has never got tired of making them. It may be that He has the eternal appetite of infancy; for we have sinned and grown old, and our Father is younger than we.

[4]1 Cor 15:43–44.

[5]In a speech he gave in 1958, Tolkien said that in looking about the world, "I see that Saruman has many descendants" (quoted in Humphrey Carpenter, *J. R. R. Tolkien: A Biography* [Boston: Houghton Mifflin, 1977], p. 228). Four years earlier, Tolkien commented, "I am not a 'reformer' (by exercise of power) since it seems doomed to Sarumanism" (Tolkien to Naomi Mitchison, September 25, 1954, in J.R.R. Tolkien, *The Letters of J. R. R. Tolkien*, ed. Humphrey Carpenter [New York: Houghton Mifflin, 2000], p. 197).

[6]Alexis de Tocqueville, *Democracy in America*, trans. Gerald E. Bevan (1835, 1840; New York: Penguin, 2003), pp. 805–6.

[7]Tolkien to Michael Straight, drafts, probably January or February 1956, in *Letters*, p. 235.

[8]Ralph C. Wood, *The Gospel according to Tolkien: Visions of the Kingdom in Middle-Earth* (Louisville, Ky.: Westminster/John Knox Press), p. x.

[9]Hal G.P. Colebatch beautifully recounts this story in his entry "Communism", in the *J. R. R. Tolkien Encyclopedia: Scholarship and Critical Assessment*, ed. Michael D. C. Drout (New York: Routledge, 2007), p. 109.

[10]The quotation is variously attributed, most commonly to Alexander Fraser Tytler, but it has not been found in Tytler's extant writings. The quotation's earliest known appearance is the *Daily Oklahoman*, December 9, 1951, in a letter signed "Elmer T. Peterson". It reads: "Two centuries ago, a somewhat obscure Scotsman named Tytler made this profound observation: 'A democracy cannot exist as a permanent form of government. It can only exist until the majority discovers it can vote itself largess out of the public treasury. After that, the majority always votes for the candidate promising the most benefits with the result the democracy collapses because of the loose fiscal policy ensuing, always to be followed by a dictatorship, then a monarchy.'" For more on the history of the quotation and its various appearances in speeches and the media, see Loren Collins, "The Truth about Tytler", http://www.lorencollins.net/tytler.html.

[11]Tolkien to Joanna de Bortadano, draft, (undated, April 1956), in *Letters*, p. 246.

[12]Hal G.P. Colebatch, *The Return of the Heroes:* The Lord of the Rings, Star Wars, Harry Potter, *and Social Conflict*, 2nd ed. (Christchurch, New Zealand: Cybereditions Corporation, 2003), p. 153.

[13]Tolkien to Colin Bailey, May 13, 1964, in *Letters*, p. 344.

[14]Tolkien to Christopher Tolkien, September 23–25, 1944, in *Letters*, pp. 92–94.

INDEX